PRAISE FOR THE FIRST EDITION OF *THE BOOK OF CSS3*

"I can honestly say I will never need another book on this subject, and I doubt anyone else will either."
—DEVON YOUNG, WRITER FOR CSS3.INFO

"One of the best technology books I've read."
—CRAIG BUCKLER, OPTIMALWORKS LTD

"An absolutely fantastic resource for developers and serious designers."
—VISUAL SWIRL

"A book you more than likely should have, even if you think you already have a pretty good handle on everything CSS."
—456 BEREA STREET

"An excellent introduction to CSS3—both what you can do with it now and what is proposed for the future."
—STEPHEN CHAPMAN, FELGALL.COM

"There are entire sections of the CSS3 spec that I never really appreciated until I read this book."
—DESIGNORATI

THE BOOK OF CSS3
2ND EDITION

A Developer's Guide to the Future of Web Design

by Peter Gasston

**no starch
press**

San Francisco

Printed in USA

First printing

18 17 16 15 14   1 2 3 4 5 6 7 8 9

ISBN-10: 1-59327-580-3
ISBN-13: 978-1-59327-580-8

Text stock is SFI certified

Publisher: William Pollock
Production Editor: Serena Yang
Cover Illustration: Octopod Studios and Garry Booth
Interior Design: Octopod Studios
Developmental Editor: William Pollock
Technical Reviewer: Patrick Lauke
Copyeditor: LeeAnn Pickrell
Compositor: Lynn L'Heureux
Proofreader: James Fraleigh
Indexer: Nancy Guenther

For information on distribution, translations, or bulk sales, please contact No Starch Press, Inc. directly:

No Starch Press, Inc.
245 8th Street, San Francisco, CA 94103
phone: 415.863.9900; info@nostarch.com
www.nostarch.com

The Library of Congress has catalogued the first edition as follows:

Gasston, Peter.
 The book of CSS3 : a developer's guide to the future of web design / Peter Gasston.
       p. cm.
 Includes index.
 ISBN-13: 978-1-59327-286-9
 ISBN-10: 1-59327-286-3
 1. Web sites--Design. 2. Cascading style sheets. I. Title.
 TK5105.888G376 2011
 006.7--dc22

                                      2011010098

For Sarah, my sister.
Your courage is inspiring.

BRIEF CONTENTS

CONTENTS IN DETAIL

14
TRANSITIONS AND ANIMATIONS   165

15
FLEXIBLE BOX LAYOUT   185

16
VALUES AND SIZING   199

17
GRID LAYOUT   209

18
BLEND MODES, FILTER EFFECTS, AND MASKING   225

19
THE FUTURE OF CSS
245

A
CSS3 SUPPORT IN CURRENT MAJOR BROWSERS
257

B
ONLINE RESOURCES   263

PREFACE

This book is the culmination of eight years' writing about CSS3, both on the Web and in print. The browser and CSS landscape has changed a lot in that short time and continues to change today, bringing new features and implementations at a rate that's difficult to keep up with. The CSS3 specification is written in (often dense) technical language that's intended for implementers rather than end users, and my intent in writing this book was to bridge the gap between specification and web developer.

The book follows a loose order based on stability of implementation: In the earlier chapters, I cover the CSS properties that are well implemented and used on a daily basis, but as the book progresses, the technologies become more experimental and are implemented in fewer browsers. As a result, in the final few chapters I sometimes rely on interpretation of the CSS3 specification to explain how future properties should behave. I would hope that there are few mistakes, but I accept that any that exist are based on my own misunderstanding.

In addition to the various modules of the CSS3 specification itself, an invaluable resource for me while writing the book was the Mozilla Developer Network (*https://developer.mozilla.org/*), a peerless collection of articles about anything web related—not least CSS—which is all the more amazing for being written by volunteers.

The text used in many of the code examples is taken from books in the public domain that are available from Project Gutenberg (*http://www.gutenberg.org/*). All images in the book that are not my own creations are credited in the relevant chapters.

This book would not have been possible without the guidance of the team at No Starch Press, especially Serena Yang and my editors, Keith Fancher (first edition) and Bill Pollock (second edition); between them they made me write more clearly and helped me transition from blogger to author. I'd also like to thank my technical editors: Patrick Lauke's rigorous eye for detail and understanding of technical specifications was instrumental in helping me find focus in the expanded scope of the second edition, and Joost de Valk not only acted as my technical editor for the first edition but also gave me my first opportunity to write about CSS3 when he created CSS3.info eight years ago.

I'd also like to thank my colleagues at Preloaded, Poke, Top10, and rehabstudio for their support and encouragement in writing two editions of this book; everyone at the many London web community meet-ups; my mum for teaching me the value of hard work; and my dad for buying me my first computer almost thirty years ago—I promised I'd pay him back one day, and hopefully this book will go some way toward that debt.

INTRODUCTION

Let me tell you a little about who I think you are: You're a web professional who's been hand-coding HTML and CSS for a few years; you're pretty comfortable with creating complex layouts, and you know not only your div from your span but also your bold from your strong; you've read a little about CSS3 and may even have started experimenting with some of its more decorative features like rounded corners, but you want to gain a deeper understanding of the fundamentals.

The Book of CSS3 helps you leverage the excellent knowledge you have of CSS2.1 in order to make learning CSS3 easier. I won't explain the fundamentals of CSS (except for the occasional reminder), as I assume you know them already. I won't talk you through step-by-step demonstrations of using CSS to make a listed navigation or an image gallery, because I assume you can apply the examples in this book to anything you want to build on your own.

I'll introduce you to what you can do with CSS3 now and show you what you'll be able to do with it in the future. At the same time, I'll take the dense technical language of the CSS3 specification and translate it into language that's plain and practical.

In short, I hope to give you some new tools for your toolkit that will let you make even cooler stuff.

The Scope of This Book

CSS can be used across many types of media; in fact, almost any device that can display HTML or XML can also display CSS rules, though sometimes in a limited form. CSS3 has modules devoted exclusively to paged media, such as PDF or printed materials, and it supports braille, handheld mobile devices (that is, cell phones rather than smartphones), teletypes, and televisions. The range and breadth of possibilities is so vast that I can't possibly cover them all.

This book focuses on CSS for the computer screen. All of the demonstrations are written for (and tested in) the most common desktop browsers, and are optimized for users of desktop and laptop computers. Almost all of the new CSS features covered in this book should work whether you're developing for smartphones, tablets, or other devices, but I can't guarantee that everything will display exactly as shown in the examples you'll find here.

Chapter by Chapter

Here's a brief idea of what will be covered in this book:

Chapter 1 introduces CSS3, explains its history, and looks at the W3C standardization process. It also describes the syntax I use for my demonstration code.

Chapter 2 covers media queries, the technology that's critical to the adaptive and responsive web design methods.

Chapters 3 and 4 introduce new selectors: attribute selectors in Chapter 3 and pseudo-classes in Chapter 4.

Chapter 5 shows how to choose custom web fonts and properties that give you more control over font rendering.

Chapter 6 continues the typographic theme, with coverage of a new property for adding shadows to text and controlling the way blocks of text are displayed.

Chapter 7 is also about text, this time explaining how you can flow it across multiple columns.

Chapters 8 and 9 cover the Background and Borders Module, including extensions to existing background properties and brand-new ways to add decorative effects to element borders.

Chapter 10 explains how to use opacity and transparency, and introduces some new color models.

Chapter 11 introduces CSS gradients, a method of transitioning between two or more colors to make unique background decorations.

Chapters 12 and 13 show how to visually transform elements, changing their appearance in two and three dimensions.

Chapter 14 introduces animation, such as transitional changes between two values and complex timed animations.

Chapter 15 covers Flexbox, a new way of laying out elements based on the space available.

Chapter 16 is also about page layout, covering new value units and how to perform dimension calculations and size elements based on their contents.

Chapter 17 is the last of the layout chapters, introducing the new CSS Grid Layout Module.

Chapter 18 looks at visual effects, such as blending an element's background layers or blending one element with another, using graphical filters, and how to clip an element using simple shapes.

Chapter 19 closes the book with a look to the (possible) future of CSS: new properties and features that are currently fairly experimental but may become fully implemented across browsers at a later date.

The Appendices and Further Resources

There are two appendices at the end of the book. The first is a quick reference to the browser support of the CSS features discussed in this book, and the second is a list of online resources, useful tools, and interesting demonstrations.

In addition, on the website for this book at *http://www.thebookofcss3.com/* you'll find up-to-date versions of both appendices and all examples and demonstrations used in this book. And if I've made any mistakes, you'll find a full list of errata there, too.

In addition to the accompanying website, you'll find more of my writing about CSS3 (and other emerging web technologies) at my blog, Broken Links (*http://www.broken-links.com/*). Feel free to comment or get in touch with me through either of these websites.

Introduction to the Second Edition

I began work on the first edition of this book in 2010. It's been only four years, but how the landscape has changed in that time! In 2010, the iPad had been out for only a few months, Android had yet to explode, and looking at visitor statistics for my own website, visits from all mobile devices accounted for 11.6 percent of sessions—compare that to the 54.8 percent count at the time of this writing.

Since publication of the first edition of this book, we've seen four major versions of Safari and three of Internet Explorer. Firefox has become an auto-updating "evergreen" browser, Chrome has switched from the Web-Kit engine to its own Blink, and Opera has discontinued work on its own Presto engine to also use Blink.

In addition, the rise of preprocessors such as Sass and LESS has brought the power of programming languages into our stylesheets and dramatically changed the way we write CSS. Most professional developers now use a preprocessor as a core component of the website authoring tool set.

Many CSS specifications have changed since the first edition, too. Some have been discontinued, and many more have been created. And the CSS3 of 2010 had many more cross-browser implementation differences, but the differences are much fewer today as browser vendors have placed more importance on adhering to standards.

In other words, this second edition is not simply a light edit of the first; every chapter has been fully revised to reflect changes to the specification and to remove outdated implementation information and experimental properties not in the specification. Certain chapters (those on media queries, Flexbox, grids, and the future of CSS in particular) are almost entirely new, and I've added new chapters on values and sizing as well as blend modes, filter effects, and masking.

Here's to the next four years of change.

1

INTRODUCING CSS3

In this first chapter, I'll cover the code conventions used in this book and discuss some syntax that's unique to CSS3, but before getting to that, let me explain a little about the history of CSS3. Obviously, you don't need to know its history to use CSS3, but I think having some context about the current state of CSS3 is important.

CSS3 is a specification in flux. Some parts of the spec are considered stable and have been well implemented in modern browsers; other parts should be considered experimental and have been partially implemented to varying degrees; yet others are still theoretical proposals and have not been implemented at all. Some browsers have created their own CSS properties that aren't described in any CSS3 specification and perhaps never will be.

All of this means that knowing how the standardization process works and the levels of implementation for each new property is vital to understanding how you can use CSS3 in your code both now and in the future.

What CSS3 Is and How It Came to Be

First, I want to discuss what CSS3 is—and isn't—and the form it takes. The W3C's approach to CSS3 is quite different from its approach to CSS2, so this overview should help you understand how and when you can use CSS3 and why it has such varied implementation across different browsers.

A Brief History of CSS3

The last major version of CSS was CSS2.1, a revision of the CSS2 specification that was originally published in 1997. Despite ongoing development and review since that time, many people are surprised to learn that CSS2 only became an "official" recommendation of the W3C in 2011. (I talk more about the recommendation process shortly.) More surprising still is the fact that Internet Explorer 8 (IE8)—released in 2009—lays claim to being the first browser to support the entire CSS2.1 specification fully.

In the last few years, the talk has been about the new revision—CSS3. I say "new," but in fact work on CSS3 began back in 1998, the year after CSS2 was published. Browser implementation of CSS2 continued to be so frustratingly inconsistent, however, that the W3C decided to halt work on any new revision and work on CSS2.1 instead, standardizing the way CSS had been implemented in the real world. In 2005, all of the CSS3 modules were moved back to Working Draft status, and the editing and review process began again.

For many years, Internet Explorer dominated the ever-expanding market of Internet users and showed no sign of wanting to implement CSS3. But over the last ten years or so, a whole new range of browsers has appeared to compete for users, and this plethora of choice has led to a features arms race. One beneficiary of that arms race has been CSS3. Each of the browsers wants to offer developers and users the latest in web technologies, and with the CSS3 spec already mostly written, implementing and even adding new features has been a no-brainer.

So here we are today, with the CSS3 specification under active development, a broad range of browsers implementing it, and a community of interested developers building with it, studying it, and writing about it. A healthy situation, and one we couldn't have foreseen just a few years ago.

CSS3 Is Modular

Creating the default styling language for every markup-based document in the world is an enormous undertaking, and the W3C was aware that it would take many years to come to fruition. W3C members, conscious that they didn't want to hold up some of the more obvious, in-demand features while they were considering and debating some of the more esoteric ones, made the decision to split CSS3 into various modules. Each of the modules could then be worked on by different authors at different paces, and the implementation and recommendation process—which I discuss shortly—could be staggered.

This is why, instead of a single, monolithic CSS3 specification document, you have CSS3 Basic User Interface Module, Selectors Level 3, Media Queries, and so on. Some of these modules are revisions of CSS2.1, and some are newly created, but all fall under the banner of CSS3.

One of the few things I find irritating (I'm an easy-going guy) is that on many blogs you'll hear people complaining, "I want to use CSS3, but it won't be ready for years." This is nonsense; some CSS3 modules already have quite stable implementation in all modern browsers, and many more are just months away from prime time. If you want to wait until all of the modules are 100 percent implemented across every browser in existence, you'll be waiting forever.

So CSS3 is here, and some of it is ready to use right now—you just have to be mindful about how you use it.

There Is No CSS3

Okay, I realize that's a pretty provocative statement, but it is technically true. As CSS has become modular, each module is designated a level number to mark how many revisions it has been through. Some of the more mature modules, such as Selectors, are already at Level 4; many of the modules featured in this book, such as Fonts, are at Level 3; whereas some very new modules, such as Flexbox, are only at Level 1 or possibly moving into Level 2.

What this means is that CSS is a living standard: As I mentioned earlier, there will be no more monolithic versions; each module will move at its own pace; and new modules will be added as new features are scoped. CSS3 is merely a convenient shorthand to mean "CSS features developed since CSS2.1." CSS4 will never exist. Eventually the numbering will fall away, and we'll just have CSS, with modules at different levels.

But let us not be deterred! I'll continue to refer to CSS3 in this book in the sense that it's defined above, as a convenient shorthand for new CSS features. This label eases understanding and means I don't have to change the title of this book!

Module Status and the Recommendation Process

As I move through this book and discuss each of the different modules, I'll sometimes refer to that module's status. Status is set by the W3C, and it indicates the module's progress through the recommendation process; note, however, that status is *not* necessarily an indication of a module's degree of implementation in any browser.

When a proposed document is first accepted as part of CSS3, its status is designated *Working Draft*. This status means the document has been published and is now ready for review by the community—in this case, the community being browser makers, working groups, and other interested parties. A document may stay as a Working Draft for a long period, undergoing many revisions. Not all documents make it past this status level, and a document may return to this status on many occasions.

Before a document can progress from a Working Draft, its status changes to *Last Call*, which means the review period is about to close and usually indicates the document is ready to progress to the next level.

That next level is *Candidate Recommendation*, which means the W3C is satisfied the document makes sense, the latest reviews have found no significant problems, and all technical requirements have been satisfied. At this point, browser makers may begin to implement the properties in the document to gather real-world feedback.

When two or more browsers have implemented the properties in the same way and if no serious technical issues have come to light, the document may progress to being a *Proposed Recommendation*. This status means the proposal is now mature and implemented and ready to be endorsed by the W3C Advisory Committee. When this endorsement has been granted, the proposal becomes a *Recommendation*.

To reiterate what I briefly touched on before, the recommendation process and the implementation process do not always work in the same way. A module can be well-implemented across all browsers, yet still hold Working Draft status—as I write this, the Transitions module (Chapter 14) has exactly that status. Conversely, a module may hold Candidate Recommendation status yet have only limited implementation—CSS Shapes (Chapter 19) fits this description right now.

As a result, I've written this book in a loose order of implementation, rather than based on recommendation status. Earlier chapters discuss features that have full implementation across all browsers (or should by the time this book is released); later chapters cover features that are implemented in some browsers only—often with browser-specific prefixes; and chapters toward the end of the book deal with potential, speculative, or partial implementations of properties.

Introducing the Syntax

With the introductions and explanations out of the way, let's get to the meat of CSS3. Throughout this book, I use a certain syntactical convention to demonstrate each of the new rules and properties. It looks something like this:

```
E { property: value; }
```

In this code example, the selector is represented with E. Of course, in HTML, this selector doesn't exist; I'm merely using it to indicate the selector is irrelevant; any selector could be used here.

Next, you have the property itself; in this case, I've used a made-up property, called property. Following this is the value of the property. For this, I use an italicized alias to refer to the value, which in this case I've called value.

If a property accepts multiple values, I'll list each with a unique alias. So a new property that requires three values might be defined like this:

```
E { property: first second third; }
```

With all that said, let's pretend we have a new property called monkeys (I've always wanted a monkeys property), which accepts only a single value. Using this book's syntax, I would introduce it like this:

```
E { monkeys: value; }
```

And when it came to providing a practical example of it, I might show it with a valid value—say, a number value—like this:

```
E { monkeys: 12; }
```

Vendor Prefixes

When a module is still under active review, as much of CSS3 is, a lot is subject to change; a property's syntax may be revised, or a property may be dropped entirely. On occasion, even the wording of the draft itself is perhaps a little nebulous and open to interpretation.

At the same time, browsers need to implement these features so we can see how they work in practice. But consider the difficulties that would occur if two separate browsers implemented the same property but interpreted it inconsistently: The result of your code would appear differently—perhaps radically so—in each of the browsers. To prevent this from happening, each of the browser vendors began to prefix a short code to the beginning of experimental properties. Let's imagine our much-desired monkeys property has been newly defined in a specification, and that all of the major browser vendors have decided to implement it to see how it works. In this case, you would use the following code:

```
E {
    -moz-monkeys: value; /* Firefox */
    -ms-monkeys: value; /* Internet Explorer */
    -webkit-monkeys: value; /* Chrome/Safari */
}
```

The amount of repetition may seem somewhat unnecessary, but the repetition is for our own good; the last thing you want is for all the browsers to implement the monkeys property differently, leading to total chaos.

Although well-intentioned, the use of vendor prefixes has led to many problems—developers used them in their production websites but did not remove them later when the browser implementation had changed. This, in turn, meant that browser vendors have to continue to support experimental features forever to avoid breakages on websites that use them. Because of this, Chrome and Firefox are now backing away from using prefixed properties, preferring instead to implement new features that are disabled, by default, and must be opted into by developers until they are stable enough for widespread use. That said, plenty of prefixed properties are still out there, and I'll note in the book when you must use them.

Let's Get Started

That should be everything you need to get started with this book—except, of course, an inquisitive nature. I have a lot of ground to cover in CSS3, so I'll move fairly quickly, but each chapter should give you the knowledge you need to build your own tests, demonstrations, and sites that take advantage of the flexibility and rich features that CSS3 provides.

We'll begin with a look at one of the simplest—and yet potentially the most disruptive (and I mean that in a good way)—new features: Media Queries.

2

MEDIA QUERIES

Back when the World Wide Web was something you only accessed via a browser on your desktop or laptop, writing CSS was fairly straightforward. Although you had to consider cross-browser and cross-platform issues, at least you knew with reasonable certainty that everyone was using fundamentally similar devices to view your website. Over the last few years, however, we've seen an explosion of new devices for accessing the Web—from game consoles to mobile devices such as smartphones and tablets. Presenting your content to everybody in the same way no longer makes sense when they could be viewing your website on a widescreen desktop monitor or a narrow handheld screen.

CSS has had a way to serve different styles to different media types for quite some time, using the media attribute of the link element:

```
<link href="style.css" rel="stylesheet" media="screen">
```

But this approach has a number of flaws—not least of which is that using it is like wielding a pretty blunt instrument when the screen in question can be between 3.5 inches and 32 inches in size. The list of types is too broad, and many aren't supported by the devices they're aimed at—for example, I don't know of a single web-enabled television that responds to the tv type. Unsurprisingly, given this, the W3C has begun to deprecate the use of media types.

The CSS3 solution to this problem is to use *media queries,* defined in the Media Queries Module (*http://www.w3.org/TR/css3-mediaqueries/*). These queries extend the media types by providing a query syntax that lets you serve far more specific styles to your user's device, giving users a tailored experience. This description may sound quite dry, but this feature is actually one of the most revolutionary in the entire CSS3 specification. Media queries give you the freedom to make websites that are truly device-independent, offering your users the best possible experience no matter how they choose to visit your site.

The Media Queries Module has W3C Recommendation status, so it is considered a standard. The module is already well implemented in all major browsers, including Internet Explorer from version 9.

The Advantages of Media Queries

As a quick demonstration of the power and flexibility of media queries, I'll show an example of how websites can be optimized for mobile browsers without requiring a great deal of extra development.

People visiting your site on a mobile device may well struggle to use it: The text may appear too small, and zooming in means a lot of scrolling to find navigational elements; those navigational elements may involve drop-down functionality that is triggered by hovering over them, an action that often doesn't exist on mobile devices; large images may take a long time to download over a weak data connection and use a substantial portion of a user's monthly bandwidth allowance. Some sites plan for this by providing mobile-friendly versions, but these generally involve a lot of development work. A subdomain has to be set up with style sheets and HTML templates that differ from the parent site; images have to be resized to better fit small screens; and a script has to be created to detect whether a mobile browser is being used and to redirect to the mobile site accordingly. This approach can cause problems: Your script has to be kept up to date with all mobile browser versions, and maintenance often involves duplication to keep both mobile and desktop versions in sync.

Media queries address many of these issues. For a start, they detect devices based on their attributes, so no browser-sniffing scripts are required. They allow you to target style sheets directly for a device's capabilities, so if a device with a small screen is detected, CSS rules will be tailored to that screen size, removing extraneous elements, serving smaller images, and making text clearer.

For example, take a look at the technology website The Next Web (*http://thenextweb.com/*), as shown in Figure 2-1.

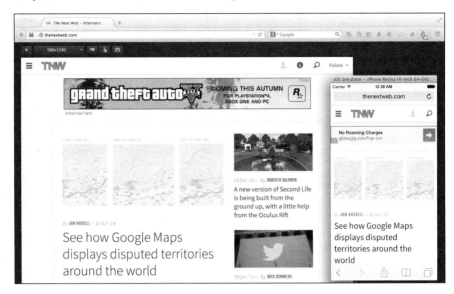

Figure 2-1: The Next Web website viewed in a desktop browser and a mobile browser (inset)

When viewed in a desktop browser, the site features a long horizontal top navigation, related content on the left of the page, and main content laid out in a grid. Through the power of media queries, when you view the same site in a narrower browser—such as an iPhone would use—the navigation is more compact with sharing options hidden away, the related content has been moved off screen, and the main content on the page is moved into a single column, which is ideal for scrolling down.

Of course, the Web now appears on more than just desktop and smartphone devices, and we really need to be working toward the common goal of websites optimized for any device. See "Responsive Web Design" on page 10 for more on this.

And if you want to see what other people have been doing with media queries, you'll find a great gallery online at *http://www.mediaqueri.es/*, which showcases some of the better examples of what's possible.

Syntax

A media query sets a parameter (or series of parameters) that enables associated style rules if the device used to view the page has properties that match that parameter. You can use media queries in three ways, all of which match the different ways that CSS can be applied to a document. The first is to call an external style sheet using the link element:

```
<link href="file" rel="stylesheet" media="logic media and (expression)">
```

RESPONSIVE WEB DESIGN

In 2010, Ethan Marcotte wrote an article titled "Responsive Web Design" (*http://www.alistapart.com/articles/responsive-web-design/*), in which he cleverly consolidated contemporary thinking on making websites that adapt to the devices used to view them through the power of media queries. Here is what he said:

> Now more than ever, we're designing work meant to be viewed along a gradient of different experiences. Responsive web design offers us a way forward, finally allowing us to "design for the ebb and flow of things."

Since then, responsive design has fast become the norm; the majority of developers think this way, and more sites every year are launched or relaunched using responsive design methods. This sort of design is not without its challenges—designing fluid, responsive sites especially has had to be reconsidered, as most design tools are simply not up to the job—but we can safely say we're on the path to creating a Web that can be consumed by anyone, anywhere, in a way that's been carefully considered to work with any device.

The second is to call an external style sheet using the `@import` directive:

```
@import url('file') logic media and (expression);
```

The third is to use media queries in an embedded style element or in the style sheet itself with the extended `@media` rule:

```
@media logic media and (expression) { rules }
```

This method is the one I'll use throughout the rest of this chapter, as it's clearer for demonstration purposes. Which method you use largely depends on your own preference and the demands of your existing stylesheet structure.

Now that I've introduced the declaration methods, let's explore the syntax. You should already be familiar with the `media` attribute—it declares the media types that the styles are applied to, just as in the HTML `link` tag:

```
<link href="style.css" rel="stylesheet" media="screen">
```

The most common media type values are `screen` and `print`, and as with the current syntax, you can use a comma-separated list to choose multiple media queries (although that's becoming less necessary as the other media types become deprecated). If omitted, the media type defaults to all, so if you're writing rules that will apply to all media types you won't need to specify them in the media query constructor; that being the case, these examples are functionally identical:

```
@media all and (expression) { rules }
@media (expression) { rules }
```

NOTE *To make the code examples in the rest of this book more concise, I'll omit the media type where not essential.*

The first new attribute for the @media rule is *logic*. This optional keyword can have the value of either only or not:

```
@media only media and (expression) { rules }
@media not media and (expression) { rules }
```

The only value is mainly useful if you want to hide the rule from older browsers that don't support the syntax; for browsers that do support it, only is effectively ignored. The not value is used to negate the query; you use not to apply the styles if the parameters you set are *not* met.

If you use *logic* or *media* in your query, you also need to use the and operator, as in the previous examples, to combine them with the required *expression* attribute. This attribute is used to set parameters that offer functionality beyond the media type. These parameters are known as *media features*, and they're critical to the power of media queries. That being the case, let's explore them in detail.

Media Features

Media features are information about the device that's being used to display the web page: its dimensions, resolution, and so on. This information is used to evaluate an *expression*, the result of which determines which style rules are applied. That *expression* could be, for example, "apply these styles only on devices that have a screen wider than 480 pixels" or "only on devices that are orientated horizontally."

In media queries, most media feature expressions require that a value be supplied:

```
@media (feature: value) { rules }
```

This value is needed to construct the example expressions I just mentioned. In a few cases, however, you can leave out the value and just test the existence of the media feature itself against the expression:

```
@media (feature) { rules }
```

Expressions will become clearer as I talk through the different media features and explain when values are required or optional.

With the syntax covered, let's meet some of the more prominent media features. The ones I introduce next are the most applicable to color display screens used for accessing the Web and are the ones you're most likely to use on a day-to-day basis. Other media features are available, but you're more likely to use them for alternative devices such as TVs or fixed-grid terminals (if they're supported on those devices at all).

Width and Height

The width media feature describes the width of the rendering viewport of the specified media type, which, in practice, usually means the current width of the browser (including the scroll bar) for desktop operating systems. The basic syntax requires a length value:

```
@media (width: 600px) { rules }
```

In this case, the rules are applied only to browsers that are set to be exactly 600px wide, which is probably far too specific. width also accepts one of two prefixes, max- and min-, which allows you to test for a minimum or maximum width:

```
@media (max-width: 480px) { rules }
@media (min-width: 640px) { rules }
```

The first query applies the rules in browsers that are no wider than 480px, and the second in browsers that are at least 640px wide.

Let's look at a practical example. Here, I'll take advantage of browser window sizes by providing a decorative header for wider windows (some rules have been left out for clarity):

```
@media (min-width: 400px) {
    h1 { background: url('landscape.jpg'); }
}
```

This media query tests for browser viewports that are at least 400px wide and applies a background image to the h1 element when that is the case.

If my browser window is at least 400px wide, I see the image; if I resize it to be narrower, only a text header is shown. You can see this example illustrated in Figure 2-2.

Figure 2-2: Different style rules applied with the width media feature, displayed in a desktop browser and mobile (inset)

The height media feature works in the same way, except it targets browsers based on their height instead of width. The syntax is the same as width and also permits using max- and min- prefixes:

```
@media (height: value) { rules }
@media (max-height: value) { rules }
@media (min-height: value) { rules }
```

Because of the prevalence of vertical scrolling, however, height is used much less frequently than width.

Pixel Ratio

In general, the CSS pixel unit (px) is a measurement of a single pixel on the computer screen—if your browser viewport is 1024 pixels wide and you give an element a width of 1024px, you expect it to fill the horizontal length of the viewport. Many new devices, however, especially smartphones and tablets, have super-high resolution screens, which would make an element with a width of 1024 pixels seem quite small and hard to read when displayed.

To get around this, these newer devices often have a notional CSS pixel, separate from the physical pixels of the device, allowing for zooming in and out of the content and for high graphical fidelity on the small screen. The ratio of physical pixels to CSS pixels is known as the *device pixel ratio (DPR)*. The iPhone 5S, for example, has a DPR of 2, which means that one CSS pixel is equal to 4 physical pixels—2 horizontally and 2 vertically.

You can see this illustrated in Figure 2-3. The example on the left shows one CSS pixel on a "normal" screen with a 1:1 pixel ratio. The example in the middle shows the same CSS pixel on a screen with a DPR of 2, like the iPhone; there are 4 physical pixels in the same space. Finally, the example on the right shows how this would appear on a screen with a DPR of 3, like the Nexus 5; now there are 9 physical pixels in the space of a single CSS pixel.

Figure 2-3: A CSS pixel with a 1:1 pixel ratio (left), a DPR of 2 (middle), and 3 (right)

What that means in practice is that, although the iPhone 5S (for example) has a physical resolution of 640×1136, it has a CSS resolution of 320×568—exactly half the dimensions, as every CSS pixel is equivalent to two physical pixels, both horizontally and vertically (although only when the device is in "mobile mode"; see "Device Width and Height" on page 15 for an explanation of this).

Although this high DPR makes scalable content—such as text and vector graphics—sharp and clear, bitmap images can suffer badly from a loss of quality when viewed on high resolution screens. To get around this problem, a new media feature, called resolution, is available that lets you target devices based on their DPR:

```
@media media and (resolution: value) { rules }
```

The value of resolution is a number with a unit of resolution: *dots per inch (DPI)*, *dots per centimeter (DPCM)*, or, most pertinently to us, *dots per pixel (DPPX)*. The DPPX unit maps to the DPR of the device, so to apply a rule to devices that have a DPR value of 1.5, you use this:

```
@media (resolution: 1.5dppx) { rules }
```

As with the other media features, you can also detect maximum and minimum pixel ratios:

```
@media (max-resolution: number) { rules }
@media (min-resolution: number) { rules }
```

This flexibility makes serving higher-resolution background images to browsers with higher pixel density easier, as you can see in this code:

```
❶ E { background-image: url('image-lores.png'); }
❷ @media (min-resolution: 1.5dppx) {
       background-image: url('image-hires.png');
❸      background-size: 100% 100%;
  }
```

The first rule (❶) means browsers on devices with a "standard" (or low-resolution) pixel ratio will use the standard image (*image-lores.png*), whereas devices with a DPR of at least 1.5 will use the high-resolution image (*image-hires.png*) instead (❷). Note the use of the unfamiliar background-size property here (❸); this property should be used with high-resolution images to ensure they aren't displayed larger than the element they are applied to (I introduce background-size fully in Chapter 8).

Chrome, Firefox, and Internet Explorer 10+ all support the resolution media feature, although IE unfortunately hasn't implemented the DPPX value; to accommodate IE, you should use DPI, multiplying the required DPR by 96 (the DPI value of a standard screen). Here's an example:

```
@media (resolution: 1.5dppx), (resolution: 144dpi) { rules }
```

Safari doesn't support resolution, instead using a proprietary media feature called -webkit-device-pixel-ratio (along with max- and min- variants), which takes as a value a single, unitless number that is the targeted DPR. So to accommodate all modern browsers, use this rule:

```
@media (resolution: 1.5dppx), (resolution: 144dpi), (-webkit-device-pixel-ratio: 2) { rules }
```

The resolution rule was implemented in the WebKit engine at the end of 2012, so I'm disappointed to not see it released in Safari at the time of writing, almost two years later. Hopefully this oversight will be rectified in the near future.

Device Width and Height

The width and height media features are related to the dimensions of the browser viewport, but that viewport isn't always as big as the screen it's displayed on. If you need to target the physical screen size rather than the viewport size, you can use the device-width and device-height properties and their related min- and max- variants. You won't use these too often, but to explain why, I need to digress.

In the previous section, I explained the difference between CSS pixels and physical pixels. The width media feature is measured in CSS pixels, and `device-width`, in physical pixels. To make content readable and "natural sized" on a small screen, both dimensions need to match. You do this by adding the *viewport meta tag* into the head of the document, like this:

```
<meta name="viewport" content="width=device-width">
```

When the viewport meta tag with these values is present in the head of a page, mobile browsers go into "mobile mode," in which the viewport is sized to ideal dimensions for that device. The result is that content is displayed at a more appropriate size for the device.

NOTE   *For a more in-depth explanation of mobile viewports and pixels, see Dutch developer PPK's "A Pixel Is Not a Pixel Is Not a Pixel"* (http://www.quirksmode.org/blog/archives/2010/04/a_pixel_is_not.html).

The viewport of a browser on a mobile device tends to be as large as the screen itself, so the two are basically equivalent; and on desktop browsers, you will most likely want to make your content relative to the width of the viewport rather than that of the screen. For these reasons, the `device-width` media feature becomes less useful than `width`, and you probably won't use it too much in practice.

The viewport meta tag is being standardized in CSS as the `@viewport` rule; see "Device Adaptation" on page 252 for a brief walkthrough.

Orientation

If you're less concerned with the actual dimensions of the viewing device but want to optimize your pages for either horizontal (like a typical desktop/laptop web browser) or vertical (like a mobile phone or ebook reader) viewing, the media feature you need is `orientation`. Here is its syntax:

```
@media (orientation: value) { rules }
```

value can be one of two keyword options: `landscape` or `portrait`. The `landscape` value applies when the width of your browser is greater than its height, and the `portrait` value applies when the opposite is true. Although `orientation` can certainly be applied to desktop browsers, you'll find it most useful when dealing with handheld devices that the user can easily rotate, such as smartphones and tablets.

For example, you can use `orientation` to display a navigation menu horizontally or vertically, depending on the visitor's browser orientation. The code looks like this:

```
ul { overflow: hidden; }
li { float: left; }
@media (orientation: portrait) {
  li { float: none; }
}
```

By default, the `li` elements have a float value of `left`, making them stack horizontally across the page. If the same page is viewed in a `portrait` orientation—either by resizing the browser to be taller than it is wide or by viewing the page in a device with a portrait orientation—the float is removed and the `li` elements stack vertically instead. You can see the result in Figure 2-4.

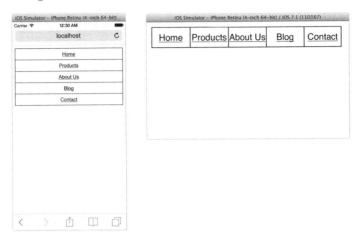

Figure 2-4: The orientation media feature in use on a mobile browser: portrait (left) and landscape (right)

As only two values are possible for the `orientation` feature, if you apply differentiating rules using one value, then the other tacitly becomes the opposite. In this example, I only used the `portrait` value, so, by default, all of the rules outside of that function apply to the `landscape` orientation.

Aspect Ratio

You can also create queries that apply when a certain width-to-height ratio is met. Use `aspect-ratio` to test the browser's aspect ratio or `device-aspect-ratio` to test the device's aspect ratio. Here is the syntax for these two features:

```
@media (aspect-ratio: horizontal/vertical) { rules }
@media (device-aspect-ratio: horizontal/vertical) { rules }
```

The *horizontal* and *vertical* values are positive integers that represent the ratio of the width and height (respectively) of the viewing device's screen, so a square display would be 1/1 and a cinematic widescreen display would be 16/9.

NOTE   *Some devices—notably the iPhone—always report the aspect ratio of the device in portrait orientation, even when being viewed in landscape.*

Selecting by aspect ratio is potentially fraught with caveats. For example, some device manufacturers define widescreen as 16/9, some as 16/10, and others as 15/10. And a device may not have the exact stated aspect ratio; the iPhone 5S, for example, claims to have a 16/9 aspect ratio but actually reports as having the slightly larger 40/71 ratio (the portrait orientation). Using the max- and min- variations of aspect-ratio and device-aspect-ratio to apply the rules may be preferable. Consider this code in which the rules in the query are applied to any element that has an aspect ratio of greater than 16/9:

```
@media (min-device-aspect-ratio: 16/9) {...}
```

Multiple Media Features

You can chain multiple queries together on the same media type by adding expressions with the and operator:

```
@media logic media and (expression) and (expression) { rules }
```

This syntax tests that both expressions are matched before applying the selected rules. For example, to test for a narrow screen on a device with an aspect ratio no greater than 15/10, you use this query:

```
@media (max-device-aspect-ratio: 15/10) and (max-width: 800px) {...}
```

You can also use a conditional "or" expression by adding extra queries in a comma-separated list:

```
@media logic media and (expression), logic media and (expression) { rules }
```

This applies rules when any of the stated cases is true; in the following example, the rules are applied to a screen in landscape orientation or to a printed document in portrait orientation:

```
@media screen and (orientation: landscape), print and (orientation: portrait) {...}
```

You can also, of course, create any combination of these syntaxes.

Mobile-First Web Development

The common best-practice method of building websites today uses a method known as *mobile-first development*, where we start developing for smaller screens before adding larger assets and more complexity for users accessing the site on larger devices.

The reason this method was adopted is because of the way that some browsers load page assets, such as images, that are included in style sheets.

Problems arose because some early adopters of media queries would, for example, apply large background images to elements and then write rules to hide them from mobile devices:

```
E { background-image: url('huge-image.jpg'); }
@media (max-width: 600px) {
    E { display: none; }
}
```

But those background images, despite being hidden, were still downloaded by the browser and held in the cache even though they weren't displayed. This method increases the page's load time and consumes bandwidth allowances—neither of which is good for mobile device users without wireless connections.

The mobile-first way to create your pages is to first make a basic style sheet, which is applied to all browsers, including mobile, and to then progressively add assets and features for users with larger screens, loaded using a media query with the min-width feature:

```
@media (min-width: 600px) {
    E { background-image: url('huge-image.jpg'); }
}
```

This change means the background image in question never gets loaded on devices with smaller screens. This approach can be extrapolated to loading entire style sheets:

```
<link href="basic.css" rel="stylesheet">
<link href="desktop.css" rel="stylesheet" media="(min-width: 600px)">
```

When the style sheets are separated in this way, some browsers will optimize the way the style sheets are loaded; in Chrome, for example, as the file *desktop.css* doesn't apply to devices with a screen width of less than 600px, its loading is delayed until after more high-priority assets have been downloaded—a quite useful optimization.

This mobile-first approach works for the great majority of browsers from the past few years; any really old browsers will get the basic style sheet instead, which is probably better for them as they won't be able to cope with the advanced features I'll be teaching you throughout the rest of this book.

Summary

Their syntax may be simple, but media queries have the capacity to be extraordinarily powerful. With the mobile web explosion of recent years, designers and developers are beginning to realize they have the power to tailor their content to the user without employing the old techniques of browser sniffing or separate (and completely different) mobile versions of their sites.

The rise of the responsive web design movement in the past few years has been fueled by the power of media queries, and in just a short space of time, they've become one of the most powerful tools at a web developer's disposal. With careful consideration and clever use of media queries, you can create websites that scale perfectly for users, however they access the Web.

Media Queries: Browser Support

	Chrome	Firefox	Safari	IE
Media queries	Yes	Yes	Yes	Yes

3

SELECTORS

Selectors are the heart of CSS, and although the original CSS1 specification had only 5 or 6, CSS2 expanded the range with 12 more. CSS3 goes further still, roughly doubling the number of available selectors.

Selectors can be broadly separated into two categories. The first are those that act directly on elements defined in the document tree (p elements and href attributes, for example); this category contains *class*, *type*, and *attribute* selectors. For the sake of expediency, I'll group these together under the banner of *DOM selectors*. The second category contains *pseudo-selectors* that act on elements or information that sits outside of the document tree (such as the first letter of a paragraph or the last child of a parent element). I cover pseudo-selectors in Chapter 4—here I discuss DOM selectors.

CSS3 provides three new attribute selectors and one new *combinator*— that is, a selector that joins other selectors together, such as the child combinator (>) from CSS2. These are defined in the Selectors Level 3 Module (*http://www.w3.org/TR/css3-selectors/*), which is a *W3C Recommendation* and has widespread and stable implementation across browsers. Unless you specifically need to support IE6, you can start using these CSS3 selectors right away—many sites already do.

Attribute Selectors

Attribute selectors were introduced in CSS2, and, as you may expect from the name, they allow you to specify rules that match elements based on their attributes—such as href or title—and the values of those attributes. The four selectors defined in CSS2 are:

```
E[attr] {...} /* Simple Attribute Selector */
E[attr='value'] {...} /* Exact Attribute Value Selector */
E[attr~='value'] {...} /* Partial Attribute Value Selector */
E[attr|='value'] {...} /* Language Attribute Selector */
```

Before moving on to the new selectors in CSS3, a quick recap of how each selector is utilized is worthwhile. For this, I'll use the following markup, which is a (very short) contact list:

```
<ul>
❶ <li><a href="" lang="en-GB" rel="friend met">Peter</a></li>
❷ <li><a href="" lang="es-ES" rel="friend">Pedro</a></li>
❸ <li><a href="" lang="es-MX" rel="contact">Pancho</a></li>
</ul>
```

The *Simple Attribute Selector* applies rules to elements that have the specified attribute defined, regardless of that attribute's value. So given the following code:

```
a[rel] { color: red; }
```

all of the a elements in my markup have a rel attribute, despite their having different values. In this case, therefore, all elements have the rule applied. If you want to be more specific, you can use the *Exact Attribute Value Selector* to define a value:

```
a[rel='friend'] { color: red; }
```

This code applies the rule only to the second a element in the markup (❷) because it selects only elements that have the exact value of friend. If you want to select both of the elements that have this value, you would use the *Partial Attribute Value Selector*:

```
a[rel~='friend'] { color: red; }
```

This code looks for the value of friend as part of a space-separated list (in most cases, a word) in any rel attribute and so applies the rule to elements ❶ and ❷.

The final selector, the *Language Attribute Selector*, applies rules to elements that have an attribute matching the first argument in the selector, the value of which is the second argument in the selector followed immediately by a hyphen. If that sounds weirdly specific, it's because this selector is really only intended to match language subcodes. The example markup has two Spanish names, each of which has a lang attribute beginning with es- although one is for Spain (es-ES) and the other is for Mexico (es-MX). To select both of these, you use this code:

```
a[lang|='es'] { color: red; }
```

This selects all elements with lang attributes whose value begins with *es*, regardless of their country values—that is, elements ❷ and ❸. You could use this selector for any attributes with hyphen-separated values, but in the great majority of cases, those will be language codes.

NOTE   *The attribute names used here aren't taken from the spec but from Eric Meyer's book* CSS Pocket Reference *(O'Reilly Media, 2011).*

New Attribute Selectors in CSS3

You've seen how useful attribute selectors can be for finding exact or partial values, but what if you want even more flexibility? CSS3's new selectors provide flexibility with the power to match substrings within an attribute value. This feature makes them especially great for applying rules to XML documents, which can often have more varied attribute values than HTML—though they are still quite useful for HTML developers as well.

Beginning Substring Attribute Value Selector

The first new attribute selector—which, to avoid having to repeat that mouthful of a title, I'll refer to as the *Beginning Selector*—finds elements whose chosen attribute begins with the string supplied to it as an argument. It uses the caret (^) symbol to modify the equals sign in the selector. Here's the full syntax:

```
E[attr^='value'] {...}
```

This code looks for the supplied value at the beginning of the specified attribute. To illustrate, consider the following example markup, showing a list of three items, each of which contains a hyperlink with different (albeit similar) values for the title attribute:

```
<li><a href="http://example.com/" title="Image Library">Example</a></li>
<li><a href="http://example.com/" title="Free Image Library">Example</a></li>
<li><a href="http://example.com/" title="Free Sound Library">Example</a></li>
```

I'll apply this selector to the example markup:

```
a[title^='image'] {...}
```

In this case, the rule will be applied to the a element in the first list item because the title attribute string begins with the word *image*. The rule will not be applied to the a element in the second item, however, because, although its title attribute contains that string, it doesn't begin with it. Nor will it be applied to the third string, as that string doesn't match.

In HTML documents, the attribute selector value is case insensitive; for XML documents, however, the value is case sensitive.

The Beginning Selector is especially handy when you want to add visual information to hyperlinks. Here's an example of a typical hyperlink to an external website:

```
<p>This is a <a href="http://example.com/">hyperlink</a>.</p>
```

When you see this link in your browser, you can't immediately tell whether it's a link to a page on the same website or to an external URI. With this new attribute, however, you can pass the protocol (*http*) as the argument and add an icon to signify external links clearly:

```
a[href^='http'] {
    background: url('link.svg') no-repeat left center;
    display: inline-block;
    padding-left: 20px;
}
```

The result is shown in Figure 3-1.

Figure 3-1: An icon applied with the Beginning Selector

You can extend this to cover many other web protocols, some of which—*mailto, ftp,* and *https*—are shown in the following example and illustrated in Figure 3-2.

```
a[href^='mailto'] { background-image: url('email.svg'); }
a[href^='ftp'] { background-image: url('folder.svg'); }
a[href^='https'] { background-image: url('lock.svg'); }
```

Figure 3-2: More examples of link icons with the Beginning Selector

Of course, the Beginning Selector also has many applications with attributes—such as alt, cite, and title—that accept more verbose values. And with the introduction of HTML5 and a whole range of new form elements and attributes, this selector and its soon-to-be-introduced siblings will become even more useful.

Consider, for example, the proposed datetime attribute, which accepts date-string values such as 2015-03-14:

```
<time datetime="2015-03-14">March 14/time>
```

This means that you could use the Beginning Selector to apply styles to all elements meeting a supplied year value, which is quite handy for calendar or archiving applications:

```
[datetime^='2015'] {...}
```

Ending Substring Attribute Value Selector

The *Ending Selector*, as I call it, works exactly like the Beginning Selector—just the other way around! That is, you use it to select attributes that *end* with the supplied value. The syntax differs by just one character: This time you use the dollar sign character ($) to modify the equal sign (=). Here's the full syntax:

```
E[attr$='value'] {...}
```

Let's look at the markup example from the previous section again, only this time apply the Ending Selector along with a new value:

```
a[title$='library'] {...}
```

This time the rule applies to all of the list items, as all of their title attribute values end with the string library.

Just like the Beginning Selector, you can use this selector to provide visual clarity to hyperlinks. But this time, instead of using the protocols at the beginning of the href attribute, you use the file types at the end. The code here shows rules for many popular file-type extensions:

```
a[href$='.pdf'] { background-image: url('pdf.svg'); }
a[href$='.doc'] { background-image: url('word.svg'); }
a[href$='.rss'] { background-image: url('feed.svg'); }
```

Figure 3-3 shows examples of these rules applied.

Figure 3-3: Link icons applied with the Ending Selector

To achieve this effect using CSS2, you would have to apply set class values to the markup (class="pdf", for example). The advantage of using the Ending Selector is that links to files can be detected automatically, without requiring you to apply a particular class. The disadvantage is that sometimes the file-type suffix is not at the end of the URI. But the next new selector helps get around that situation.

Arbitrary Substring Attribute Value Selector

The final new attribute selector—which I call the *Arbitrary Selector*—works in the same way as the previous two, but it searches for the provided substring value *anywhere* inside the specified attribute string. This selector uses the asterisk (*) character. Here's the new syntax:

```
E[attr*='value'] {...}
```

To demonstrate this selector, I'll once again use the same markup that I used for the Beginning and Ending Selectors, only this time applying the Arbitrary Selector:

```
a[title*='image'] {...}
```

This rule is applied to the first and second list items because they both contain the text string image in their title attributes, even though the string appears in a different position in each example.

You may notice that this selector is somewhat similar to the Partial Attribute Value Selector from CSS2, and, indeed, in this example, they are interchangeable:

```
a[title~='image'] {...}
```

But the two selectors differ in a major way. In the example markup, with CSS3, you could match this element using just a substring:

```
a[title*='im'] {...}
```

The Partial Attribute Value Selector, however, requires that you enter a value that matches a full item in a space-separated list—in the example that would be either free, image, or library—so the im value would not be matched anywhere in the markup when using the CSS2 selector.

To continue with the examples provided for the first two attribute selectors, the Arbitrary Selector is also handy for adding file-type icons to URIs that have parameters at the end. Consider this fairly typical URI:

```
<a href="http://example.com/example.pdf?foo=bar">Example</a>
```

If you use the Ending Selector with a value of pdf, this element would not be recognized as a valid target, even though the file type is a PDF, because the value does not appear at the very end of the string. Providing the same value using the Arbitrary Selector does the trick, however; the .pdf substring value occurs within the specified attribute, so the icon is applied.

```
a[href*='.pdf'] { background-image: url('pdf.svg'); }
```

This selector is the most flexible of the three new attribute selectors as it can match substrings no matter where they appear within strings. But this extra flexibility means you must take more care when defining the values provided to the selector; simple combinations of letters are far more likely to occur when you can match anywhere within a string—which is the reason I used it to search for .pdf (the file extension) rather than pdf (the common abbreviation).

Multiple Attribute Selectors

You can also chain multiple selectors together, which allows you to be really specific. Using multiple selectors, you can create rules to apply to attributes with values defined for the start, end, and anywhere in between. Imagine, for example, that you had links to two files with identical names but that were located in different folders:

```
<p><a href="http://example.com/folder1/file.pdf">Example</a></p>
<p><a href="http://example.com/folder2/file.pdf">Example</a></p>
```

If you want to specify a rule to apply to only the second p element, you can chain some selectors together:

```
a[href^='http://'][href*='/folder2/'][href$='.pdf'] {...}
```

This code looks for a elements that have an href attribute beginning with http://, ending with .pdf, and with /folder2/ contained within it. That's specific!

The General Sibling Combinator

Our final new DOM selector in CSS3 is a combinator, which you'll recall means that it joins together more than one selector. The General Sibling Combinator is an extension of the Adjacent Sibling Combinator, which was introduced in CSS2. The syntaxes differ by just a single character:

```
E + F {...} /* Adjacent Sibling Combinator */
E ~ F {...} /* General Sibling Combinator */
```

The difference between the two is subtle but important: Adjacent Sibling selects any element (F) that is immediately preceded by element (E) on the same level of the document tree, but General Sibling selects any element (F) that is preceded by element (E) on the same level of the tree, regardless of whether it is immediately adjacent.

If that still sounds confusing, I'll explain with an example. Let's start with this CSS:

```
h2 + p { font-weight: bolder; } /* Adjacent Sibling */
h2 ~ p { font-style: italic; } /* General Sibling */
```

And apply it to the following markup (truncated for clarity):

```
❶ <p>Next we're going to discuss...</p>
  <h2>Ren&eacute; Descartes</h2>
❷ <p>A highly influential French philosopher...</p>
❸ <p>He once famously declared:</p>
  <blockquote>
❹    <p>I think, therefore I am.</p>
  </blockquote>
❺ <p>However, this presumes the existence of the thinker.</p>
```

You can see the outcome in Figure 3-4. In the CSS, I'm using the Adjacent Sibling Combinator to bold the p element immediately adjacent to the h2 element—that is, element ❷. I'm also using the General Sibling Combinator to italicize all the p elements following the h2 element, which applies to elements ❷, ❸, and ❺.

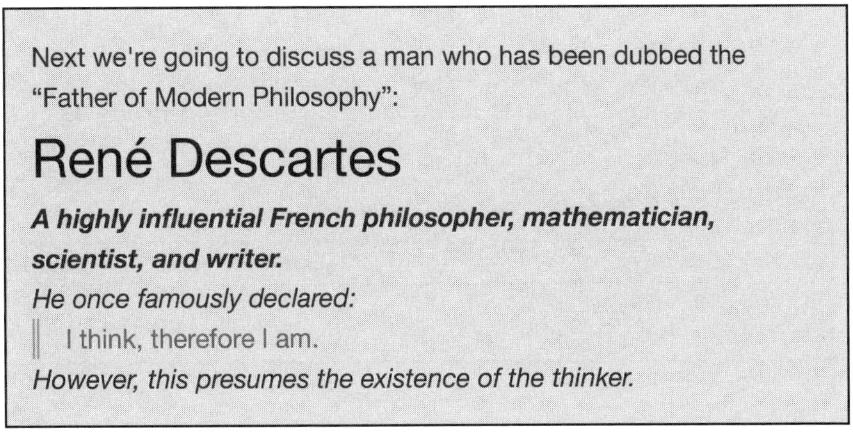

Next we're going to discuss a man who has been dubbed the "Father of Modern Philosophy":

René Descartes

A highly influential French philosopher, mathematician, scientist, and writer.

He once famously declared:

> I think, therefore I am.

However, this presumes the existence of the thinker.

Figure 3-4: The difference between the Adjacent Sibling and General Sibling Combinators

The paragraph elements ❶ and ❹ have neither bold nor italic rules applied to them. Why not? Because element ❶ precedes the h2, and element ❹ is inside a blockquote and, therefore, on a different level (the level below) in the document tree, so neither is affected by the rules.

To achieve the desired effect of only italicizing the paragraphs on the same level as the h2 element in CSS2, without the General Sibling Combinator, you would need to set all p elements to display in italic and then add an extra rule for the p inside the blockquote to overrule the inheritance:

```
p { font-style: italic; }
blockquote p { font-style: normal; }
```

You probably won't need to use the General Sibling Combinator often because much of its function overlaps with the basic DOM selectors. That said, you will still discover plenty of occasions where this combinator can save you a little bit of code (and time).

Summary

Although attributes are a key feature of HTML4, most of them accept only a limited range of values, so many of them do not really require the attribute selectors I've introduced in this chapter. Aside from the href attribute, only a handful of attributes accept more verbose values (alt, class, id, rel, and title are the ones that spring to mind). But, as I mentioned before, HTML5 introduces attributes like datetime and pubdate that allow you to be more creative with selectors.

The new selectors introduced in this chapter, along with those from previous versions of CSS, provide ways to apply style rules based on defined elements and attributes. Of course, on occasion, styling elements and attributes only isn't sufficient for your purposes. That's when you need to add classes or nonsemantic elements to act as hooks to hang your styles on. In Chapter 4, you'll discover how CSS3 removes that need.

Selectors: Browser Support

	Chrome	Firefox	Safari	IE
New attribute selectors	Yes	Yes	Yes	Yes
General sibling combinator	Yes	Yes	Yes	Yes

4

PSEUDO-CLASSES AND PSEUDO-ELEMENTS

The very first CSS specification, CSS1, introduced the concepts of *pseudo-classes* and *pseudo-elements*. These are selectors that act on information about elements that extends (or sits outside of) the document tree. A pseudo-class differentiates among an element's different states or types; these include—but are not limited to—those that provide information about link states: `:hover`, `:visited`, `:active`, and so on. A pseudo-element provides access to an element's subpart, which includes those pseudo-elements that select portions of text nodes; for instance, `:first-line` and `:first-letter`.

The selectors just mentioned have been around since the first CSS specification, but a handful more were added in CSS2.1—although pseudo-element support has not been well implemented until relatively recently. CSS3 builds on these foundations with an expanded range of pseudo-classes, as well as a (slightly) tweaked syntax to differentiate pseudo-elements.

The advantage of having more methods for traversing documents should be clear: Fewer styling hooks are required. You are most likely familiar with markup like this:

```
<ul>
    <li class="❶first ❷odd">❸<span>L</span>orem ipsum</li>
    <li>Lorem ipsum</li>
    <li class="odd">Lorem ipsum</li>
    <li class="❹last">Lorem ipsum</li>
</ul>
```

The markup contains class names to describe each element's position in the document tree: first (❶) and last (❹) show that the li elements are the first and last children of the ul element, and odd (❷) is used for the odd-numbered li elements. An extra span (❸) is included around the first letter of the initial li element.

You mark up code like this when you want to add styles to alternating elements, set different values on the first and last elements, or add special formatting to the first letter of a text node. This markup detracts from the clarity and semantic meaning of your code, but in many cases you need it to provide the hooks to hang your styles on.

CSS3's new methods allow you to achieve the same visual results without muddying the markup with unnecessary classes and nonsemantic elements, making for cleaner and more maintainable code:

```
<ul>
    <li>Lorem ipsum</li>
    <li>Lorem ipsum</li>
    <li>Lorem ipsum</li>
    <li>Lorem ipsum</li>
</ul>
```

The other major advantage of the new selectors is that if new elements are added to the markup, class names don't have to be updated to accommodate them while still keeping order. This change takes CSS a big step closer to achieving its stated goal: the separation of content and presentation.

Structural Pseudo-classes

As I stated in the introduction to this chapter, a pseudo-class provides a way to select an element based on information that is not specified in the document tree. Various subtypes are available, the most common of which is the *structural pseudo-class*. These subtypes are used to select elements that are not accessible using simple selectors.

Take, for example, the following markup:

```
<div>
    <p>Lorem ipsum.</p>
    <p>Dolor sit amet.</p>
</div>
```

The first of the two p elements is the first child of the div element. That's obvious from the document tree, but the document tree doesn't provide any information that would allow you to apply a rule only to that element. CSS2 introduced the :first-child pseudo-class for exactly that reason:

```
E:first-child {...}
```

This pseudo-class allows you to make a selection based on information that exists but isn't provided as an attribute of the element—the exact purpose of a pseudo-class. Since :first-child was introduced in CSS2, it has been the only pseudo-class of its type. But CSS3 extends the range greatly with the introduction of 11 new structural pseudo-classes.

The :nth-* Pseudo-classes

Four of the new pseudo-classes are based on a count value used to find an element's position in the document tree; for this count, you use the syntax :nth-*. Note that I've used the asterisk here in place of a number of different values, each of which I'll introduce throughout the rest of this chapter.

The basic syntax of the :nth-* pseudo-classes is quite straightforward. By default, n represents a number that begins at 0 and increments by 1 (1, 2, 3, etc.). Another integer can be passed into it as a multiplier. For example, 2n is every multiple of 2 (2, 4, 6, etc.), 3n is every multiple of 3 (3, 6, 9, etc.), and so on:

```
E:nth-*(n) {...}
E:nth-*(2n) {...}
E:nth-*(3n) {...}
```

The first example uses the default value n, so all elements of type E would be selected; in practice, this is the same as using a simple element selector. The next example selects every other E element, and the final example selects every third element of type E.

You may also use the mathematical operators for plus (+) and minus (−). So 2n+1 selects every multiple of two plus one (1, 3, 5, etc.), and 3n-1 selects every multiple of three minus one (2, 5, 8, etc.):

```
E:nth-*(n+1) {...}
E:nth-*(2n+1) {...}
E:nth-*(3n-1) {...}
```

The first example selects every element of type *E* except for the first instance; the count for this would be 2, 3, 4, 5, and so on. The next example selects every odd-numbered *E* element (1, 3, 5, and so on). The final example, as just mentioned, selects elements in the sequence 2, 5, 8, and so on.

Two special keyword values, even and odd, are also available; you can use these to replace 2n and 2n+1, respectively:

```
E:nth-*(even) {...}
E:nth-*(odd) {...}
```

Finally, it's also acceptable to use 0n (that's zero) as a value. It has no use of itself but is very useful when combined with a mathematical operator, as it allows you to pinpoint a single element without any recurrence. In fact, for brevity, you can supply only the value after the mathematical operator. For example, to select only the third element in a selector list, both of these values are valid:

```
E:nth-*(0n+3) {...}
E:nth-*(3) {...}
```

With the basic syntax out of the way, let's move on to the pseudo-classes themselves.

:nth-child() and :nth-of-type()

Most of the new structural pseudo-classes allow you to select elements based on either their position in the document tree in relation to their parent element (-child) or their classification (-of-type). Often these definitions overlap, but there are crucial differences between them.

The simplest examples of these pseudo-classes are :nth-child() and :nth-of-type(). The first, :nth-child(), selects an element based on its position in a count of the total number of children in its parent element; :nth-of-type() bases its count not on the total children, but only on those of the specified element type.

```
❶ E:nth-child(n) {...}
❷ E:nth-of-type(n) {...}
❸ E:nth-child(2n) {...}
❹ E:nth-of-type(2n) {...}
```

In this example, rules ❶ and ❷ are equivalent because the count value (n) is left at the default; both of these simply select all child elements of type *E*. The difference reveals itself in the later examples: in ❸, :nth-child(2n) selects all elements of type *E* from a count that includes all its siblings but only where those elements are even-numbered. In ❹, by comparison, :nth-of-type(2n) selects all even-numbered elements of type *E* from a count that includes only those elements.

These rules are much easier to demonstrate than they are to explain. I'll demonstrate the difference between them with the following example (text has been truncated for clarity):

```
<div>
    <h2>The Picture of Dorian Gray</h2>
    <p>The artist is the creator...</p>
    <p>To reveal art and conceal the artist...</p>
    <p>The critic is he who can translate...</p>
</div>
```

And in my style sheet I'll use these two rules:

```
❶ p:nth-child(2n) { font-weight: bolder ; }
❷ p:nth-of-type(2n) { font-weight: bolder; }
```

You can see the differing result of the two rules in Figure 4-1. In the example markup, the div element has a total of four child elements: one h2 and three p. The :nth-child(2n) selector in rule ❶ makes bold every second child (the first and third paragraphs), as seen in the box on the left. Compare that to the box on the right, which has rule ❷ applied; the :nth-of-type(2n) selector ignores the h2 and applies a bold weight to every second instance of the three elements of type p—that is, only the second paragraph.

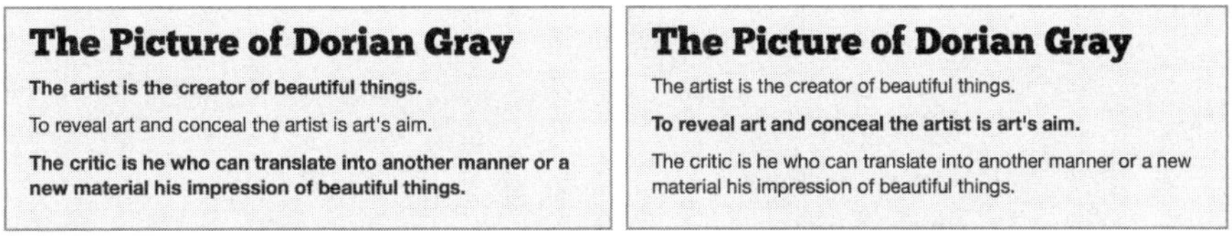

Figure 4-1: Comparing the result of using the :nth-child() selector (left) with :nth-of-type() (right)

As I mentioned before, and as you can no doubt deduce from the previous examples, :nth-child() and :nth-of-type() have a fair bit of overlap, and you can often use them interchangeably, as I do in the following example.

The table on the left of Figure 4-2 shows the five-day weather forecast for London (so temperatures are given in degrees Celsius—0°C equals 32°F). These figures were taken in January—it's not *always* this cold here! All of the information I want to convey is in the table, but without any definition of rows, I find the table difficult to read.

Now compare this table to the one on the right in the same Figure 4-2. Here, I used the technique known as *zebra striping* to aid the eye along the row, making the data much more readable to me.

Day	Weather	Max. Day (°C)	Min. Night (°C)	Wind (mph)
Sun	Sunny	8	4	8
Mon	Grey Cloud	7	4	6
Tue	Grey Cloud	5	2	13
Wed	Sleet	2	1	8
Thu	Heavy Rain	4	2	7

Day	Weather	Max. Day (°C)	Min. Night (°C)	Wind (mph)
Sun	Sunny	8	4	8
Mon	Grey Cloud	7	4	6
Tue	Grey Cloud	5	2	13
Wed	Sleet	2	1	8
Thu	Heavy Rain	4	2	7

Figure 4-2: Weather forecast table (left) and better formatted for readability (right). Weather data from http://bbc.co.uk/weather/

I achieved this technique with a single CSS3 declaration:

```
tbody tr:nth-of-type(even) { background-color: #DDD; }
```

In this example, I could have used :nth-child() instead, as in the markup all of the child elements of tbody are of the same type: tr. Where every child is of the same type, :nth-child() and :nth-of-type() are interchangeable.

:nth-last-child() and :nth-last-of-type()

The :nth-last-child() and :nth-last-of-type() pseudo-classes accept the same arguments as :nth-child() and :nth-of-type(), except they are counted from the last element, working in reverse. For example, say I want to use some visual shorthand to show in my weather table that the forecasts for days four and five are less certain than for the preceding days. You can see how this would look in Figure 4-3.

Day	Weather	Max. Day (°C)	Min. Night (°C)	Wind (mph)
Sun	Sunny	8	4	8
Mon	Grey Cloud	7	4	6
Tue	Grey Cloud	5	2	13
Wed	*Sleet*	*2*	*1*	*8*
Thu	*Heavy Rain*	*4*	*2*	*7*

Figure 4-3: Extra formatting using :nth-last-child()

Here I italicized the characters in the last two rows by using the :nth-last-child() pseudo-class (although, once again, :nth-last-of-type() would serve just as well in this example), passing an argument of -n+2:

```
tbody tr:nth-last-child(-n+2) { font-style: italic; }
```

I used the negative value (-n) to increment the count negatively, which has the effect of acting in reverse. Because :nth-last-child() and :nth-last-of-type() count backward through the tree, using a negative value here makes the count go forward! The count starts at the last tr element in the table and counts up in reverse order, so the last and penultimate lines are the first two counted and are, therefore, italicized. This may seem counter-intuitive, but it'll become second nature as you traverse the document tree.

:first-of-type, :last-child, and :last-of-type

If you take a look at the tables in Figure 4-2, you'll notice that the text in the Weather column is left-aligned, whereas the other columns are center-aligned. I did this using the :first-of-type pseudo-class, which is similar to the :first-child selector introduced in CSS2, but with the same difference in type and child that you've seen so far in this chapter.

As you're no doubt aware, the :first-child pseudo-class is a selector used to apply rules to an element that is the first child of its parent. As with :nth-of-type(), however, :first-of-type is more specific, applying only to the element that is the first child of the named type of its parent. A pair of counterpart pseudo-classes is also available, :last-child and :last-of-type, which—as you might have guessed—select the last child element or the last child element of that type, respectively, of the parent.

In the weather table examples in the previous section, the markup for each row in the table body is structured like this:

```
<tr>
    <th>Sun</th>
    <td>Sunny</td>
    <td>8</td>
    <td>4</td>
    <td>8</td>
</tr>
```

I want to left-align the content of the second column, so I can't use :first-child here as the first child is a th. Instead, I use the :first-of-type selector:

```
tbody td:first-of-type { text-align: left; }
```

I'll show two more examples to demonstrate the difference clearly. I'll apply both of the examples to the same chunk of markup (I've truncated the text for clarity):

```
<div>
    <h2>Wuthering Heights</h2>
    <p>I have just returned...</p>
    <p>This is certainly...</p>
    <p>In all England...</p>
    <h3>By Emily Bronte</h3>
</div>
```

In the first example, I use :first-child and :last-child, as shown here:

```
:first-child { text-decoration: underline; }
:last-child { font-style: italic; }
```

The result is shown in Figure 4-4. The h2 element is the first child of the div, so it has an underline applied to it. The last child of the div is the h3 element, so that is italicized. All quite straightforward.

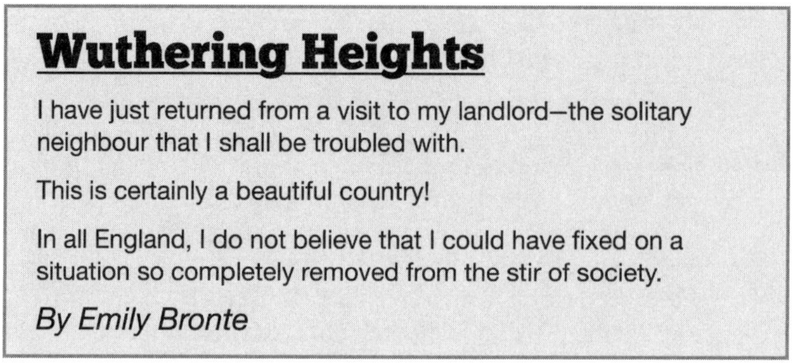

Wuthering Heights

I have just returned from a visit to my landlord—the solitary neighbour that I shall be troubled with.

This is certainly a beautiful country!

In all England, I do not believe that I could have fixed on a situation so completely removed from the stir of society.

By Emily Bronte

Figure 4-4: Applying the `:first-child` and `:last-child` selectors

Now let's see the difference when we use the `:first-of-type` and `:last-of-type` selectors:

```
:first-of-type { text-decoration: underline; }
:last-of-type { font-style: italic; }
```

Take a look at the result in Figure 4-5. You'll notice that three elements—h2, h3, and the first p—are underlined. This is because they are the first instance of that element type. Likewise, the h2, h3, and last p are all italicized. Again, this is because they are all the last element of that type; the h2 and h3 are both the first and last of their type, and so both rules are applied to them.

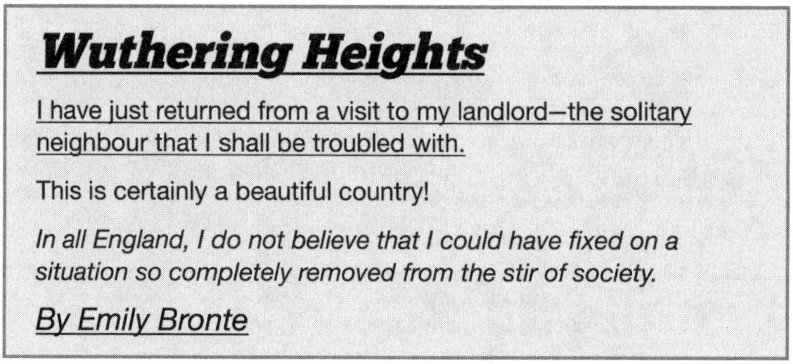

Wuthering Heights

I have just returned from a visit to my landlord—the solitary neighbour that I shall be troubled with.

This is certainly a beautiful country!

In all England, I do not believe that I could have fixed on a situation so completely removed from the stir of society.

By Emily Bronte

Figure 4-5: Applying the `:first-of-type` and `:last-of-type` selectors

As with all of the *-type and *-child pseudo-classes, the distinction is subtle, and sometimes the last child element is also the last of its type, so the selectors are interchangeable. But as I've just shown, at times, they have different applications.

:only-child and :only-of-type

These two pseudo-classes are used to select elements in the document tree that have a parent but either no sibling elements (:only-child) or no siblings of the same type (:only-of-type). As with many of the previous pseudo-classes, these two overlap substantially in function, but this next example illustrates the difference between them. Take the following style rules:

```
p:only-of-type { font-style: italic; }
p:only-child { text-decoration: underline; }
```

and then apply them to this markup:

```
<h2>On Intelligence</h2>
<p>Arthur C. Clarke once said:</p>
<blockquote>
    <p>It has yet to be proven that intelligence has any survival value.</p>
</blockquote>
```

You can see the result in Figure 4-6.

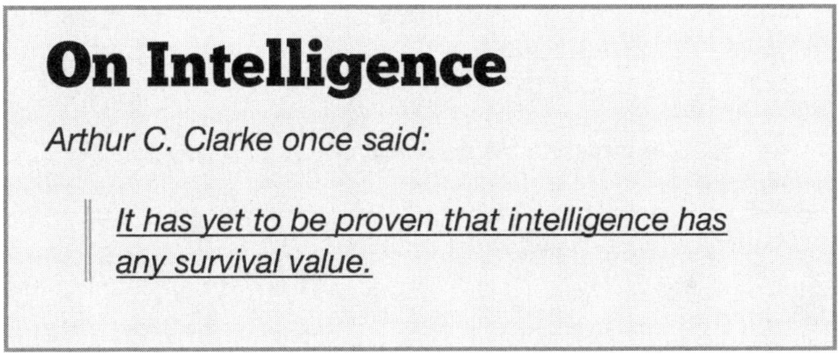

Figure 4-6: Comparing :only-child and :only-of-type

Both p elements are the only elements of their type in their level of the document tree, so the :only-of-type rule selects both and italicizes them. The p element inside the blockquote, however, is also the only child in its level, so it's also subject to the :only-child rule that applies the underline.

Using :only-of-type allows you to pick an element from among others, whereas :only-child requires the element to sit alone.

Other Pseudo-classes

In addition to the structural pseudo-classes discussed so far in this chapter, CSS3 introduces a number of pseudo-classes that allow you to select elements based on other criteria. These include link destinations, user interface elements, and even an inverse selector that permits selection based on what an element *isn't*!

:target

On the Web, sites don't just link between pages but also provide internal links to specific elements. A URI can contain a reference to a unique ID or a named anchor. For example, if you had this markup in a page:

```
<h4 id="my_id">Lorem ipsum</h4>
```

you could refer to it with this link:

```
<a href="page.html#my_id">Lorem</a>
```

The :target pseudo-class allows you to apply styles to the element when the referring URI has been followed. In this example, if you want to apply styles to the h4 element when the URI is followed, you use:

```
#my_id:target {...}
```

A popular practice is to highlight the subject of an internal link visually to provide a clear cue to the user. Consider, for example, the standard pattern for blog comments, which are somewhat like this simplified markup:

```
<div class="comment" id="comment-01">
    <p>Thanks for this scintillating example!</p>
    <p class="author">N.E. Boddy, April 13</p>
</div>
```

And another fairly common pattern is to include links to individual comments:

```
<p><a href="#comment-02">Latest comment</a></p>
```

Using the :target pseudo-class, you can easily highlight the comment that the user wants to read:

```
.comment:target { background-color: #DDD; }
```

Figure 4-7 shows a list of comments in two states: on the left, as they appear before the referring link has been clicked, and on the right, as they appear after the link has been clicked—with the element that the link refers to showing a different background color thanks to the :target selector.

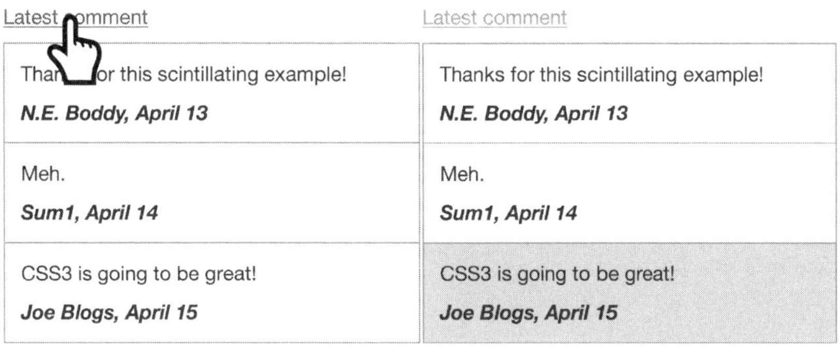

Latest comment	Latest comment
Thanks for this scintillating example! **N.E. Boddy, April 13**	Thanks for this scintillating example! **N.E. Boddy, April 13**
Meh. **Sum1, April 14**	Meh. **Sum1, April 14**
CSS3 is going to be great! **Joe Blogs, April 15**	CSS3 is going to be great! **Joe Blogs, April 15**

Figure 4-7: Highlighting applied with the :target pseudo-class

:empty

The :empty pseudo-class selects an element that has no children, including text nodes. Consider this markup:

```
<tr>
<td></td>
<td>Lorem ipsum</td>
<td><span></span></td>
</tr>
```

If you apply this CSS rule:

```
td:empty { background-color: red; }
```

the rule is only applied to the first td element, as the other two contain a text node and a child element, respectively.

:root

The :root pseudo-class selects the first element in a document tree, which is only really handy if you're adding a style sheet to XML documents—in HTML, the root will always be the html element. One small advantage of using :root in HTML is that you can use it to give a higher specificity to the html element, which could be useful if you need to override the simple type selector:

```
html {...} /* Specificity: 1; */
html:root {...} /* Specificity: 2; */
```

Let's say you're creating a base style sheet and want to set a property on the html element, which shouldn't be altered. In this case, you would use something like this:

```
html:root { background-color: black; }
```

The higher specificity gives precedence to this rule over any other rules applied to the html element, meaning the following is ignored:

```
html { background-color: white; }
```

But it's unlikely that you'll need to use this in most situations.

:not()

The negation pseudo-class :not() selects all elements *except* those that are given as the value of an argument:

```
E :not(F) {...}
```

This rule selects all children of element E except for those of type F. For example, to color all the immediate child elements of a div, except for p elements, you use this:

```
div > :not(p) { color: red; }
```

To see how useful :not() is, consider a situation where you have the following markup:

```
<div>
    <p>Lorem ipsum dolor sit amet...</p>
    <p>Nunc consectetur tempor justo...</p>
    <p>Nunc porttitor malesuada cursus...</p>
</div>
```

Now imagine you want to italicize all of the child p elements except for the first one.

To do this with CSS2, you applied a style to all the p elements and then applied a further style to reset the first element back to its previous state:

```
p { font-style: italic; }
p:first-child { font-style: normal; }
```

With :not(), you can reduce that to a single rule:

```
p:not(:first-child) { font-style: italic; }
```

The argument passed into :not() must be a simple selector—therefore combinators (such as + and >) and pseudo-elements (which I discuss in "Pseudo-elements" on page 45) are not valid values.

UI Element States

Elements relating to forms and user input can have various states; they can be disabled or checked, for example, by setting attribute values:

```
<textarea disabled="disabled"></textarea>
<input checked="checked" type="checkbox">
```

CSS3 has three UI state pseudo-class selectors, which allow you to apply rules to elements based on their current state:

```
:checked {...}
:disabled {...}
:enabled {...}
```

HTML has no enabled attribute; elements that are not disabled are, by definition, enabled.

To see the effect of these pseudo-class selectors, consider the following style rules:

```
input[type='text']:disabled { border: 1px dotted gray; }
input[type='text']:enabled { border: 1px solid black; }
```

I'll apply these rules to a form that has two text input elements, one of which has a disabled attribute (the form isn't well-structured as I don't have labels for the inputs, but I've left them out for clarity):

```
<form action="">
<fieldset>
<legend>UI element state pseudo-classes</legend>
<input type="text" value="Lorem ipsum" disabled>
<input type="text" value="Lorem ipsum">
</fieldset>
</form>
```

You can see the results in Figure 4-8.

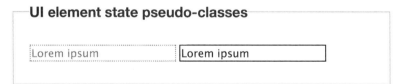

Figure 4-8: Disabled and enabled element states

As you can see, the disabled form element has grayed-out text (which is done automatically by the browser) and a gray dotted border (which I set in the style sheet). I set a solid black border around the enabled element.

I'm not giving a demonstration of the checked state here, as most browsers have different interpretations of which style rules can be applied to checkbox inputs. For a comprehensive overview of cross-browser styling of form elements, I highly recommend "Styling Form Controls with CSS" from the blog 456 Berea Street (*http://www.456bereastreet.com/lab/styling-form-controls-revisited/*).

There is a fourth UI element state, indeterminate, which is used in a limited set of circumstances; for example, a radio button input in a group where no input has been checked would be classed as indeterminate, as would a progress element with no value supplied. Although implemented in some browsers, however, it hasn't yet been fully defined, and its status is indeterminate (ha!).

Constraint Validation Pseudo-classes

HTML5 introduced a new API for client-side validation of forms, known as the *constraint validation API*, which can be used to determine if certain requirements are met before the form contents are sent to the server. The constraint validation API brings along with it an associated range of new pseudo-classes.

NOTE   *Mozilla Developer Network (MDN) has an excellent introduction to the Constraint Validation API at* https://developer.mozilla.org/docs/Web/Guide/HTML/HTML5/Constraint_validation/.

Under constraint validation, a form field can be made mandatory through use of the new required attribute:

```
<input type="text" required>
```

You can style elements depending on whether they're required or optional by using their namesake pseudo-classes:

```
:required {...}
:optional {...}
```

Each form field can be in one of two states of validation: either valid or invalid. If no specific constraints are applied, either by the browser or the author, a form field is valid by default. As before, each state has a namesake pseudo-class:

```
:valid {...}
:invalid {...}
```

WARNING   *In a form with which the user has yet to interact, fields with constraints that aren't met—such as being required—will have rules set with the :invalid pseudo-class applied already.*

Finally, some HTML5 elements can have a permitted range of values, set by using the min and max attributes. You can style these elements depending on whether the current value is in or out of range by using, once again, a pair of namesake pseudo-classes:

```
:in-range {...}
:out-of-range {...}
```

Pseudo-elements

Like pseudo-classes, pseudo-elements provide information that is not specified in the document tree. But where pseudo-classes use "phantom" conditions such as an element's position in the tree or its state, pseudo-elements go further and allow you to apply styles to elements that don't exist in the tree at all.

In CSS2, the four pseudo-elements are :first-line and :first-letter, which select subelements in text nodes, and :after and :before, which allow you to apply styles at the beginning and end of existing elements. CSS3 doesn't introduce any new pseudo-elements, but it refines the definitions slightly and introduces a new syntax to differentiate them from pseudo-classes. In CSS3, pseudo-elements are prefixed with a double colon (::), like so:

```
::first-line {...}
::first-letter {...}
::after {...}
::before {...}
```

NOTE *The single colon syntax is still accepted for reasons of backward compatibility, although it is deprecated and you shouldn't use it going forward.*

The ::selection Pseudo-element

Early versions of the CSS3 Selectors module included the definition of a ::selection pseudo-element. Although formally removed from the module, it has been well implemented across desktop browsers (less so in mobile browsers). ::selection is used to apply rules to an element that the user has selected in the browser (for example, a portion of a text node):

```
::selection {...}
```

Only a limited number of properties can be applied with ::selection: color, background-color, and the background shorthand (although not background-image). Using ::selection, you can do something like this:

```
p::selection {
    background-color: black;
    color: white;
}
```

Figure 4-9 shows a comparison of the system-native ::selection colors (top) and the colors I've applied with the ::selection pseudo-element (bottom).

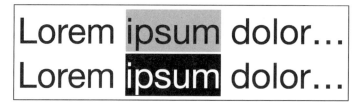

Figure 4-9: Custom colors applied with the ::selection pseudo-element

The ::selection pseudo-element is implemented in Chrome, Safari, and IE9+ without a prefix, and in Firefox with the -moz- prefix—so despite it no longer being part of the CSS3 specification, you can use it with confidence.

Summary

The new range of pseudo-classes (and any pseudo-elements that may be defined in the future) makes document traversal far more flexible and powerful with CSS3 than it ever was with its predecessors, and allows for much leaner and more maintainable markup.

The increased number of pseudo-classes based on the state of UI and form validation also gives users a much broader range of feedback, without relying on JavaScript. This is exceptionally useful for HTML5, with its increased focus on web applications.

DOM and Attribute Selectors: Browser Support

	Chrome	Firefox	Safari	IE
Structural pseudo-classes	Yes	Yes	Yes	Yes
:target	Yes	Yes	Yes	Yes
:empty	Yes	Yes	Yes	Yes
:root	Yes	Yes	Yes	Yes
:not()	Yes	Yes	Yes	Yes
Pseudo-elements (:: syntax)	Yes	Yes	Yes	Yes
UI element states	Yes	Yes	Yes	Yes
Constraint validation	Yes	Yes	Yes	IE10*
::selection	Yes	Yes	Yes	Yes

* Does not support :in-range, :out-of-range

5

WEB FONTS

The features covered in this chapter are the oldest in this book, having been introduced in CSS2 many years ago—only to be dropped from the 2.1 spec owing to a lack of implementation by browser makers. Now a new generation of browsers has revived interest in improving the typographical options available to web designers, and I, for one, welcome the return of these features in CSS3. Chief among them is the ability to specify fonts that don't already exist on the user's system—by utilizing the @font-face method—which frees designers from the yoke of the standard palette of "web-safe" system fonts that have been used for many years. Surprisingly, this capability has been available in Internet Explorer since 1997!

IE4 was the first browser to allow web fonts, but it did so with a proprietary format that prevented other browsers from following suit. Microsoft later submitted its format to the W3C for consideration as a standard, but in the meantime Firefox, Safari, and Chrome all backed a different set of formats (see "Font Formats" on page 52), so later versions of Internet Explorer eventually followed suit.

The CSS Fonts Module Level 3 (*http://www.w3.org/TR/css3-fonts/*) has Candidate Recommendation status, and most of the spec has already been implemented in modern browsers (with a couple of exceptions, which I'll cover later), so you can consider these features safe to use.

The @font-face Rule

To display web fonts on your pages, you first need to define them by using the @font-face rule. This rule sets the name and type of the font and provides the browser with the location of the file to use. Here's the basic syntax:

```
@font-face {
❶    font-family: FontName;
❷    src: ❸local('fontname'), ❹url('/path/filename.otf') ❺format('opentype');
}
```

I'll break this syntax down a little. First, I give the font a name with the font-family property (❶). This property is one you should be familiar with, although it serves a slightly different purpose inside the rule than it does when used in the declaration block for a regular selector; here, it's used to declare a font name, not to refer to one. Just like the font-family property in CSS2.1, you can use multiple, space-separated words as long as you enclose them within single quotation marks.

NOTE *When you define your font's name with font-family, you can use the same name multiple times—in fact, sometimes you need to. I'll discuss why shortly, in "Defining Different Faces" on page 49.*

Next is the src property (❷), which tells the browser the location of the font file. This property accepts a few different values: local (❸) uses the name of the source font to check if the font is already installed on the user's machine; and url (❹) provides a path to the font if it's not available locally. I've also included the optional format (❺) hint, used to specify the font type; in this example, I used OpenType, but more types are available, and I'll discuss those later in "Font Formats" on page 52.

I can supply many different values for the src property by separating the values with commas, as I've done in the code example. This utilizes the power of the cascade to allow different fall-back values, which will come in handy in a later example.

NOTE *Remember that in a font stack the browser will use the first file it encounters that can be loaded, rather than reading through all files and choosing the most recent.*

To use the font I just defined, I need only call its name in the font stack, as I'd normally do:

```
E { font-family: FontName; }
```

To illustrate a real-world example, I'll apply the Chunk font (available to download for free from *http://www.theleagueofmoveabletype.com/fonts/4-chunk/*) to an h1 element using @font-face. Here's the code I'll use in my style sheet:

```
@font-face {
❶    font-family: ChunkFive;
     src: ❷local('ChunkFive'), ❸url('ChunkFive.woff') ❹format('woff');
}
❺    h1.webfont { font-family: ChunkFive, sans-serif; }
```

The first step is to name my font; I've chosen ChunkFive (❶) because I can remember it easily, but I could use any name. Next I provide values to the src property: local (❷) uses the true name of the font, ChunkFive, to check if it's available on my system. Following that I enter a relative path to the font file I want to use (❸), and finally, I assign an argument of woff to the format value (❹). I explain the WOFF format in "Font Formats" on page 52.

NOTE   *You can usually find a font's true name by using a font management application or by right-clicking the font file to view the font information.*

In the last line (❺), I include my newly defined font in the font stack using the name value I defined inside the @font-face rule and apply it to all h1 elements with a class of webfont. To see how that displays, here's a quick comparison using the following markup:

```
<h1>Alas, poor Yorick!</h1>
<h1 class="webfont">Alas, poor Yorick!</h1>
```

You can see the output in Figure 5-1.

Alas, poor Yorick!
Alas, poor Yorick!

Figure 5-1: The ChunkFive font (the bottom row), called using the @font-face rule, compared to the page default font (the top row)

Defining Different Faces

The @font-face syntax you've seen so far in this chapter is pretty straight-forward, but it only defines one font face—that is, a single permutation of weight, slope, and so on. If you want to use a different face, such as a bolder weight or an italic type, you have to define each font face individually. To do this, you re-use the same name and add extra descriptors to the @font-face rule:

```
@font-face {
❶      font-family: 'Gentium Basic';
       src: url('❷GenBasR.woff') format('woff');
}
@font-face {
❸      font-family: 'Gentium Basic';
❹      font-style: italic;
       src: url('❺GenBasI.woff') format('woff');
}
h1 { font-family: 'Gentium Basic', sans-serif; }
```

Here, you can see that the first @font-face rule defines the font name as Gentium Basic (❶) and gives the URL of the regular font face (❷). The second @font-face rule uses the same font name (❸) but adds the font-style property with the italic value (❹), and the URL points at the font's italic face (❺). The italic style is applied automatically and appropriately, without your having to define it in the CSS, as in this example markup:

```
<h1>I knew him, Horatio</h1>
<h1><em>I knew him, Horatio</em></h1>
```

The second h1 element uses the italic font face defined in the previous rules (you can see the result in Figure 5-2).

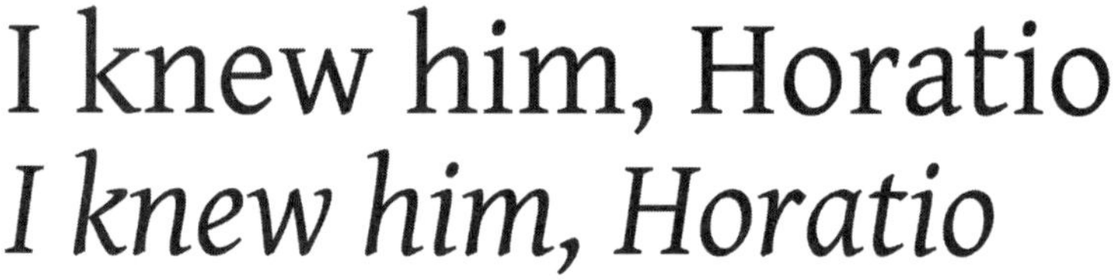

I knew him, Horatio
I knew him, Horatio

Figure 5-2: Gentium Basic Regular (top) and Italic (bottom) applied using @font-face

You can define any number of variations of a font with this method by using different font properties in the @font-face rule: font-weight to set various weights, font-variant for small caps faces, and so on.

True vs. Artificial Font Faces

One thing to be aware of when you use web fonts is that you must define a link to an appropriate file for each different font face you wish to use. If you don't, browsers will attempt to re-create the face artificially, often with ugly results.

For example, if you're going to use an italic style in your page, you must be sure to also define an italic style in @font-face. Here's an illustration of how *not* to define an italic weight:

```
@font-face {
    font-family: 'Gentium Basic';
    src: url('GenBasR.woff') format('woff');
}
h1 {
    font-family: 'Gentium Basic', sans-serif;
    font-style: italic;
}
```

You can see that my @font-face rule uses the regular face of the Gentium Basic font, but the h1 element has an italic style declared on it. You can see the effect in Figure 5-3, which compares this method with the correctly defined method from the previous section.

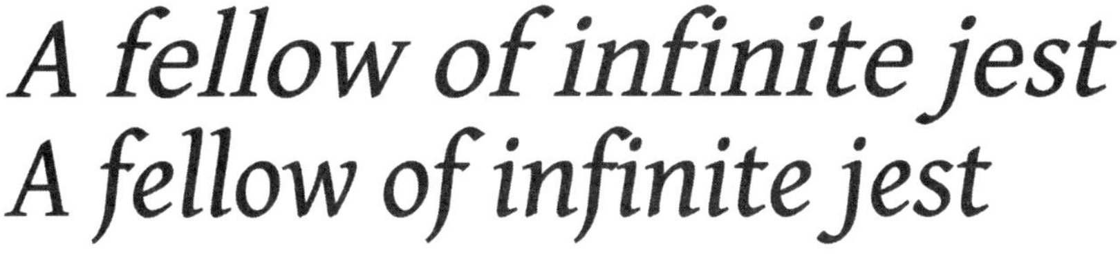

A fellow of infinite jest
A fellow of infinite jest

Figure 5-3: Comparing an artificial italic (top) with a true italic font face (bottom)

As you can see, the two examples are quite different. The first is the selected Gentium Basic font slanted to fake an italic style (using the first code example); the characters are larger, slightly distorted, and spaced inconsistently. The second is the true italic font face (using the correct method), which uses characters designed specifically for this purpose.

The same applies for all the different font faces: bold, italic, bold italic, small caps, condensed, and so on.

A "Bulletproof" @font-face Syntax

I explained at the beginning of this chapter that the @font-face rule has been around for quite a while, having been implemented in Internet Explorer as far back as 1997. This means that it carries with it some unfortunate legacy issues in older versions of IE. In addition, some historical issues around font formats can cause compatibility problems in older versions of other browsers.

Because of these issues, you need a workaround to ensure that @font-face works correctly across all browsers. Before I introduce the fully cross-browser "bulletproof" @font-face syntax, let me discuss briefly some of the problems it addresses.

Using Local Fonts

The local() value for the src property is used to check whether a user already has the defined font installed on his or her system—if the user does, the local copy can be applied rather than downloading a new copy. local() is a good idea, but it suffers from a few drawbacks. The first drawback, and not the least, is that local() isn't supported by any versions of Internet Explorer below 9!

Another drawback is that, in some cases, the @font-face rule doesn't play nicely with font management software, displaying incorrect characters or opening a dialog to ask for permissions to use a font.

For these reasons, leaving the local() value out is generally safer.

Font Formats

The next problem comes in the shape of different, and competing, formats. When @font-face was originally implemented, it supported only Microsoft's proprietary *Embedded OpenType (EOT)* format, and this is still the only font format that is supported in IE8 and below. To complicate this still further, IE9 causes the @font-face rule to break when the browser is put into compatibility mode; this is very much an edge case and becoming less relevant all the time, but it's worth noting as we can fix it simply in our bulletproof syntax.

The resurgence of interest in web fonts came about because modern browsers—first Safari and then Firefox and then others—allowed the use of the more common *TrueType* and *OpenType* formats. Unfortunately, many commercial font foundries wouldn't allow their fonts to be used in this way as it makes illegal copying of their fonts a little easier (see "Licensing Fonts for Web Use" on page 53). For this reason, Mozilla consulted with some font makers and created the *Web Open Font Format (WOFF)*, which is now supported in all major browsers, including IE9 and above, with the exception of older versions of the stock Android browser (4.3 and below).

Some browsers also accept the *Scalable Vector Graphics (SVG)* font type. This font type is a vector re-creation of the font and is considerably lighter in file size, making it ideal for mobile use. This format is really only useful, however, if you need to support older versions (4.1 and below) of Safari for iPhone.

The Final "Bulletproof" Syntax

For your chosen font to display the same in every browser on every platform, you should use code in this format:

```
@font-face {
    font-family: 'Gentium Basic';
❶  src: url('GenBkBasR.eot');
❷  src: url('GenBasR.eot?#iefix') format('embedded-opentype'),
❸  url('GenBkBasR.woff') format('woff'),
❹  url('GenBkBasR.ttf') format('truetype');
}
```

Let me explain what's happening here. The first font to be specified is the EOT (❶) for Internet Explorer 8 and below. This font is in a rule of its own, as the next rule contains the optional `format()` hint; this hint is unfamiliar to old IE8, and so the whole rule will be ignored. But the EOT font needs to be included again (❷) to deal with the IE9 compatibility problem. Next, the WOFF format is defined (❸) for the majority of browsers, followed by the TTF format (❹) for older browsers, including Android 4.3 and below (remember that browsers will ignore formats they don't understand and therefore can't load).

As the IE9 compatibility problem is really becoming less important, you can leave out the second line (❷) at your discretion.

For this to work, the major requirement is that your chosen font be available in three different formats. To make this easier, I strongly recommend using the `@font-face` Generator by Font Squirrel (*http://www .fontsquirrel.com/fontface/generator/*). Simply upload the font file you want to use and `@font-face` Generator converts it into all the relevant formats—as well as generating the CSS you need to use in your pages. This tool is invaluable. Font Squirrel also has a library of fonts that are ready to use with `@font-face` embedding, saving you the task of converting.

NOTE   *For a full explanation of why the IE trick is required and how it works, read* http://www.fontspring.com/blog/the-new-bulletproof-font-face-syntax/.

Licensing Fonts for Web Use

As mentioned previously in "Font Formats" on page 52, many font foundries expressly forbid embedding their web fonts in your pages using `@font-face`. They forbid this because linked OpenType or TrueType fonts are easy to locate and download and can then be used illegally in both on- and offline applications. The WOFF file type was created in response to this; WOFF is a web-only format and can contain licensing information to help track down a copyright infringer. Many foundries have already committed to selling this format, and I hope many more will follow.

In general, the best policy is to check that the font you choose has a license explicitly allowing you to use it for web embedding; don't assume that because a font is free to download, it is free to use online. That said, many good-quality free fonts that do allow embedding are available online; some resources are given in Appendix B.

While the licensing situation is in a state of flux, many web font service providers have created mechanisms to embed fonts legally in your pages. By adding JavaScript to your pages, the provider is authorized to serve the font files from their network, so you can call the font families in your stacks. The method is known as *Fonts as a Service (FaaS)*.

Most FaaS providers are commercial, allowing a limited set of fonts for free but charging a monthly or annual fee for the majority. The two biggest players in this category are probably Fontdeck (*http://fontdeck.com/*) and Typekit (*https://typekit.com/*). Other providers supply only free fonts—Google Fonts (*http://www.google.com/fonts/*) being a notable example of this. Each provider has its own way of including the licensed fonts on your site, usually through the inclusion of an external CSS or JS file, or both.

A Real-World Web Fonts Example

Having discussed the intricacies and niceties of fonts, licensing, and multiple syntaxes, let's see a real-world example of @font-face in action. I'll use an example that compares text displayed in a standard sans-serif font (Arial) to the same text displayed in three different font families (all from Font Squirrel).

Here's the CSS for this example. Bear in mind that, for the sake of clarity, I've simplified this snippet to show only a single font format (WOFF), although the accompanying example file has the full code:

```
@font-face {
    font-family: 'CartoonistHand';
    src: url('CartoonistHand.woff') format('woff');
}
@font-face {
    font-family: 'CartoonistHand';
    font-style: italic;
    src: url('CartoonistHand-Italic.woff') format('woff');
}
@font-face {
    font-family: 'CartoonistHand';
    font-weight: bold;
    src: url('CartoonistHand-Bold.woff') format('woff');
}
@font-face {
    font-family: 'ChunkFiveRegular';
    src: url('Chunkfive.woff') format('woff');
}
@font-face {
    font-family: 'AirstreamRegular';
    src: url('Airstream.woff') format('woff');
}
.font-face h1 { font-family: ChunkFiveRegular, sans-serif; }
.font-face h2 { font-family: AirstreamRegular, cursive; }
.font-face p { font-family: CartoonistHand, sans-serif; }
```

I also left out some color and size adjustments to keep the code as readable as possible. Here's the markup I used:

```
<h1>Great Expectations</h1>
<h2>By Charles Dickens</h2>
<p>My father's family name being <em>Pirrip</em>, and my Christian name
<em>Philip</em>, my infant tongue could make of both names nothing longer or
more explicit than <strong>Pip</strong>. So, I called myself <strong>Pip
</strong>, and came to be called <strong>Pip</strong>.</p>
```

You can see the output in Figure 5-4.

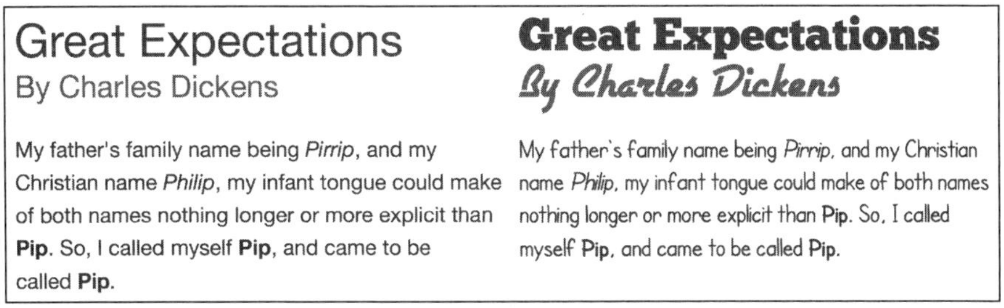

Figure 5-4: Text using "web-safe" fonts (left) and using different web fonts (right)

In the example on the right, I mixed three fairly distinctive font families—many designers will probably tell you mixing isn't a good idea on a production site, but it works well to illustrate my point. Whatever you think of my font choices, I hope you'll at least agree that the text looks more dynamic and enticing with those choices applied.

Despite the long and winding route we've had to take to get a cross-browser syntax, using @font-face isn't complicated; you'll expend some overhead in the form of extra setup time to declare the font faces and variants you want to use, but after that you can call them in your font stacks and style them in exactly the same way as system fonts.

Controlling Font Loading

Web fonts are loaded as external assets and must be downloaded by the browser before they can be displayed. Before the file has loaded, no font at all will be visible on the elements the font is to be applied to. You may then see a slight "flash" that occurs as the font loads and is applied. This is known as the *Flash of Unstyled Text (FoUT)*.

Many FaaS providers offer ways to work around this problem using configuration files, but if you're hosting your own fonts, you may want to investigate the Web Font Loader library (*https://github.com/typekit/webfontloader/*), which provides an event system that allows you to control the appearance of your page dynamically as fonts are loaded.

More Font Properties

The CSS3 Web Fonts Module doesn't just re-introduce the @font-face rule; it also revives two other font properties that were first proposed for CSS2. These properties are potentially quite useful for giving you granular control over your fonts—I say *potentially* because, as of this moment, they aren't widely implemented.

font-size-adjust

The only drawback to using font stacks in CSS is that fonts can vary so much in size; your first choice font may look great at 16px, but if that font isn't available, the next fallback may appear smaller or have different proportions and be harder to read at that size. To combat this, the font-size-adjust property lets you dynamically alter the font-size property to ensure a regular appearance no matter which font is used from the stack. The font-size-adjust property takes a single decimal value; here's the syntax:

```
E { font-size-adjust: number; }
```

The *number* value is the proportion of the total height that is occupied by a lowercase *x* character (known as the *x-height*). In other words, a font might be 16px high in total, but the height of the lowercase *x* might be half that (8px), which gives an x-height ratio of 0.5 (8 divided by 16):

```
p { font-size-adjust: 0.5; }
```

By using font-size-adjust, you can ensure that no matter which font is displayed, the x-height always has the same value, and legibility does not suffer. To illustrate, consider the following code:

```
h1.adjusted { font-size-adjust: 0.517; }
h1.impact { font-family: Impact, serif; }
```

Then, in the following three h1 elements, all with the same values for font-size, I apply different values to them using their class names, which you can see in this markup:

```
<h1>Of most excellent fancy</h1>
<h1 class="impact">Of most excellent fancy</h1>
<h1 class="adjusted impact">Of most excellent fancy</h1>
```

The first h1 is rendered in the default Helvetica Neue font, the second in Impact, and the third also in Impact but with the font-size-adjust property applied using the value 0.517, which is the x-height of Helvetica Neue. You can see the results in Figure 5-5.

Of most excellent fancy
Of most excellent fancy
Of most excellent fancy

Figure 5-5: The effect of font-size-adjust on the Impact font (third line)

You can clearly see the difference between the Helvetica Neue (first line) and Impact (second line) fonts in the first two h1 elements. (Of course, you are unlikely to ever use these two in the same font stack, but because they have quite different x-heights, they're good for illustrative purposes.) As I mentioned, Helvetica Neue has an x-height ratio of 0.517, which means the lowercase x is about half the height of the font. By contrast, Impact has an x-height ratio of 0.7, which means less contrast in height between upper- and lowercase letters.

The first two lines in the example are not adjusted in any way, so Impact's lowercase characters in the second line are considerably taller than Helvetica Neue's in the first line—the fonts have the same size, but their metrics are different. In the third line, however, I set the font-size-adjust value to 0.517 to match the x-height ratio of Helvetica Neue:

```
h1.adjusted { font-size-adjust: 0.517; }
```

This adjusts the font size so Impact displays at a smaller size—just over 18.6px, which is slightly more than half of the 36px height set by font-size. You can see this more clearly if I directly compare the two elements, as shown in Figure 5-6. Here, the characters without *ascenders* (lines that rise above the x-height)—that is, *e*, *x*, *c*, and *n*—of the adjusted Impact font are the exact same height as those of the Helvetica Neue font.

excellent excellent

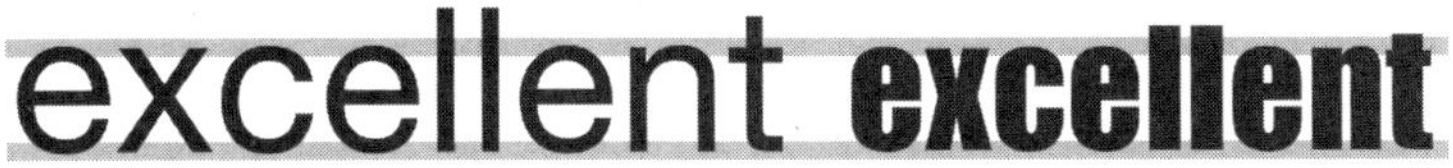

Figure 5-6: Characters from the Helvetica Neue font (left) compared to characters from the Impact font adjusted with font-size-adjust (right)

Unfortunately, a font's x-height ratio isn't easily available; you can either use a graphics package to measure it manually or try to find an online resource. (I found a calculator made by the online fonts service, Fontdeck, which works with the fonts installed on your system: *http:// fontdeck.com/support/fontsizeadjust/*.)

The major drawback of this property is that, at the time of writing, Firefox is the only browser that supports it.

font-stretch

Some font families contain condensed or expanded variants, and the font-stretch property allows access to these. Here's the syntax:

```
E { font-stretch: keyword; }
```

According to the specification, the keyword value can be any one of the following: normal (the default), ultra-condensed, extra-condensed, condensed, semi-condensed, semi-expanded, expanded, extra-expanded, and ultra-expanded. Each keyword relates to a font variant within a family, such as Frutiger Condensed or Nova Ultra Expanded.

In the following example, I use font-stretch to display two different faces of the font PT Sans, using the following code:

```
h1 { font-family: 'PT Sans', sans-serif; }
h1.narrow { font-stretch: condensed; }
```

The h1 element is displayed twice, both times using the font PT Sans. In the second instance, I've used the font-stretch property with the value condensed, which tells the browser to display the PT Sans Condensed face. You can see the results in Figure 5-7.

Lorem Ipsum Dolor
Lorem Ipsum Dolor

Figure 5-7: The second example uses the narrow font face because of the effect of the font-stretch property.

The font-stretch property is implemented in Firefox and IE9 and above, but you could also replicate the effect by using the @font-face rule (introduced at the beginning of this chapter) to specify a condensed or expanded face in your font stack:

```
@font-face {
    font-family: 'PT Sans Condensed';
    src: url('PT-Sans-Narrow.woff') format('woff');
}
```

OpenType Features

Although web typography takes a great leap forward in CSS3, it still just scratches the surface of the possibilities of type. If you compare the options available to you in a browser with what's available in a desktop publishing application such as Adobe InDesign, you'll see that the latter is much richer than the former.

OpenType font formats are capable of much more than face or weight variations; they have a range of ligatures, swashes, special numeric characters, and much more. (If none of those terms makes any sense to you, I recommend Magnet Studio's Beginners Guide to OpenType at *http://www.magnetstudio.com/words/2010/opentype-guide/*).

Enabling Font Features

Many browsers have implemented a property that allows you to explore the extra features afforded by OpenType and other similar formats. The new property is called font-feature-settings, and here's its syntax:

```
E { font-feature-settings: "parameters"; }
```

The *parameters* value is a series of strings containing shorthand codes for each font feature, plus an optional binary value to enable or disable the feature. Here's an example:

```
E { font-feature-settings: "dlig" on; }
```

The first parameter is dlig, the short code for discretionary ligatures, plus the value of on to show it's being enabled—the default state is on, so you can safely omit that value in this example.

If you want to disable a feature, you use the alternative binary value, off; in the following example, I'm disabling the small caps OpenType feature:

```
E { font-feature-settings: "smcp" off; }
```

You can, as I mentioned, have more than one parameter—just create a comma-separated list. The following example enables common ligatures and disables tabular numbers:

```
E { font-feature-settings: "liga", "tnum" off; }
```

Let's look at some examples that show the advantage of using Open-Type features. In "True vs. Artificial Font Faces" on page 50, I showed why you should always use a true italic font rather than letting the browser create one artificially. In this example, you'll see that the same principle holds when using the small caps font variant. Here are the relevant style rules:

```
.smallcaps { font-variant: small-caps; }
.ot-smallcaps { font-feature-settings: "smcp"; }
```

Here, I use two h1 elements: I apply the font-variant property with the small-caps value to the first; for the second, I use font-feature-settings, with the parameter used to toggle small caps, smcp. You can see the difference in Figure 5-8.

Lorem Ipsum
Lorem Ipsum

Figure 5-8: The lower example uses OpenType's own small caps feature

In the first h1 element, which uses simulated small caps, the proportions are off; the difference between the large and small capitals is barely noticeable. Compare that with the second h1 element, which has more obvious proportions and looks more pleasing to the eye.

Now I'll demonstrate the use of ligatures, which are used to join certain pairs of characters to make them appear more harmonious. As with kerning, most browsers automatically use common ligatures unless instructed not to, so, in this example, I'll compare text with no ligatures, common ligatures, and discretionary—that is, more decorative—ligatures.

Here's the code:

```
.lig-none { font-feature-settings: "liga" off; }
.lig-common { font-feature-settings: "liga"; }
.lig-disc { font-feature-settings: "dlig"; }
```

This code is applied to three h1 elements. The first has the parameter string "liga" off, so common ligatures are disabled. The second uses the same parameter string except without the off value, so common ligatures are enabled. The third has the string "dlig", which enables discretionary ligatures. Figure 5-9 compares the three.

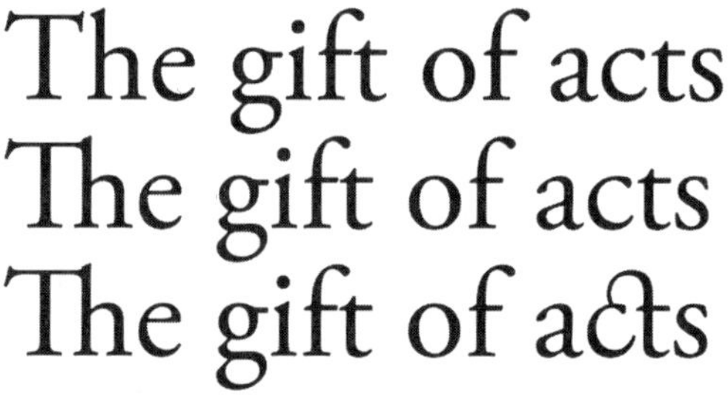

The gift of acts
The gift of acts
The gift of acts

Figure 5-9: Comparing OpenType ligatures: (from top) none, common, and discretionary

Pay attention to the character pairs *Th* and *ct*. In the first h1 element, without ligatures, they are rendered as separate characters. In the second, with common ligatures, the *Th* pair is joined together at the point where the characters almost meet. In the third h1 element, the ligatures are discretionary, so the *ct* pair is also joined with an extravagant flourish.

At the time of writing, `font-feature-settings` are implemented in IE10+ and in Chrome and Firefox with appropriate vendor prefixes. You can also get access to these properties in Safari, but in a slightly different way; read on to find out how.

These features are all suggestions to the browser, not commands; some browsers will choose how fonts are rendered considering the platform and potential performance, and these feature suggestions may be ignored.

Font Feature Properties

The individual features enabled or disabled by `font-feature-settings` are also specified to be implemented as individual properties, known as the `font-variant-*` properties. For example, to work with ligatures, you use the `font-variant-ligatures` property with a keyword value representing the ligatures you wanted to set; the following code disables discretionary ligatures:

```
E { font-variant-ligatures: no-discretionary-ligatures; }
```

You can also use `font-variant-position` for super- or subscript, `font-variant-caps` for titling capitalization, `font-variant-numeric` for numerical forms, and `font-variant-alternates` for swashes, ornaments, and so on.

Chrome and Safari are the only browsers to support the `font-variant-*` properties currently, with the `-webkit-` prefix, and the examples in Figures 5-7, 5-8, and 5-9 should all work in Safari using these properties instead of `font-feature-settings`.

One other related property is `font-kerning`, which (fairly obviously) controls the kerning of a font. This accepts values of `normal`, where kerning is applied; `none`, where kerning is disabled; and `auto` (the default), which lets the browser make the decision of whether to kern.

```
E { font-kerning: normal; }
```

In Figure 5-10, you can see this property in action. The upper heading has kerning disabled, whereas the lower has it applied. I've added some background lines to make it easier to see.

Figure 5-10: Text with kerning disabled (top) and enabled (bottom) using the `font-kerning` property

Summary

While `font-size-adjust` and `font-stretch` will surely come in handy in the future, for now `@font-face` is the killer feature of the Web Fonts Module. `@font-face` is not without its drawbacks, however, not least that every extra font you use adds to the page's load time. Also be aware that misuse or over-use of different typefaces can lead to decreased legibility. Your site lives or dies on its content, so make sure your visitors can read it by choosing your fonts carefully and checking them closely across different browsers.

Despite those caveats, you can use this simple rule to amazing effect. In Chapter 6, I'll show you some ways to further enhance your typography.

Web Fonts: Browser Support

	Chrome	Firefox	Safari	IE
@font-face	Yes	Yes	Yes	Yes
font-size-adjust	No	Yes	No	No
font-stretch	No	Yes	No	Yes
font-feature-settings	Yes	Yes	No	IE10
font-variant-*	Yes*	No	Yes*	No

* Requires vendor prefix

6

TEXT EFFECTS AND TYPOGRAPHIC STYLES

Text content has been the backbone of the Web since its creation, yet for years we've had to make do with a limited set of tools. CSS3 hugely expands its typographic toolset by introducing a range of new and updated features in the Text Module.

Chief among these new features is the ability to add shadows to text. Although this addition doesn't sound particularly revolutionary—print typographers have been using shadows for a long time—the new syntax is flexible enough to allow for some very nice effects. A similar feature is text-outlining (or text-stroking), which, although not widely implemented, does increase the variety of options available when creating decorative headlines. In addition to these are some less flashy effects but ones that can do wonders for your text's readability.

The CSS Text Level 3 Module (*http://www.w3.org/TR/css3-text/*) currently has Last Call Working Draft status; however, some elements are well implemented and ready for you to use straightaway.

Before I introduce the first new property in this module, I'll briefly introduce the concepts of coordinates and axes. If you're already familiar with these, feel free to skip this section; otherwise, read on.

Understanding Axes and Coordinates

One syntax concept that's new to CSS3 is that of the *axis* (or *axes* when you have more than one). You may know all about axes if you remember your math lessons, but if you're reading this section, I assume you need a refresher.

CSS uses the *Cartesian coordinate system*, which consists of two lines, one horizontal and one vertical, that cross each other at a right angle. Each of these lines is an axis: The horizontal line is known as the *x-axis*, and the vertical line is known as the *y-axis*. The point where the two lines meet is called the *origin*. You can see this illustrated in Figure 6-1.

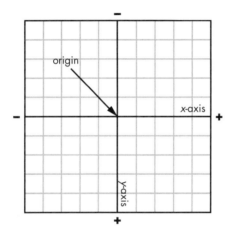

Figure 6-1: The x- and y-axes and the point of origin

For onscreen items, you measure the lengths of these axes in pixels. In Figure 6-1, you can see the axes and origin are overlaid on a grid. Imagine that each square corresponds to a single pixel. You'll also notice positive (+) and negative (–) labels at either end of each axis; these tell you that the distance away from the origin will be measured either positively or negatively in this direction.

Now that you understand this concept, you can find the coordinates of any point relative to the origin. The *coordinates* are a pair of values—one for each axis—that indicate the distance from the origin. The origin has coordinates (0, 0). For example, given the coordinates (3, 4), you would find the point by moving 3 pixels along the *x*-axis, and 4 pixels along the *y*-axis (remember the first line on each axis is 0 and is not counted). Likewise, the coordinates (–3, –1) indicate a point 3 pixels in a negative direction away from the origin along the *x*-axis and 1 pixel away from the origin in a negative direction along the *y*-axis. You can see both of these values plotted on the chart in Figure 6-2.

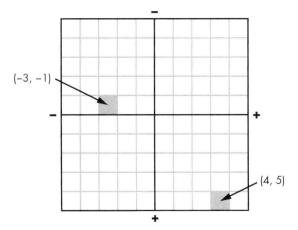

Figure 6-2: Two sets of coordinates

If this all sounds terribly complicated, don't worry—you've been using the Cartesian coordinate system already with properties like background-position; you just didn't realize it.

In CSS, all elements have a height and a width, each of which is a stated number of pixels in length (even when using other length units such as em or a percentage). The height and width together create a *pixel grid*; for example, an element that is 10px by 10px in size has a pixel grid of 100px. If you consider that the origin of the element is at the top-left corner, then the two positional values for properties like background-position correspond exactly to the *x*- and *y*-coordinates.

NOTE   *In CSS, the default origin is the top-left corner of an element, but that isn't always fixed; some CSS properties allow you to change the origin's position. For instance, you could set the origin at the dead center of an element or at the bottom-right corner or anywhere you wish. We'll see this later in this book, for example when dealing with 2D Transformations in Chapter 12.*

Applying Dimensional Effects: text-shadow

The ability to apply drop shadows to text using the text-shadow property has been around for a long time; Safari first implemented it in version 1.1, which was released in 2005. So you might be wondering why I am discussing it in a book on CSS3. As with the font properties in Chapter 5, text-shadow was dropped from CSS2.1 owing to lack of implementation, but this property has been reinstated in the CSS3 spec and is well implemented in browsers today.

The position of the shadow is set using the *x*- and *y*-coordinates that I just introduced. The simplest form of the syntax accepts two values: *x* to set the horizontal distance from the text (known as the *x-offset*) and *y* to set the vertical distance (the *y-offset*):

```
E { text-shadow: x y; }
```

By default, the shadow will be the color that it inherited from its parent (usually black), so if you want to specify a different color, you need to provide a value for that, such as:

```
E { text-shadow: x y color; }
```

Here's an example of a gray (hex code #BBB) drop shadow located 3px to the right and 3px down from the original text:

```
h1 { text-shadow: 3px 3px #BBB; }
```

You can see the output of this code in Figure 6-3.

Figure 6-3: Simple text-shadow

You aren't limited to positive integers as offset values; you can use both 0 (zero) and negative numbers to get different effects. Here are a few examples:

```
❶ .one { text-shadow: -3px -3px #BBB; }
❷ .two { text-shadow: -5px 3px #BBB; }
❸ .three { text-shadow: -5px 0 #BBB; }
```

You can see the output of these examples in Figure 6-4.

Figure 6-4: Different axis offset values for text-shadow

The first example (❶) uses negative values for both axes, so the shadow is rendered above and to the left of the text. The next (❷) uses a negative value for the *x*-axis and a positive value for the *y*-axis, so the shadow renders below and to the left. The final example (❸) has a negative value for the *x*-axis and a value of 0 for *y*-axis, so the shadow renders to the left and on the same baseline.

The `text-shadow` property also has a fourth option: *blur-radius*. This option sets the extent of a blur effect on the shadow and must be used after the offset values:

```
E { text-shadow: x y blur-radius color; }
```

The blur radius value is, like the two offset values, also an integer with a length unit; the higher the value, the wider (and lighter) the blur. If no value is supplied (as in the examples shown in Figure 6-4), the blur radius is assumed to be 0. Here are a couple of examples:

```
.one { text-shadow: 3px 3px 3px #BBB; }
.two { text-shadow: 0 0 3px #000; }
```

You can see the output of these examples in Figure 6-5.

Figure 6-5: Different blur values for text-shadow

In the first example, I set the same offset values as in Figure 6-4, but with a blur radius of 3px. The result is a much softer, more "natural" shadow. In the second example, I've set 0 values for the offsets and a 3px blur radius, matching the text to the background and creating the illusion that the text is raised.

Multiple Shadows

You don't have to limit yourself to a single shadow—text-shadow's syntax supports adding multiple shadows to a text node. Just supply extra values to the property, using commas to separate them, like this:

```
E { text-shadow: value, value, value; }
```

The shadows are applied in the order you supply the values. Figure 6-6 shows two examples of multiple shadows in action.

Figure 6-6: Using multiple values with text-shadow

The CSS for these examples is shown here. The first example has a class of one, and the second has a class of two. Note that I've indented them for clarity.

```
.one {
    text-shadow:
    0 -2px 3px #FFF,
    0 -4px 3px #AAA,
    0 -6px 6px #666,
    0 -8px 9px #000;
}
.two {
    color: #FFF;
    text-shadow:
    0 2px rgba(0,0,0,0.4),
    0 4px rgba(0,0,0,0.4),
    0 6px rgba(0,0,0,0.4),
    0 8px 0 rgba(0,0,0,0.4);
}
```

In the first example, I've kept the x-offset at 0 while increasing the y-offset's negative value from –2px to –8px. The blur radius increases from 3px to 9px, and the color gets gradually darker, creating a ghostly pale outline behind the characters, which becomes a darker shadow as it gets farther from the characters.

In the second example, the x-offset also remains consistent, but this time the y-offset increases its value positively. Because the *blur-radius* value isn't specified, it stays at 0. Here, I've used the rgba() color function (which I explain in Chapter 10), so the color stays the same but is partially transparent, creating an overlapping effect. Although the value changes are fairly small, the visual difference between the two elements is quite profound.

As I said earlier, text-shadow is well implemented in browsers, with support in IE10+ and all other major browsers, including mobile.

Restricting Overflow

Under certain circumstances—perhaps on mobile devices where screen space is limited—you may want to restrict text to a single line and a fixed width, perhaps when displaying a list of links to other pages, where you don't want the link text to wrap onto multiple lines. In these circumstances, your text being wider than its container and getting clipped mid-character can be quite frustrating.

A new property called `text-overflow` is available in CSS3 for just those circumstances. Here's its syntax:

```
E { text-overflow: keyword; }
```

The permitted keyword values are `clip` and `ellipsis`. The default value is `clip`, which acts in the way I just described: Your text is clipped at the point where it flows out of the container element. But the new value that's really interesting is `ellipsis`, which replaces the last whole or partial character before the overflow with an ellipsis character—the one that looks like three dots (...).

Let's walk through an example using the following CSS:

```
p {
    overflow: hidden;
    text-overflow: ellipsis;
    white-space: nowrap;
}
```

On this `p` element, I set the value of `overflow` to `hidden` to prevent the content showing outside of the border, the value of the `white-space` property to `nowrap` to prevent the text from wrapping over multiple lines, and a value of `ellipsis` on the `text-overflow` property. You can see the result, compared with the default behavior, in Figure 6-7.

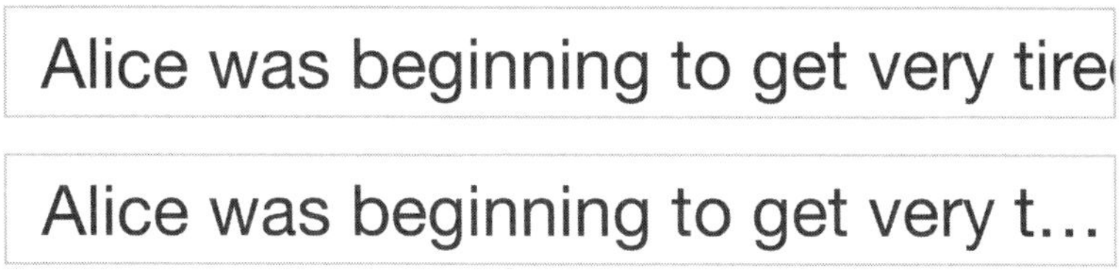

Alice was beginning to get very tire

Alice was beginning to get very t...

Figure 6-7: The text-overflow property with a value of ellipsis (bottom)

The last word in the sentence has been truncated and an ellipsis used in place of the removed characters, signifying that the line has been truncated.

The `text-overflow` property was originally specified in the Text Module, but has since been moved to the Basic User Interface Module (*http://www .w3.org/TR/css3-ui/*). This property is implemented in all major browsers.

The specification also extends the basic syntax in two ways. First, you can provide two values to the property—a first for overflow at the end of a line and a second for overflow at the start. For example, if you negatively indented text that also overflowed its container, you could put ellipses on both ends:

```
E { text-overflow: ellipsis ellipsis; }
```

The second extension offers a third possible keyword value, which is a string of characters to be used instead of the ellipsis, like in this example where I use a tilde to show the overflow:

```
E { text-overflow: '~'; }
```

These extensions are currently implemented only in Firefox and are marked in the spec as being at risk of being removed at a later date.

Aligning Text

The `text-align` property has been around for a long time, but CSS3 adds two new values to it: `start` and `end`. For people who read left-to-right, they are equivalent to the values `left` and `right` (respectively). Their real usefulness is on internationalized sites that may also use right-to-left text, however. You can use these new values in most modern browsers, with the exception of Internet Explorer.

New to CSS3 is the `text-align-last` property, which lets you set the alignment of the last (or only) line of text in a justified block. This property accepts the same values as `text-align`:

```
E { text-align-last: keyword; }
```

So if you want to justify a block of text but also align the last line to the right, you would use

```
p {
    text-align: justify;
    text-align-last: right;
}
```

At the time of writing, this extension is implemented in Internet Explorer (although, again, without the `start` and `end` keyword values), Firefox with the `-moz-` prefix, and Chrome.

Controlling Line Wrapping

An issue that's frequently encountered when working with dynamic text is line wrapping in inappropriate places. For example, if you're providing details about an event, you want the start time and end time to appear next to each other on the same line, but with a dynamic line break, the end time may be pushed to the subsequent line. CSS3 gives you more control over these kinds of issues with a pair of properties that lets you define more clearly how you want your content to wrap.

Breaking Words

The first property is `word-wrap`, which specifies whether the browser can break long words to make them fit into the parent element. The syntax for it is simple:

```
E { word-wrap: keyword; }
```

This property allows the keyword values `normal` or `break-word`. The former allows lines to break only between words (unless otherwise specified in the markup), and the latter allows a word to be broken if required to prevent overflow of the parent element.

So, for example, if I want to allow long words to be wrapped instead of overflowing their containing element, I might use:

```
p.break { word-wrap: break-word; }
```

Figure 6-8 shows this effect. The left block doesn't use word wrapping, and the right block does.

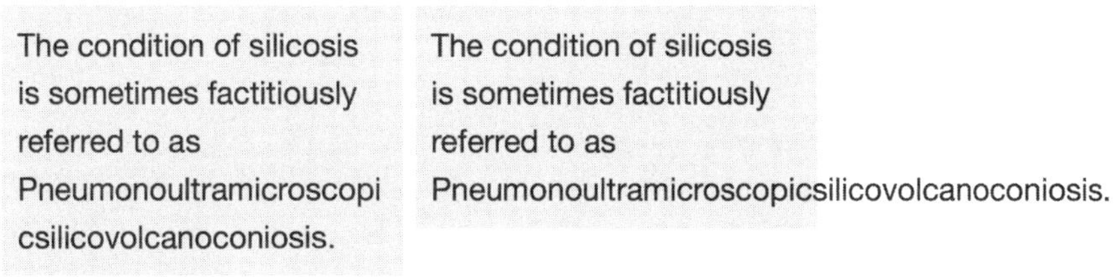

The condition of silicosis is sometimes factitiously referred to as Pneumonoultramicroscopi csilicovolcanoconiosis.

The condition of silicosis is sometimes factitiously referred to as Pneumonoultramicroscopicsilicovolcanoconiosis.

Figure 6-8: Example of text with (left) and without (right) a break-word value for word-wrap

The `word-wrap` property is widely implemented across all major browsers, including Internet Explorer. Recent versions of the Text Module have renamed `word-wrap` to `overflow-wrap`, however, and some browsers—Chrome and Safari, for example—have implemented the new name, although the old name will also be supported for legacy reasons.

Hyphenating Words

If you'd prefer an extra option for breaking words over multiple lines, you can use hyphenation. Long a standard of print, hyphens indicate where the break in a word occurs. You can hyphenate your text already in HTML, using the soft-hyphenation symbol entity, ­—although this requires that you mark up all of your content, which is not always an option.

CSS3 makes this somewhat easier through the hyphens property:

```
E { hyphens: keyword; }
```

---

hyphens has three possible keyword values: manual hyphenates words only where a hyphenation suggestion exists in the markup—that is, using the soft-hyphenation symbol mentioned in the previous paragraph; auto hyphenates words at an appropriate point even if no hyphenation suggestions are present; and none never hyphenates words, even if suggestions are present.

WARNING *Automatic hyphenation only occurs when the language of a document has been specified, and the browser has access to a hyphenation dictionary of that language.*

You can see an example of hyphenation in Figure 6-9. The paragraph on the left has no hyphenation applied, whereas the paragraph on the right has a value of auto; the word "conversations" (highlighted) has been hyphenated and broken over two lines by the browser.

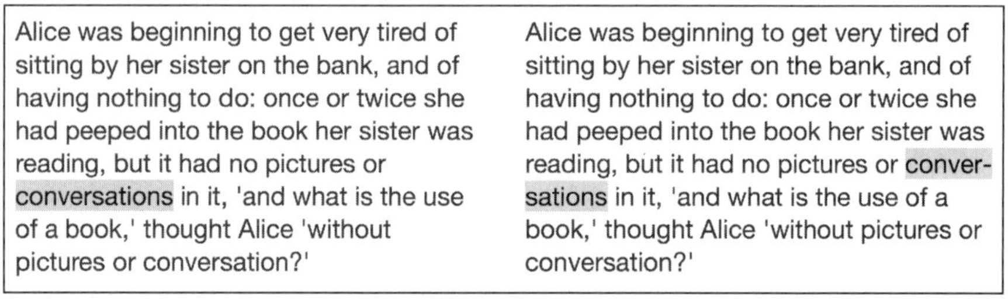

Figure 6-9: The paragraph on the right has automatic hyphenation enabled

The hyphens property currently has a rather piecemeal implementation: it's in IE10+, Firefox, and Safari, with the relevant vendor prefix for each, but has recently been pulled from Chrome (where automatic hyphenation was not supported anyway). It's also in Safari for iOS.

Resizing Elements

Another new property that's useful for elements whose contents are wider than their container is the resize property. This property lets you control an element's dimensions by providing a handle with which you can drag the element out to a different size.

The property has the following syntax:

```
E { resize: keyword; }
```

The keyword value states in which direction the element can be dragged: horizontal or vertical, both, or none. In the following example, I'll show a p element with the value of both on the resize property, using this code:

```
p {
    overflow: hidden;
    resize: both;
}
```

Figure 6-10 shows how a resizable element is displayed in Firefox on the Mac.

On a certain afternoon, in the late springtime, the bell

Figure 6-10: A resizable text box has a striped handle in the lower-right corner

The resize property is supported in Chrome, Firefox, and Safari—although the implementation can be somewhat shaky in mobile browsers, which have coarser input controls. Also be aware that resizing elements may not be keyboard-accessible, so don't make resizing a required activity.

Summary

The last few years have seen a noticeable upturn in the quality of typography on the Web, although the limited range of CSS text properties hasn't made that easy. But I believe that browser makers have noticed the push for better implementation and, slowly but surely, more typographic control is being placed in our hands.

In Chapter 5, I looked at ways to increase the range and variety of fonts, and in this chapter, I've discussed methods to make those fonts more decorative, flexible, and—most importantly—readable. Chapter 7 will complete the trio of chapters on fonts and typography by introducing a whole new way to lay out text content. Well, new to the Web, that is; printers have been doing it for centuries.

Text Effects and Typographic Styles: Browser Support

	Chrome	Firefox	Safari	IE
text-shadow	Yes	Yes	Yes	IE10
text-overflow	Yes	Yes	Yes	Yes
text-align (new values)	Yes	Yes	Yes	No
text-align-last	Yes	Yes[*]	No	Yes[†]
overflow-wrap	Yes	Yes[‡]	Yes	Yes[‡]
hyphens	No	Yes[*]	Yes[*]	IE10[*]
resize	Yes[§]	Yes	Yes[§]	No

[*] With vendor prefix
[†] Without the start and end values
[‡] As word-wrap
[§] Not in mobile browsers

7

MULTIPLE COLUMNS

Although desktop and laptop screens have gotten wider in recent years, studies still show that people have difficulty reading long lines of text. (Roughly 65 to 75 characters per line is generally considered a comfortable length to read.) This convention has led to restricted layouts and websites that don't take advantage of the opportunities presented by wider screens.

For years, magazines and newspapers have used multiple columns to flow content—addressing both the issue of long text lines and how to pack a lot of copy into limited spaces. Now, with the advent of the Multi-column Layout Module in CSS3 (*http://www.w3.org/TR/css3-multicol/*), websites can take advantage of multiple columns, too.

The Multi-column Layout Module currently has Candidate Recommendation status, meaning the module is considered mostly complete and is well implemented in IE10+ and other modern browsers (albeit with some minor caveats), so you have plenty of opportunities to experiment with multiple columns.

Column Layout Methods

You can divide your content into columns using two methods: either prescriptively, by setting a specific number of columns, or dynamically, by specifying the width of columns and allowing the browser to calculate how many columns will fit into the width of the parent element.

Note that, although Chrome, Firefox, Safari, and IE10+ all support the properties in this chapter at the time of writing, the latter browser is the only one to do so without a vendor prefix. The different browsers also have a few implementation quirks, which I'll point out as I go along.

Prescriptive Columns: column-count

The simplest way to divide your content into equally distributed columns is to use the `column-count` property:

```
E { column-count: columns; }
```

The element `E` is the parent of the content you want to divide, and the `columns` value is an integer that sets the number of columns. For example, to flow content inside a `div` element into two columns, you would use:

```
div { column-count: 2; }
```

Let's move on to a real-world example. I'll demonstrate a few paragraphs of copy displayed twice, the first distributed over two columns and the second over three columns. Here's the code I'll use:

```
div[class*='-2'] { column-count: 2; }
div[class*='-3'] { column-count: 3; }
```

NOTE   *I've used the Arbitrary Substring Attribute Value Selector in these examples, which I introduced in Chapter 3.*

You can see the results of this code in Figure 7-1.

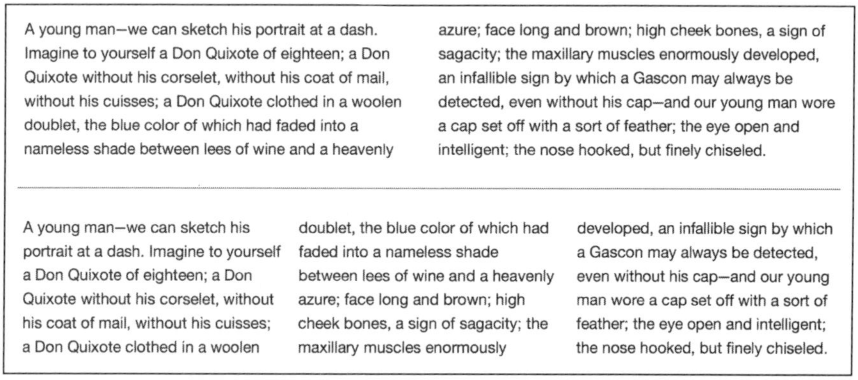

> A young man—we can sketch his portrait at a dash. Imagine to yourself a Don Quixote of eighteen; a Don Quixote without his corselet, without his coat of mail, without his cuisses; a Don Quixote clothed in a woolen doublet, the blue color of which had faded into a nameless shade between lees of wine and a heavenly azure; face long and brown; high cheek bones, a sign of sagacity; the maxillary muscles enormously developed, an infallible sign by which a Gascon may always be detected, even without his cap—and our young man wore a cap set off with a sort of feather; the eye open and intelligent; the nose hooked, but finely chiseled.

> A young man—we can sketch his portrait at a dash. Imagine to yourself a Don Quixote of eighteen; a Don Quixote without his corselet, without his coat of mail, without his cuisses; a Don Quixote clothed in a woolen doublet, the blue color of which had faded into a nameless shade between lees of wine and a heavenly azure; face long and brown; high cheek bones, a sign of sagacity; the maxillary muscles enormously developed, an infallible sign by which a Gascon may always be detected, even without his cap—and our young man wore a cap set off with a sort of feather; the eye open and intelligent; the nose hooked, but finely chiseled.

Figure 7-1: Text broken over two and then three columns

Here's the markup I used for the example shown in Figure 7-1 (edited for brevity):

```
<div class="columns-2">
    <p>A young man...</p>
</div>
<div class="columns-3">
    <p>A young man...</p>
</div>
```

The syntax is extremely simple, and the browser takes care of distributing the content equally.

Dynamic Columns: column-width

The second method for dividing content into columns is perhaps a better choice for flexible layouts. Instead of specifying the number of columns, you use the column-width property to specify the width of each column, and the browser fills the parent element with as many columns as can fit along its width. The syntax is just as easy:

```
E { column-width: length; }
```

As with column-count, E is the parent element of the content you want to divide into columns. But column-width differs in that it requires a *length* value: either a unit of length (such as px or em) or a percentage. Here's an example:

```
div { column-width: 150px; }
```

This code divides the child elements of the div into columns that are 150px wide and repeats the columns along the width of the div. Let's see how this works, using the following style rules:

```
.columns {
    column-width: 150px;
    width: 710px;
}
```

Here, I have an element with a class name of columns, which is 710px wide; the content inside it will be distributed into 150px-width columns. You can see how this renders in Figure 7-2.

With the column-width set to 150px, the browser has created four columns to fill the parent element. But all is not as it seems. Remember, the parent element is 710px wide, and even with a 12px-gap between each column (we'll talk about that shortly), the total width comes to only 636px, so where is the extra white space?

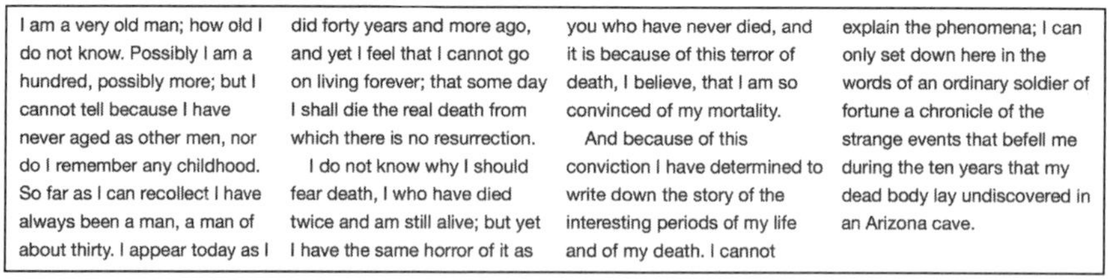

I am a very old man; how old I do not know. Possibly I am a hundred, possibly more; but I cannot tell because I have never aged as other men, nor do I remember any childhood. So far as I can recollect I have always been a man, a man of about thirty. I appear today as I	did forty years and more ago, and yet I feel that I cannot go on living forever; that some day I shall die the real death from which there is no resurrection. I do not know why I should fear death, I who have died twice and am still alive; but yet I have the same horror of it as	you who have never died, and it is because of this terror of death, I believe, that I am so convinced of my mortality. And because of this conviction I have determined to write down the story of the interesting periods of my life and of my death. I cannot	explain the phenomena; I can only set down here in the words of an ordinary soldier of fortune a chronicle of the strange events that befell me during the ten years that my dead body lay undiscovered in an Arizona cave.

Figure 7-2: Text broken across dynamically created, equally spaced columns

The algorithm that creates the columns is actually quite intelligent and resizes the columns automatically so they better fit the parent. It uses the 150px as a *minimum* value, making each column wider until the total width matches that of its parent—in this case, each column is resized to 168.5px.

Varying Distribution of Content Across Columns

By default, content that's flowed into multiple columns will be balanced as equally as possible across the columns, so no one column is longer than any of the others. If the browser can't arrange the content so there are an equal number of lines in each column, the last column will be made shorter. This is probably easier to show than to explain, so Figure 7-3 shows text distributed over three columns using the default layout method.

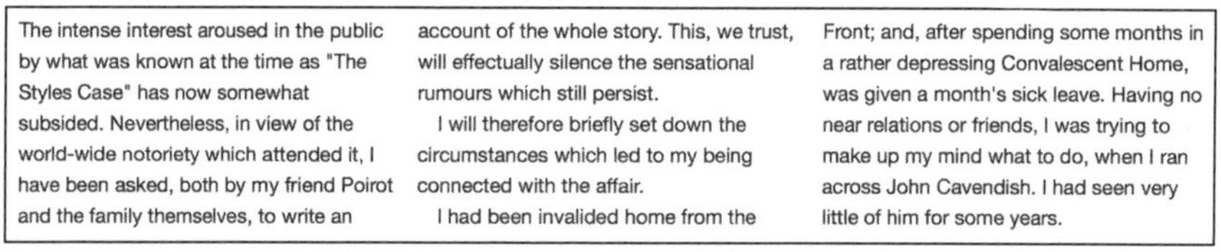

The intense interest aroused in the public by what was known at the time as "The Styles Case" has now somewhat subsided. Nevertheless, in view of the world-wide notoriety which attended it, I have been asked, both by my friend Poirot and the family themselves, to write an	account of the whole story. This, we trust, will effectually silence the sensational rumours which still persist. I will therefore briefly set down the circumstances which led to my being connected with the affair. I had been invalided home from the	Front; and, after spending some months in a rather depressing Convalescent Home, was given a month's sick leave. Having no near relations or friends, I was trying to make up my mind what to do, when I ran across John Cavendish. I had seen very little of him for some years.

Figure 7-3: Text dynamically distributed over three columns

You can see that all three columns have the same number of lines. If you want to change this default behavior, you can do so with the `column-fill` property:

```
E { column-fill: keyword; }
```

This property has two possible keyword values: the default is `balance`, which tries to make all the columns equal length, as in Figure 7-3; and the alternative is `auto`, which fills columns sequentially.

The auto value takes effect only when the parent element has a fixed height. The content is flowed into the first column to fill the height and then into the next column until that one is filled, and so on.

When using the auto value, it may appear that you have fewer columns than are specified in the column-count property, but that won't be the case; it's just that some columns would be empty.

You can see an example of the auto value for column-fill in Figure 7-4; the first two columns have an equal number of lines and the third has three fewer, as the text is simply flowed into the columns without the browser trying to balance them.

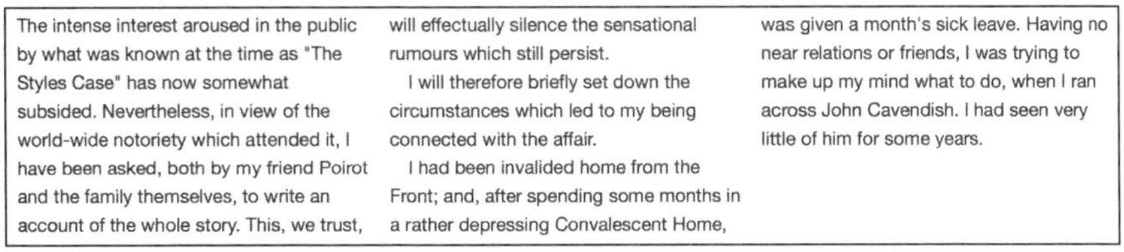

The intense interest aroused in the public by what was known at the time as "The Styles Case" has now somewhat subsided. Nevertheless, in view of the world-wide notoriety which attended it, I have been asked, both by my friend Poirot and the family themselves, to write an account of the whole story. This, we trust,	will effectually silence the sensational rumours which still persist.
	
	    I will therefore briefly set down the circumstances which led to my being connected with the affair.
	    I had been invalided home from the Front; and, after spending some months in a rather depressing Convalescent Home,
		was given a month's sick leave. Having no near relations or friends, I was trying to make up my mind what to do, when I ran across John Cavendish. I had seen very little of him for some years.

Figure 7-4: Content flowed into columns with the auto value for the column-fill property

Firefox and IE10+ are the only browsers to implement this property currently, although Chrome and Safari automatically act as if the auto value were applied when a height is fixed on the parent.

Combining column-count and column-width

You can set both column-count and column-width properties on an element, though, at first, you might think doing so would create a conflict. This possibility has been taken into consideration, however: If both properties are applied to the same element, the column-count value acts as a maximum. To illustrate, let's refer to Figure 7-2 but change the CSS to also include the column-count property:

```
.columns {
    column-count: 3;
    column-width: 150px;
}
```

Here is the logic behind this: divide the text into columns of 150px each, unless that would create three or more columns, in which case make three columns with a minimum width of 150px.

If you refer back to the example shown in Figure 7-2, you'll remember that, given the parent element's width of 710px, the column-width property rendered four columns. As you're applying both properties on the same element, however, the column-count property takes precedence and only three columns are distributed, with their widths dynamically altered to best fit the parent element. You can see the result in Figure 7-5.

I am a very old man; how old I do not know. Possibly I am a hundred, possibly more; but I cannot tell because I have never aged as other men, nor do I remember any childhood. So far as I can recollect I have always been a man, a man of about thirty. I appear today as I did forty years and more ago, and yet I feel that I cannot go on living forever; that some day	I shall die the real death from which there is no resurrection. I do not know why I should fear death, I who have died twice and am still alive; but yet I have the same horror of it as you who have never died, and it is because of this terror of death, I believe, that I am so convinced of my mortality. And because of this conviction I have	determined to write down the story of the interesting periods of my life and of my death. I cannot explain the phenomena; I can only set down here in the words of an ordinary soldier of fortune a chronicle of the strange events that befell me during the ten years that my dead body lay undiscovered in an Arizona cave.

Figure 7-5: When combining column properties, column-count acts as a maximum.

If you want to use these two properties together, a shorthand property is available:

```
E { columns: column-width column-count; }
```

So if you were to use the values from Figure 7-5 with this shorthand property, it would look like this:

```
div { columns: 150px 3; }
```

Column Gaps and Rules

When using a prescriptive multi-column layout, the browser should place a default 1em gap between each column. You can, however, alter that default and specify your own distances by using two new properties: column-gap and column-rule.

The first property, column-gap, sets the space between columns, and its syntax is simple:

```
E { column-gap: length; }
```

The *length* value is any number with a standard CSS length unit. Here's an example that puts a 2em gap between each of your generated columns (though not on the outside of either the first or last column):

```
div { column-gap: 2em; }
```

The second property, column-rule, draws a line, similar to a border, equidistantly between columns. The syntax for column-rule is actually shorthand for three subproperties: column-rule-width, column-rule-style, and column-rule-color. These subproperties take values in exactly the same way as their equivalent border-* properties from CSS2. Here's the syntax:

```
E {
    column-rule-width: length;
    column-rule-style: border-style;
    column-rule-color: color;
    column-rule: length border-style color;
}
```

If you added real values, you would have something like this:

```
div {
    column-rule-color: silver;
    column-rule-style: double;
    column-rule-width: 0.3em;
}
```

You can then use the `column-rule` shorthand to set all three subproperties at once:

```
div { column-rule: 0.3em double silver; }
```

Let's see the `column-gap` and `column-rule` properties in action. The following example combines them with `column-count`:

```
.columns {
    column-count: 3;
    column-gap: 2em;
    column-rule: 0.3em double silver;
}
```

This example splits the element's children into three columns, each with a gap of 2em between the columns, and a 0.3em rule. The thickness of the rule has no effect on layout—no matter how thick you make the rule, the gap will always stay the same width. You can see the result of this example in Figure 7-6.

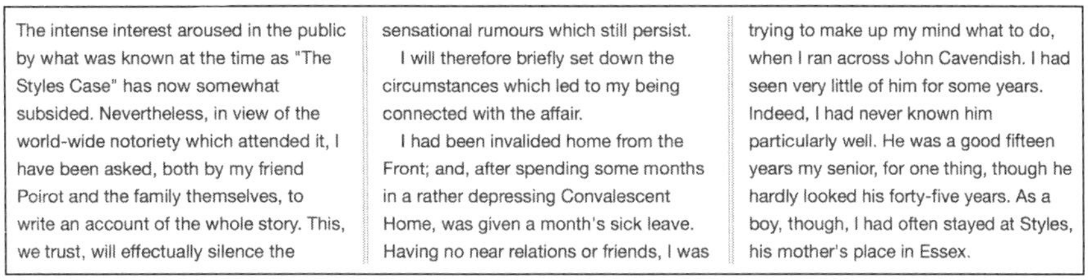

| The intense interest aroused in the public by what was known at the time as "The Styles Case" has now somewhat subsided. Nevertheless, in view of the world-wide notoriety which attended it, I have been asked, both by my friend Poirot and the family themselves, to write an account of the whole story. This, we trust, will effectually silence the | sensational rumours which still persist. I will therefore briefly set down the circumstances which led to my being connected with the affair. I had been invalided home from the Front; and, after spending some months in a rather depressing Convalescent Home, was given a month's sick leave. Having no near relations or friends, I was | trying to make up my mind what to do, when I ran across John Cavendish. I had seen very little of him for some years. Indeed, I had never known him particularly well. He was a good fifteen years my senior, for one thing, though he hardly looked his forty-five years. As a boy, though, I had often stayed at Styles, his mother's place in Essex. |

Figure 7-6: Inter-column gaps and rules

Containing Elements Within Columns

So far in these examples I've only used blocks of text, which flow neatly into columns. But what happens with larger elements, like images, that could have a width greater than the column that contains them? Let's see what happens when I add an image that's wider than a single column inside a column layout, using the `img` element. The result is displayed in Figure 7-7.

| The intense interest aroused in the public by what was known at the time as "The Styles Case" has now somewhat subsided. Nevertheless, in view of the world-wide notoriety which attended it, I have been asked, both by my friend Poirot and the family themselves, to write an account of the whole story. This, we trust, will effectually silence the sensational rumours which still persist. | Front; and, after spending some months in a rather depressing Convalescent Home, was given a month's sick leave. Having no near relations or friends, I was trying to make up my mind what to do, when I ran across John Cavendish. I had seen very little of him for some years. Indeed, I had never known him particularly well. He was a good fifteen years my senior, for one thing, though he hardly looked his forty-five years. |

I will therefore briefly set down the circumstances which led to my being connected with the affair.

I had been invalided home from the

Figure 7-7: An *img* element wider than a column[1]

As you can see, the image is displayed in the second column, but the overflow is clipped at a point halfway inside the column-gap. The only browser that differs from this behavior (at the time of writing) is Firefox, which (unfortunately) keeps the width of the image but flows the content of subsequent columns over it, as shown in Figure 7-8.

The intense interest aroused in the public by what was known at the time as "The Styles Case" has now somewhat subsided. Nevertheless, in view of the world-wide notoriety which attended it, I have been asked, both by my friend Poirot and the family themselves, to write an account of the whole story. This, we trust, will effectually silence the sensational rumours which still persist.

I will therefore briefly set down the circumstances which led to my being

connected with the affair.

I had been invalided home from the Front; and, after spending some months in a rather depressing Convalescent Home, was given a month's sick leave. Having no near relations or friends, I was trying to make up my mind what to do, when I ran across John Cavendish. I had seen very little of him for some years. Indeed, I had never known him particularly well. He was a good fifteen years my senior, for one thing, though he hardly looked his forty-five years.

Figure 7-8: Firefox differs from all other browsers in the way it displays wide elements in columns.

Hopefully, this issue will be fixed in a future release (perhaps even by the time you read this).

To work around the problem entirely, I could set a value of 100% on the max-width property of the image, as the width is calculated from that of its containing column, rather than the parent element.

Elements Spanning Multiple Columns

On occasion, you may want certain elements to span multiple columns—for example, a subheading that will be used to break up sections of a story. To deal with these elements, the module introduces the column-span element. Here's the syntax:

```
E { column-span: value; }
```

---

1. The landscape image is by Flickr user Nicholas_T (*http://www.flickr.com/photos/nicholas_t/1426623052/*) and is used under license.

In this case, *value* can be only one of two possibilities: all or none. The default is none, which keeps the element in the column flow. The alternative value, all, provides a break in the flow—all content before the element will be distributed into columns, and all content after the element will be distributed into columns, but the element itself—known as the *spanning element*—will not.

In the following example, the h2 element has a column-span value of all, so it spans multiple columns, causing a break in the text flow. You can see the result in Figure 7-9.

```
h2 { column-span: all; }
```

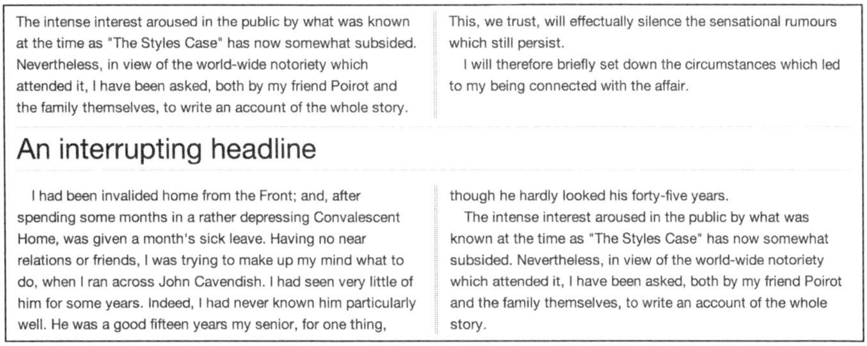

The intense interest aroused in the public by what was known at the time as "The Styles Case" has now somewhat subsided. Nevertheless, in view of the world-wide notoriety which attended it, I have been asked, both by my friend Poirot and the family themselves, to write an account of the whole story.

This, we trust, will effectually silence the sensational rumours which still persist.

I will therefore briefly set down the circumstances which led to my being connected with the affair.

An interrupting headline

I had been invalided home from the Front; and, after spending some months in a rather depressing Convalescent Home, was given a month's sick leave. Having no near relations or friends, I was trying to make up my mind what to do, when I ran across John Cavendish. I had seen very little of him for some years. Indeed, I had never known him particularly well. He was a good fifteen years my senior, for one thing,

though he hardly looked his forty-five years.

The intense interest aroused in the public by what was known at the time as "The Styles Case" has now somewhat subsided. Nevertheless, in view of the world-wide notoriety which attended it, I have been asked, both by my friend Poirot and the family themselves, to write an account of the whole story.

Figure 7-9: An h2 element spans two columns

Firefox is the only browser not to support this property at the time of writing.

Summary

Although CSS3 makes flowing your content into columns easy, the challenges it presents are not so much technical as they are practical: What happens if you want to use images that are wider than a column or if you want to use long headlines in narrow columns?

Although using multiple columns is definitely appropriate in certain situations, think twice about whether your content is suitable. Make sure you have full control over your content before using these properties, and don't design websites that rely on multiple columns if your client doesn't have a dedicated and conscientious web content team.

Also, bear in mind that screen resolutions can vary dramatically, and content that looks readable to you may not be readable to the visitors of your website. If they have to scroll up and down too frequently, which can cause lots of confusion, they may be put off from visiting your site altogether. But with all that said, clever use of columns can make your content much more readable.

In the last three chapters, I've described how CSS3 provides methods to format and present your text copy, giving you better control over your typography and layout. Next, I introduce ways you can improve the overall visual presentation of your websites, starting with new background and border effects.

Multiple Columns: Browser Support

	Chrome	Firefox	Safari	IE
column-count	Yes*	Yes*	Yes*	IE10
column-width	Yes*	Yes*	Yes*	IE10
columns	Yes*	Yes*	Yes*	IE10
column-fill	No	Yes*	No	IE10
column-gap	Yes*	Yes*	Yes*	IE10
column-rule	Yes*	Yes*	Yes*	IE10
column-span	Yes*	No	Yes*	IE10

* With vendor prefix

8

BACKGROUND IMAGES

Adding decorative elements to make our websites more visually appealing used to be surprisingly resource- and time-intensive. Even seemingly simple graphical effects, such as two background images on the same element, required a lot of unnecessary markup, and this in turn made pages slower to render and harder to maintain.

CSS3 introduces a number of new and extended properties that are aimed at decorating elements much more simply, and the browser makers have been quick to implement them and to add a number of their own implementations as well. Over the next few chapters, we'll take a look at the new range of features that we can use to prettify our pages, from background images to decorative borders and new color effects.

I'll begin by taking you on a walk through the Backgrounds and Borders Module (*http://www.w3.org/TR/css3-background/*). Because of high demand from web developers, the new properties it brings are already well implemented by browsers. Internet Explorer 9 fully implemented the properties and changes listed in this chapter, as have—in most cases—all of the other major modern browsers, so unless otherwise stated in the text you can presume widespread support.

As the Backgrounds and Borders Module is quite extensive, I'll break it over two chapters and start with a look at background image properties. Background images have been part of CSS for many years, but unlike previous versions, in CSS3, you can apply multiple images to elements, and you can resize those images on the fly. Just these two new features alone would be enough to please most of us, but the specification goes further to provide more control over image placement and tiling.

Updates to Existing Background Properties

Many of the other CSS3 modules bring new properties and even whole new concepts to CSS, but the strength of the Backgrounds and Borders Module is the way it extends existing properties to make them more powerful and useful. That's not to say this module has no novelties—it certainly does, and I'll come to them shortly. But the subtleties shine, and in this section, I want to talk about the extensions and changes to properties you'll be familiar with from CSS2.1.

background-position

The background-position property in CSS2.1 accepts two values: either a keyword for each side of the box (top, right, and so on), or length or percentage values that set a position relative to the top-left corner of the element to which it's applied. This is okay for many tasks but doesn't really provide the fine control that we desire when laying out pages.

In CSS3, the property now accepts up to four values: you can use keywords to specify a side and then length or percentage values for relative distance from that side. Take a look at this example code:

```
.foo { background-position: right 10em bottom 50%; }
```

The background image on the element .foo will be positioned 10em from the right and 50% from the bottom. This positioning would have been very difficult in CSS2.1; you had to know the widths of all the elements involved and that they didn't change.

background-attachment

The way that a background image scrolls in the viewport is determined by the background-attachment property. The permitted values in CSS2.1 are scroll (the default), which means the image doesn't scroll with the element it's applied to but does scroll with the viewport, and fixed, which means the image doesn't scroll with either its element or the viewport.

A new value of `local` is introduced in CSS3; this value allows an image to scroll with both its element and the viewport. This is nigh-impossible to demonstrate in a static book, so I urge you to take a look at example file 8-a on the book's companion website (*http://thebookofcss3.com/*).

The new value is supported in IE9+ and all other major modern desktop browsers. Mobile browsers, however, tend to use different viewport layout mechanisms in which fixed elements don't really work, so you'll likely get unexpected (or, no) behavior in those.

background-repeat

In CSS2.1, the `background-repeat` property accepts one of four possible values: `no-repeat`, `repeat`, `repeat-x`, and `repeat-y`. With these values, you can tile images either horizontally or vertically (or both) across an element, but they don't allow for any finer control than that. CSS3, however, extends the usefulness of the property in two ways: a pair of new properties and a tweak to the syntax.

The first of the new properties is `space`, which sets the background image to repeat across its containing element as many times as possible without clipping the image. All of the repetitions (except the first and last) are then equally spaced, so the image is evenly distributed.

The second is `round`, which likewise sets the background image to repeat as many times as possible without clipping, but instead of equally spacing the repetitions, the images scales so a whole number of images fills the containing element.

To compare the difference between the two, I've put together an example in which a different `background-repeat` value is applied to two elements, using the following code:

```
.space { background-repeat: space; }
.round { background-repeat: round; }
```

Figure 8-1 displays the results. The element on the left is for reference; it has the default `background-repeat` value of `repeat` and shows the behavior you would currently expect. The element in the middle has a value of `space`, and the maximum number of images that can be tiled without clipping or scaling are displayed with empty space between them. Finally, the element on the right has a value of `round`, which calculates the maximum whole number that can fit in the containing element both horizontally and vertically, scaling the image as required.

Internet Explorer 9+ and Chrome are currently the only browsers to implement these keywords correctly. Safari recognizes them but makes them both behave incorrectly, as if `no-repeat` were applied. Firefox ignores them and uses the previous cascaded or inherited value.

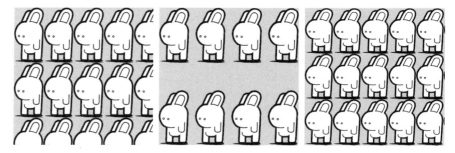

Figure 8-1: background-repeat values: repeat (left), space (center), and round (right)[1]

I also mentioned a change to the syntax. You can control tiling on the two different axes independently, as the property now accepts two values. The first value controls tiling on the horizontal axis, the second on the vertical. So if you want a background image to repeat with rounding on the vertical and spacing on the horizontal, you use this code:

```
.foo { background-repeat: round space; }
```

The result is shown in Figure 8-2.

Figure 8-2: Different background-repeat values applied to the horizontal and vertical

Multiple Background Images

The first new feature in the Backgrounds and Borders Module isn't a new property but an extension of an existing one—or, rather, several existing ones. Using CSS2.1, you could only apply a single background image to an element, but in CSS3, (almost all of) the background-* properties now accept multiple values, so you can add many background images to one element.

---

1. The bunny image is by Flickr user Andrew Mason (*http://www.flickr.com/photos/a_mason/ 42744470/*) and is used under license.

To do this, you need just list the values separated by commas. For example, here's the syntax with background-image:

```
E { background-image: value, value; }
```

For each background layer you create, you can add appropriate values to all of the relevant background-* properties. Here's a real-world example:

```
h2 {
    background-image: url('monkey.svg'), url('landscape.jpg');
    background-position: 95% 85%, 50% 50%;
    background-repeat: no-repeat;
}
```

You can see how this looks in Figure 8-3. The layers are created in reverse order—that is, the first layer in the list becomes the topmost layer, and so on. In my example code, *monkey.svg* is a layer above *landscape.jpg*. The background-position property follows the same order: The landscape is positioned at 50% left and 50% top (the horizontal and vertical center) of its containing element and the monkey at 95% left and 85% top.

Figure 8-3: Two background images on the same element[2]

Note that I've only given background-repeat one value; if a property has fewer values than there are background layers, the values will repeat. In this example that means no-repeat will be applied to all background layers.

You can use multiple values with the background shorthand property; as with the individual properties, you only need to provide a comma-separated list. To get the same result seen in Figure 8-3, I can also use this code:

```
h2 {
    background:
    url('monkey.svg') no-repeat 95% 85%,
    url('landscape.jpg') no-repeat 50% 50%;
}
```

---

2. The monkey image is by rachelps on openclipart (*https://openclipart.org/detail/2876/cheeky-monkey-by-rachelps*) and is used under license.

I mentioned at the start of this section that almost all background properties can have multiple values. `background-color` is the exception, however, as the color layer will always be stacked below all other background layers. If you want to specify a background color when using the shorthand property, you must place it in the last instance of the comma-separated list. In the case of my example code that would be in the instance with the landscape picture:

```
h2 {
    background:
    url('monkey.svg') no-repeat 95% 85%,
    url('landscape.jpg') no-repeat 50% 50% #000;
}
```

Dynamically Scaled Background Images

A new property to CSS3 is `background-size`. This property, as you can probably guess, allows you to set the size of the background images. Here's the syntax:

```
E { background-size: value; }
```

This property's value can be a pair of lengths or percentages, a single length or percentage, or a keyword. If a pair is used, the syntax is as follows:

```
E { background-size: width height; }
```

To resize a background image to be 100px wide and 200px high, you use:

```
div { background-size: 100px 200px; }
```

The length can be any standard unit of measurement. If you use percentages, the dimension is based on the containing element, *not* the background image. So a width and height of 100%, for example, will stretch the background image to fill the container. To make the image appear at its natural size, use the `auto` keyword.

If you only specify a single value, that value is considered the width, and the height is then assigned the default value of `auto`. Therefore, these two examples are exactly equivalent:

```
div { background-size: 100px auto; }
div { background-size: 100px; }
```

You can use your newly learned multiple background method with background-size as well. For example, let's revisit Figure 8-3, but repeat the monkey image a few more times, adding different values to the background-position and background-size properties. Here's the code:

```
h2 {
background:
    url('monkey.svg') no-repeat 95% 85%,
    url('monkey.svg') no-repeat 50% 80%,
    url('monkey.svg') no-repeat 10% 100%,
    url('landscape.jpg') no-repeat 50% 50%;
    background-size: auto 80%, auto 15%, auto 50%, auto;
}
```

Figure 8-4 shows this method in action. One monkey has a vertical background-size of 80%, the next 15%, and the last, 50%; in all cases, the horizontal size has been set to auto to keep the image in proportion.

Figure 8-4: Example of multiple resized background images

As well as length values, two keywords are available: contain and cover. The contain keyword sets the image to scale (proportionately) as large as possible, without exceeding either the height or width of the containing element; cover sets the image to scale to the size of either the height or width of the containing element, whichever is larger.

Take a look at the following code to see what I mean:

```
.monkey-1, .monkey-2 {
    background-image: url('monkey.svg');
    background-position: 50% 50%;
}
.monkey-1 { background-size: contain; }
.monkey-2 { background-size: cover; }
```

I used two elements, with classes of monkey-1 and monkey-2, and set different keyword values for background-size on each. The result is shown in Figure 8-5.

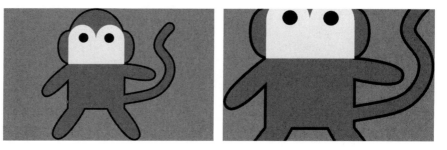

Figure 8-5: background-size keywords: contain (left) and cover (right)

The box on the left has the contain keyword value, so the background image fills the box vertically (the shortest length); the box on the right has the cover keyword value, so the background image fills the box horizontally (the longest length) and is cropped at the top and bottom.

Background Clip and Origin

In CSS2, the position of a background image is defined relative to the outer limit of its containing element's padding, and any overflow extends underneath its border. CSS3 introduces two new properties that provide more granular control over this placement.

The first property is background-clip, which sets the section of the box model that becomes the limit of where the background (either color or image) is displayed. Here's the syntax:

```
E { background-clip: box; }
```

The *box* value can be one of three keywords: border-box, content-box, or padding-box. border-box, the default value, displays the background behind the border (you can see it if you use a transparent or semi-opaque border color). A value of padding-box displays the background only up to, and not behind, the border. content-box means the background stops at the element's padding.

I'll illustrate the difference using the following code:

```
h2 {
    background: url('landscape.jpg') no-repeat 50% 50% #EFEFEF;
    border-width: 20px;
    padding: 20px;
}
h2.brdr { background-clip: border-box; }
h2.pddng { background-clip: padding-box; }
h2.cntnt { background-clip: content-box; }
```

I've used three h2 elements with classes of brdr, pdding, and cntnt, respectively. Figure 8-6 illustrates the difference between the values.

Figure 8-6: Showing the effect of different values on the background-clip property: border-box (left), padding-box (center), and content-box (right)

I've used a semi-opaque border (I'll explain how in Chapter 10) so you can see the image paint beneath it in the box on the left, which has the border-box value. The central box has the padding-box value, and as you can see, the background stops at the limit of the padding. In the box on the right, the value is content-box, so the background does not show behind the padding.

The second property that gives you more granular control is background-origin. Using background-origin, you can set the point where the background is calculated to begin. As I mentioned before, CSS2 background positions are calculated relative to the limit of the padding, but background-origin lets you change that. Here's the syntax:

```
E { background-origin: box; }
```

The box value accepts the same keywords as you've just seen in background-clip: border-box, content-box, and padding-box. I'll explain the different results using this code:

```
h2 { background: url('monkey.svg') no-repeat 0 100%;}
h2.brdr { background-origin: border-box; }
h2.cntnt { background-origin: content-box; }
h2.pddng { background-origin: padding-box; }
```

The effects of the different values are illustrated in Figure 8-7. As you can see, the monkey is in a different position in each box because the background-position is calculated relative to a different point in each box (I've added a background grid to make it a little easier to see).

The background-position is always set at 0 100%, which is the bottom left. The point from which the bottom left is measured changes depending on the background-origin value, however. In the first box, the background originates at the limit of the border; in the second, from the limit of the padding; and in the third, from the limit of the content box.

Figure 8-7: The background-origin property with values of border-box (left), padding-box (center), and content-box (right)

A couple of things to bear in mind: First, this property has no effect if the background-position is set to fixed. Second, both background-clip and background-origin accept multiple values, using the same syntax shown in "Multiple Background Images" on page 88.

Updated Background Shortcut

The background shortcut property has been updated to include values for the background-size, background-clip, and background-origin properties. Values for background-size should immediately follow those for background-position and be separated by a forward slash, like so:

```
E { background: url('bar.png') no-repeat 50% 50% / 50% auto; }
```

In this case, the background image, *bar.png*, will be positioned at the dead center of the element, with a width set to 50% of the element and an automatic height.

For background-clip and background-origin, if only one box value (border-box, padding-box, or content-box) is present, both properties will be set to that value. If two box values are supplied, the first will be set on background-origin and the second on background-clip. As an illustration, take this shorthand code:

```
E { background: url('bar.png') no-repeat padding-box content-box; }
```

In this case, the origin of the background image will be the padding box, and the image will be clipped to the content box.

Summary

The new features introduced in this chapter are a big step toward the stated aim of CSS: to separate a page's content from its presentation. More flexibility with background images means fewer required elements to create the effects we want, and the more nonessential markup we can remove from our documents, the easier our pages will be to maintain and the better it will be for semantics.

In this chapter, I've covered only half of what the Backgrounds and Borders module offers, so in the next chapter I'll cover the other half—which, as you can probably guess by the title "Border and Box Effects," relates to borders.

Background Images: Browser Support

	Chrome	Firefox	Safari	IE
background-position (edge values)	Yes	Yes	Yes	Yes
background-attachment	Yes	Yes	Yes	IE10
background-repeat (new values)	Yes	No	No*	Yes
background-repeat (two values)	Yes	Yes	Yes	Yes
Multiple background images	Yes	Yes	Yes	Yes
background-size	Yes	Yes	Yes	Yes
Updated background property	Yes	Yes	Yes	Yes
background-clip	Yes	Yes	Yes	Yes
background-origin	Yes	Yes	Yes	Yes

* The values are recognized but don't display correctly.

9

BORDER AND BOX EFFECTS

The ability to add borders to page elements has been around, almost unchanged, since the days of CSS1. What developers *wanted* to do with borders, however, outstripped what they *could* do with them years ago. Adding border effects like rounded corners or shadows has probably been responsible for more extraneous empty markup elements than almost anything else in the web development world. Things that should have been simple often involved some incredibly complex workarounds.

The second part of our look at the Backgrounds and Borders Module explores new methods of decorating elements without extra markup. You'll learn how to make rounded corners, use images for borders, and add drop shadows.

Giving Your Borders Rounded Corners

Since the earliest days of the Web, designers have been putting rounded corners on page elements. That they've had no way to create them without using images seems crazy. To create a box of flexible width with four rounded corners has meant creating four images and adding at least two extra nonsemantic elements, which made maintaining a website much harder than it needed to be.

But no more. The Backgrounds and Borders Module introduces a way to round the corners of your elements using CSS alone. Each corner is treated as a quarter ellipse, which is defined by a curve that is drawn between a point on the *x*-axis and a point on the *y*-axis (you may remember those from Chapter 6). Figure 9-1 illustrates this more clearly.

A quarter ellipse can be *regular*, which means the length along both axes is the same, or *irregular*, which means the length along each axis is different. Figure 9-2 shows examples of both.

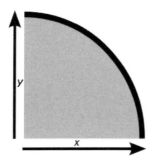

Figure 9-1: A quarter ellipse made by the curve between lengths on the x- and y-axes

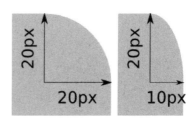

Figure 9-2: A regular curve (left) has identical values on both axes; an irregular curve has different values on each axis.

CSS3 defines these curves using the `border-radius` property. With this property, you can define the radius of the quarter ellipse simply, using the following syntax:

```
E { border-v-h-radius: x y; }
```

In this syntax, *v* is a keyword value of `top` or `bottom`; *h* is a keyword value of `left` or `right`; and the *x* and *y* values are lengths along the axes that define the curve of the quarter ellipse. That sounds like a mouthful, but here's an example that should make it clearer:

```
div { border-top-right-radius: 20px 20px; }
```

This syntax will round the top-right corner of a `div` element with a radius of 20px horizontally and vertically, which is a regular curve.

In fact, for regular curves, `border-radius` lets you simplify even further by leaving out either the *x* or the *y* value; if one value is not specified, both are assumed to be equal. So if you want to apply that radius to each corner of your element, you use this code:

```
div {
    border-top-left-radius: 20px;
    border-top-right-radius: 20px;
```

```
    border-bottom-right-radius: 20px;
    border-bottom-left-radius: 20px;
}
```

To create a shape with irregular rounded corners, you just use different values on the individual properties:

```
div {
    border-top-left-radius: 10px 20px;
    border-top-right-radius: 10px 20px;
    border-bottom-right-radius: 10px 20px;
    border-bottom-left-radius: 10px 20px;
}
```

You can compare the two different code examples in Figure 9-3: the shape on the left uses the first snippet and has four regular curved corners, and on the right is the result of the second snippet with four (equal) irregular corners.

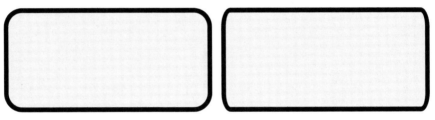

Figure 9-3: Two elements, one with regular rounded corners (left) and one with irregular corners (right)

The border-radius Shorthand

If having to write a different property for each corner strikes you as quite repetitive, you'll be happy to learn that a shorthand property is available. As with border-width, margin, and padding, you can specify one, two, three, or four values. Where those values refer to sides, however, the border-radius values refer to corners, starting at the top left:

```
E { border-radius: [top-left] [top-right] [bottom-right] [bottom-left]; }
E { border-radius: [top-left] [top-right & bottom-left] [bottom-right]; }
E { border-radius: [top-left & bottom-right] [top-right & bottom-left]; }
E { border-radius: [top-left & top-right & bottom-right & bottom-left]; }
```

So if I want to apply a value of 20px to the top-left and top-right corners of a div, and 10px to the bottom-right and bottom-left corners, here's the code I use:

```
div { border-radius: 20px 20px 10px 10px; }
```

NOTE   *Using the shorthand syntax like this only creates regular rounded corners; I'll cover the shorthand for irregular corners momentarily.*

To illustrate the shorthand property in action, I'll apply rules to three elements, each time with a different set of values:

```
.radius-1 { border-radius: 0 20px; }
.radius-2 { border-radius: 0 10px 20px; }
.radius-3 { border-radius: 0 0 20px 20px; }
```

You can see the results in Figure 9-4. The first (left) box has two values for border-radius: The top-left and bottom-right corners have a value of 0, so are square, but the top-right and bottom-left are rounded with a radius of 20px. The second (middle) box has three values: The top-left corner is once again square, but now the top-right and bottom-left corners have a 10px radius, and the bottom-right corner has a value of 20px. Finally, the third (right) box has four values: The top-left and top-right corners have a value of 0, so are squared, whereas the bottom-right and bottom-left have radii of 20px.

Figure 9-4: Effects of different values for the border-radius shorthand property

You can also use the shorthand syntax with irregular curves. To achieve this effect, you list the values separated by a slash (/):

```
border-radius: { horizontal-radius / vertical-radius; }
```

Each side of the slash can contain between one and four values, as with the shorthand for regular curves. This means, for example, you could have one value for the horizontal radius and four separate values for the vertical radii. Again, I'll illustrate what this looks like with some examples:

```
.radius-1 { border-radius: 20px / 10px; }
.radius-2 { border-radius: 20px / 10px 20px; }
.radius-3 { border-radius: 10px 20px 20px / 20px 10px; }
```

Figure 9-5 shows the results. The first (left) box has four equal corners of 20px horizontal and a 10px vertical radius. The second (middle) box has two corners of 20px/10px and two of 20px/20px. The third (right) box has a top-left corner of 10px/20px, a top-right and a bottom-left corner of 20px/10px, and a bottom-right corner of 20px/20px.

Using Percentage Values

The examples so far in this chapter use length units, but you can also define border-radius using a percentage value, which is the percentage of the length of the side of the element it's applied to. You'll find this especially handy if you want to make a perfect circle in CSS: A square element with four equal curves of half of each side creates a perfectly round element.

The next example shows two elements with the same percentage border-radius value (50%) applied to each corner. Both have the same height, but one is twice as wide as the other:

```
div {
    border-radius: 50%;
    height: 100px;
    }
.ellipse { width: 200px; }
.circle { width: 100px; }
```

The result is shown in Figure 9-6. The element on the left has the wider length, so the rounding of the corners creates an ellipse. On the right, the element has equal height and width, resulting in a perfect sphere.

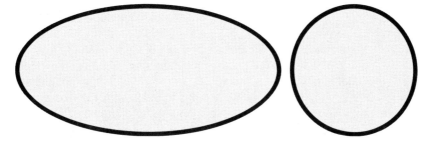

Figure 9-6: Percentage values on border-radius create an ellipse (left) and a circle (right).

Using Images for Borders

Another common way to style elements is to use background images as decorative borders. With CSS2, however, you had no way to achieve this, and you had to use a lot of extra markup to get the desired effect, with a subsequent penalty on semantics and maintainability. CSS3 introduces a series of properties that provide a simple syntax to apply decorative borders.

border-image-source

The first property, `border-image-source`, sets the source of the image that will be used for the border—but you probably guessed that. It takes a single value, which is an image data type; for most browsers that's only the `url()` function. Here's an example of `border-image-source`:

```
E { border-image-source: url('foo.png'); }
```

 This property should also accept gradient functions (see Chapter 11) as values, but currently only Chrome and Firefox support that use.

border-image-slice

Once you have the source of the image for the border, you need to slice it. The `border-image-slice` property accepts between one and four values, each of which maps to a side of an element, similar to `margin`, `padding`, `border-radius`, and so on. These values are used to set a distance from each edge of the image, marking the area used to "frame" the element.

I'm aware that's probably a little confusing, so I'll explain with an example. Take a look at this code:

```
E { border-image-slice: 34; }
```

Note here that no units are used on the number value. The number serves two purposes: for bitmap images (such as JPG or PNG), the units are pixel values; but for vector images (such as SVG), they are coordinate values. You could also use percentage values as an alternative.

In my example code, I provided only a single value, which sets the area I want to slice: 34px from the top, right, bottom, and left. Take a look at Figure 9-7, which shows how this value is used to divide the source image into nine segments: four corners (c1, c2, and so on), four sides (known as *slices*—slice1, slice2, and so on), and the central fill. Each of these slices will be placed onto the border of a target element in the equivalent positions.

With the source image and slices defined, now I just have to set a border on the element to apply a border image. The image will be applied to the area created by the border, so in the following code example, I define a 34px border on the top and bottom, and 10px on the left and right.

```
E {
    border: 34px 10px;
    border-image-slice: 34;
    border-image-source: url('foo.png');
}
```

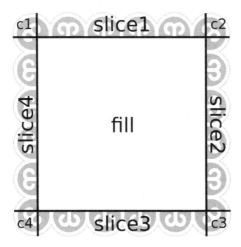

Figure 9-7: Where the specified values in border-image will slice the image

You can see in Figure 9-8 how this code is applied: the top and bottom image slices have the same height as the top and bottom borders, so the image is applied at its natural height, whereas the left and right slices are applied to borders that are less than half their width, so the image is squashed to fit. The corner slices are distorted to fit the two different dimensions.

Figure 9-8: Here, 34px image slices are applied to a border of 34px horizontally and 10px vertically.

The default behavior of border images is to use only the slices and corners on the border, leaving the center of the element blank for its own background properties to be shown. The border-image-slice property has an optional keyword value of fill, however; if the fill keyword is included, the area of the image inside the slices will be applied over the background of the element in the appropriate place.

```
E { border-image-slice: value fill; }
```

Figure 9-9 shows a comparison of an element with a border image, with and without the fill keyword.

NOTE   *Filling the element with* border-image-slice *means you have no control over the fill sizing and can leave it quite distorted, so consider carefully if you want to use this rather than* background-image.

Figure 9-9: Left to right: the source image, applied as a border image, and with the fill keyword value

border-image-width

As you saw in Figure 9-8, border image slices are stretched or condensed to fit the width of the element's border; for example, if the element has a border that's 10px wide but your slices are 40px wide, each slice will be condensed to a quarter of its height or width in order to fit. You can control this by using the border-image-width property:

```
E { border-image-width: value; }
```

Like border-width or border-image-slice, the *value* here can actually be up to four values, to match the sides of the element, and each can be a length, a percentage, or a unitless number.

The *value* creates a "virtual" border on the element, by which I mean it has no impact on page layout or flow; unlike border-width, the border that *value* creates is visual only and has no effect on the box model. To illustrate the difference, take a look at this code:

```
E { border-width: 34px; }
F {
  border-width: 1px;
```

```
  border-image-width: 34px;
}
E, F {
  border-image-slice: 34;
  border-image-source: url('foo.png');
}
```

You can see how this compares in Figure 9-10: The element on the left has a border of 34px on each side and no explicit border-image-width value, so the text content starts inside the border as you'd expect; the element on the right, however, has only a 1px border but a border-image-width value of 34px. Although the image slices are applied in the same way, the text content sits over the top of the "virtual" border in the element on the right.

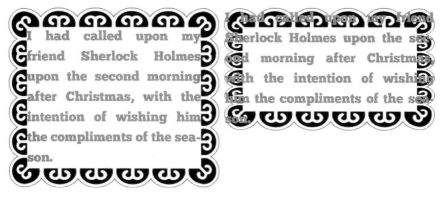

Figure 9-10: Comparing a border-width value of 34px (left) with a border-image-width value of 34px (right)

If you use a unitless number it acts as a multiplier of an existing border-width value; in the following code, the border-image-width will be equivalent to 20px:

```
E {
  border-width: 10px;
  border-image-width: 2;
}
```

border-image-outset

By default, a border image starts displaying from the outside of the border box, moving in toward the content box; but you can change this default behavior by outsetting the image to start from outside the border box. You do this with the border-image-outset property, which takes (the by now customary) four possible length values, one for each side. For example, to outset the border image by 10px from the top and bottom and 5px from the left and right, you use this rule:

```
E { border-image-outset: 15px 30px; }
```

You can see a comparison of this in Figure 9-11; the element on the left has the default border-image-outset value of 0, whereas the element on the right has the value shown in the code example; although each has an identical box size, the border image on the right is greatly outset from the content (and even overlaps the element on the left).

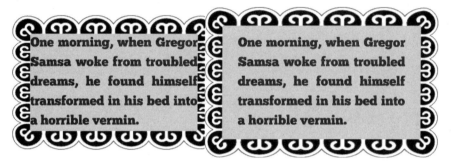

Figure 9-11: The element on the right has an outset border image.

border-image-repeat

One more property is related to border images: border-image-repeat. This property controls how the image fits the length of each side between the corners:

```
E { border-image-repeat: keyword; }
```

It accepts one of three keyword values: stretch (the default), repeat, and round. All of the example illustrations so far in this chapter used the default value (stretch), where the image slice is stretched to fill the length of the border. Using repeat applies the slice at its natural length, repeating the slice until it fills the length of the border it is applied to; so the slice could be cut off if it didn't fit into the length a whole number of times. The final value, round, behaves like repeat except it scales the slice up or down to best fit the length of the border, without being cut off.

That's easier done than said, so you can see the difference in these three values in Figure 9-12. These three elements have the same values applied to all of the border-image properties, except for border-image-repeat. For this property, the first element has the default value, stretch; the second, repeat; and the final element, round.

Figure 9-12: Different border-image-repeat values: (from left to right) stretch, repeat, round

I said a few paragraphs ago that `border-image-repeat` accepts one of three keyword values, but that's not actually correct; I only said it to make the subsequent explanation a little clearer. I hope you can forgive me for misleading you. In fact, you can use two of the three keyword values on the property; the first controls horizontal repetition, the second, vertical. So if you want to stretch your element along the top and bottom borders and round it along the left and right, you use this rule:

```
E { border-image-repeat: stretch round; }
```

The border-image Shorthand Property

To save time and keystrokes, you can use the `border-image` shorthand for all of the properties just described. The syntax looks like this:

```
E { border-image: source slice / width / outset repeat; }
```

The following code example shows all of the individual properties applied to an element and then the same properties applied to another element using the shorthand property:

```
E {
   border-image-source: url('foo.png');
   border-image-slice: 25 10 fill;
   border-image-width: 25px 10px;
   border-image-outset: 5px;
   border-image-repeat: round;
}
F { border-image: url('foo.png') 25 10 fill / 25px 10px / 5px round; }
```

That's quite the space saver.

Browser Support

All of the `border-image` properties in this section are supported in Chrome, Firefox, Safari 6+, and Internet Explorer 11+. Some older browsers—notably mobile Safari 5.1 and below, and the stock browser in Android 4.3 and below—do support border images, but only using the `border-image` shorthand and, even then, without the `border-image-width` and `border-image-outset` properties.

Drop Shadows

In Chapter 6, we looked at a way to add drop shadows to text with the `text-shadow` property, but CSS3 also has a method for adding shadows to box elements. You use the `box-shadow` property; the syntax is similar to that of `text-shadow`:

```
E { box-shadow: inset horizontal vertical blur-radius spread color; }
```

The first value, inset, is an optional keyword that sets whether the shadow sits inside or outside of the element. I explain this in more detail in the next section; for now, all you need to know is that if inset is not specified, the shadow sits outside the element. The next two values are, just as with text-shadow, lengths that set the *horizontal* and *vertical* distance of the shadow from the box; if you want to have a shadow, these values are required.

The next value sets the *blur-radius* and is another length value and, again, works exactly as in text-shadow. Then you have *spread*, yet another length value, which sets the distance the shadow spreads. A positive length makes the shadow larger than its element, and a negative length makes it smaller. Both *blur-radius* and *spread* are optional.

Finally you have the *color* value, also optional, which, if left unspecified, defaults to the inherited color (usually black).

Now I'll put these together in an example. The next code snippet creates a dark-gray shadow outside of the element, positioned at a distance of 4px, both horizontally and vertically, with a blur radius of 3px:

```
div { box-shadow: 4px 4px 3px #666; }
```

In the next code snippet, I demonstrate further examples of the effects of different values on the box-shadow property. The results are shown in Figure 9-13.

```
.shadow-one { box-shadow: 4px 4px; }
.shadow-two { box-shadow: 4px 4px 3px; }
.shadow-three { box-shadow: 12px 12px 2px -6px; }
.shadow-four { box-shadow: #999 4px -4px 2px 0; }
.shadow-five { box-shadow:
    #999 4px -4px 2px 0,
    -4px 4px 2px;
}
```

Figure 9-13: The effects of using different values for the box-shadow property

The elements in the code correspond to the boxes in Figure 9-13, moving from left to right. The first is the simplest shadow, simply distanced 4px both horizontally and vertically from the element, using the inherited color. The second has the same distance values as the first but also adds a blur radius of 3px to soften the shadow's edges. The third has a distance of 12px along both axes but a negative spread value (–6px), which makes the shadow smaller than its box. The fourth example has a medium gray–colored shadow with a negative vertical distance, meaning the shadow falls above the element instead of below it.

The fifth box has two shadows applied to it, with each set of values separated by a comma. The first value set is the same as in the fourth box, and the second makes a black (or inherited color) shadow with a negative horizontal distance, causing the shadow to fall to the left of the box.

Inset Shadows

I briefly mentioned the optional inset keyword at the beginning of the previous section. If present, this keyword draws a shadow on the interior of the box, but it also has the effect of "flipping" the shadow to the other side of the box. What I mean is that where a regular—that is, *outset*—shadow with positive *x* and *y* values would appear at the bottom right of the box, an inset shadow would appear at the top left.

To illustrate, I'll use the same code as for the previous example but add the inset keyword to each one:

```
.shadow-one { box-shadow: inset 4px 4px; }
.shadow-two { box-shadow: inset 4px 4px 3px; }
.shadow-three { box-shadow: inset 12px 12px 2px -6px; }
.shadow-four { box-shadow: inset #999 4px -4px 2px 0; }
.shadow-five { box-shadow:
    inset #999 4px -4px 2px 0,
    inset -4px 4px 2px;
}
```

The result is shown in Figure 9-14, and as you can see, it's almost the inverse of Figure 9-13; all offset, blur radius, and color values are the same, but the shadows now appear on the interior of the boxes, and in the opposite corners.

Figure 9-14: Inset shadows

The box-shadow property is broadly implemented, with unprefixed support in IE9+ and all other modern browsers. The -webkit- prefix is required for older versions of Safari for iOS and the stock Android browser.

Summary

I mentioned at the beginning of the previous chapter that the Backgrounds and Borders Module became a priority for the W3C because of the clamor from web developers. The new properties it introduces are extremely handy for removing extraneous elements used as containers for purely visual styling from markup, giving developers finer control over the way pages are presented. With a multitude of new background and border properties at our disposal, creating websites that can be viewed at many different sizes and resolutions is going to be much easier, and our sites will be more suited to the cross-platform ideal of the age.

In the next chapter, I continue with the theme of page decoration, as we take a look at the new color and opacity controls that CSS3 provides.

Border and Box Effects: Browser Support

	Chrome	Firefox	Safari	IE
border-radius	Yes	Yes	Yes	Yes
border-image	Yes	Yes	Yes	IE11
box-shadow	Yes	Yes	Yes	Yes

10

COLOR AND OPACITY

Color in CSS2 was based around the *Red, Green, Blue (RGB)* model; whether you used hexadecimal or `rgb()` function values, you had to combine those three colors to add color to your pages. Of course, designers speak in terms of shades and tints: When a designer says to use a "50 percent tint" of a certain color, developers have had to use the RGB model to match that color, which has often involved some chicanery with a graphics package to find the exact tone needed.

The CSS Color Module (*http://www.w3.org/TR/css3-color/*) has a solution to that problem—and more besides. For starters, it introduces the concepts of *opacity* through the `opacity` property and the *Alpha* color channel. In addition, the CSS Color Module adds an entirely new color model, which is more intuitive and easier to tweak to find the perfect tone.

The Color Module is a W3C Recommendation and is well implemented in IE9 and above and every other major browser, so with perhaps a bit of careful coding to provide a fallback for older versions of IE, you can begin to use its properties and values straightaway.

The opacity Property

Opacity is, strictly speaking, the measure of an object's resistance to light—the more opaque something is, the less light it lets through. An object with no opacity is fully transparent.

In CSS, opacity is measured using the opacity property. In essence, with opacity, you are setting how much of the background can be seen through the specified element. The opacity property has the following syntax:

```
E { opacity: number; }
```

The *number* value is a decimal fraction—that is, a number between 0.0 and 1.0—where 0.0 is fully transparent, 1.0 is fully opaque, and any value between those two is a blend of opacity and transparency. For example, to set an element to be 50 percent opaque (or 50 percent transparent, depending on whether your glass is half empty or half full), you use the following rule:

```
E { opacity: 0.5; }
```

To further demonstrate, I'll show a set of elements—a parent div, with a child div, which in turn has a child p—repeated three times:

```
<div class="parent">
    <div class="child">
        <p>...</p>
    </div>
</div>
```

I'll apply the same rules to each set of elements, except for a change to the opacity value. Here are the relevant rules for this example:

```
.parent { background-color: black; }
.child { background-color: white; }
.child.semi-opaque-1 { opacity: 0.66; }
.child.semi-opaque-2 { opacity: 0.33; }
```

You can see the output in Figure 10-1. The .child element in the first (left) example has no explicitly set value for opacity, so it defaults to 1.0, or fully opaque—its background is white. The next (middle) .child has a value of 0.66, so its opacity is reduced by a third, causing the white background to appear as a light gray (a blend of the black background color of the parent and the white background color of the element itself, which shows through). Finally, the last (right) .child has an opacity value of 0.33, so it can be considered two-thirds transparent, making the box a darker gray color.

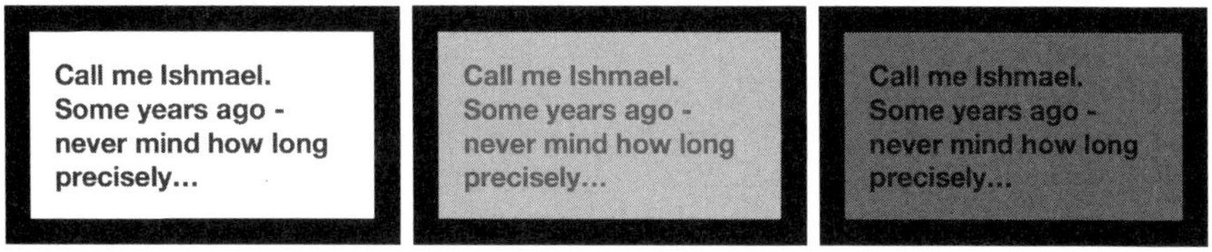

Figure 10-1: The effect of differing opacity *values on three identical elements*

Now, here's an extremely important point to remember about this property: Opacity affects not only the element it's applied to but also all of that element's children. If I set an opacity value of 0.5 on an element, its children will never be more opaque than that. This setting can't be overruled by any other property—or rather, you can never make an element more opaque than its parent, but you *can* make it less opaque.

This may make the opacity property seem somewhat limiting, as you can't apply it to elements with children without also applying it to their children. CSS3 has a new method to get around this limitation, however; it's called the Alpha channel, and I explain it in the next section.

New and Extended Color Values

CSS2.1 allowed three methods for specifying color values: keywords (black), hexadecimal notation (#000000), and RGB (0,0,0). In CSS3, the range is expanded by a completely new method of specifying colors (see "Hue, Saturation, Lightness" on page 116), as well as the introduction of opacity through the Alpha channel.

The Alpha Channel

The *Alpha channel* (*Alpha* for short) is the measure of the opacity of a color—as opposed to the opacity property, which is the measure of the opacity of an element. So, although color values using Alpha can be inherited by child elements like any other color value, the overall opacity of the element is not affected.

CSS3 introduces Alpha as a value in the *RGBA* color model. RGBA stands for *Red, Green, Blue, Alpha*, and is applied with the rgba() function. The syntax is the same as for the rgb() function value used in CSS2, but with the Alpha value specified by an extra comma-separated argument at the end:

```
E { color: rgba(red, green, blue, alpha); }
```

The value of the *alpha* argument is the same as the value provided for opacity: a decimal fraction from 0.0 to 1.0, which is once again a measure between full transparency (0.0) and full opacity (1.0). If you want an element to have a foreground color of black at 50 percent opacity, you use the following code:

```
E { color: rgba(0,0,0,0.5); }
```

As mentioned, rgba() differs from the opacity property in two ways: First, rgba() is a color value, so you couldn't, for example, use it to change the opacity of an image (or an element with a background image). Second, although the value of the rgba() function can be inherited, child elements can overrule with an rgba() value of their own.

To more precisely illustrate the difference between the two, I'll create two identical code blocks using the following markup:

```
<div class="box">
    <div class="text">
        <h1>...</h1>
    </div>
</div>
```

I'll apply the following CSS rules to this markup: both elements will get the same rules except that I'll set the opacity of one and give an rgba() value to the background-color of another, both with the same decimal fraction value of 0.5:

```
.box { background-image: url('monkey.svg'); }
.text { background-color: white; }
.opacity { opacity: 0.5; }
.rgba { background-color: rgba(255,255,255,0.5); }
```

The results are shown in Figure 10-2, and the difference is pretty clear. Both boxes have the same level of transparency, but in the first, the opacity value has been inherited by its child p element, also making the text semitransparent. In the second box, the rgba() value is applied strictly to the background-color of the .text element, so the p element retains its fully opaque black color.

Figure 10-2: Comparing opacity (left) and RGBA (right)

Having established that rgba() is not the same as opacity, let's see how it works. Being a color value, it can obviously be used for backgrounds, borders, shadows, and so on. The following code shows some examples of rgba applied to different properties:

```
❶ .shadow .text { box-shadow: 10px 10px 4px rgba(0,0,0,0.7); }
❷ .border .text { border: 10px solid rgba(0,0,0,0.5); }
❸ .text-semi p { color: rgba(0,0,0,0.6); }
❹ .text-shadow p { text-shadow: 5px 5px 1px rgba(0,0,0,0.6); }
```

Figure 10-3 shows these properties in action. Moving clockwise from top left, in the first box, rgba lowers the opacity of box-shadow; setting the Alpha value to 0.7 ❶ allows some of the background to show through, making the shadow more "realistic." The next example shows a 50 percent opaque black border ❷ (which I used in the example shown in Figure 8-6 on page 93). In the next example, the Alpha value of the color property has been set to 0.6 ❸, which makes the text appear semi-opaque. And finally the last example shows another shadow effect, this time on the text-shadow property. The Alpha value is set at 0.6 ❹, which, once again, makes for a more realistic shadow.

Figure 10-3: RGBA applied to different properties

RGBA and Graceful Degradation

Older browsers that don't support RGBA values (notably IE8) will ignore any rules that use them and default to a previously specified or inherited value. To compensate, you should specify the color twice—first without and then with an Alpha value—using the cascade to ensure the right color is implemented:

```
p {
    color: #F00;
    color: rgba(255,0,0,0.75);
}
```

In this example, browsers that don't support RGBA values ignore the second `color` property and apply the first `color` property. Of course, this result means that a fully opaque color will be used instead of a semi-opaque one, so check your design thoroughly to make sure it isn't negatively affected.

The same goes for all new color values introduced in the rest of this chapter.

Hue, Saturation, Lightness

I mentioned earlier in the chapter that CSS3 brings a new notations system for color, and that system is known as HSL. Summing up exactly what HSL is without providing a course in color theory is hard, but I'll do my best: *HSL*—which stands for *Hue, Saturation, Lightness* (sometimes called *Luminance*)—is a cylindrical-coordinate representation of color space. Still not clear? Take a look at Figure 10-4.

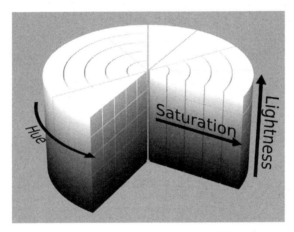

Figure 10-4: The HSL color notation method[1]

All the possible colors are arranged in a cylinder with a central axis. The angle around the axis is the *hue*; the distance from the axis is the *saturation*; and the distance along the axis is the *lightness*. The combination of those three values creates a unique color.

Hue represents the major colors, starting and ending with red (0 or 360) and including all the main colors between. Think of the colors of the visible spectrum (or the colors of the rainbow) you learned about in school—red, orange, yellow, green, blue, indigo, and violet—arranged around the circumference of a circle; the value of hue is a degree around that circumference that points to a specific color.

---

1. This image is taken from Wikimedia (*http://en.wikipedia.org/wiki/File:HSL_color_solid_cylinder_alpha_lowgamma.png*) and is published under a Creative Commons Attribution license.

Saturation is the strength or intensity of that color: 0 percent is zero intensity, which makes the color a shade of gray, and 100 percent is full strength, the most intense version of that color.

Lightness is the brightness or darkness of the color: 50 percent is the true color, 0 percent is black, and 100 percent is white.

If you've never encountered HSL before and my explanation has still left you baffled, don't worry—for our purposes, you just need to understand that HSL is applied with the hsl() color value function. It takes three arguments, with a similar syntax to rgb():

```
E { color: hsl(hue,saturation,lightness); }
```

The *hue* value is a number between 0 and 360 (the degrees around the hue wheel), and *saturation* and *lightness* accept values from 0 percent to 100 percent. Some simple color examples with their hexadecimal and RGB equivalents are shown in Table 10-1.

Table 10-1: Common Color Equivalents for Four Color Values

HSL	RGB	Hexadecimal	Keyword
0,0%,0%	0,0,0	#000000	black
360,0%,100%	255,255,255	#FFFFFF	white
0,100%,50%	255,0,0	#FF0000	red
120,100%,25%	0,128,0	#008000	green
240,100%,50%	0,0,255	#0000FF	blue

NOTE *Even if you are using a 0 (zero) value for saturation and lightness, you must still specify the value as a percentage.*

Table 10-1 doesn't actually tell the whole story—many different combinations of values allow you to create pure white, for example. Really, the best way to learn more about HSL is to get a color picker that supports it and play around for a while. Photoshop and most other graphics packages have an HSL color picker, and you should also be able to find color conversion tools online. Be careful, however, not to confuse HSL with *Hue, Saturation, Value (HSV)*—although they use an identical syntax, the color values are mapped differently so you will not get the same results.

The advantage of HSL over RGB (or hexadecimal) is that it allows you to try different variants of a color more quickly, such as making a certain color lighter/darker or more/less intense. The flexibility of HSL makes it more useful for web designers. If you're a developer coding from other people's designs, however, you may want to continue using RGB. HSL is simply a new alternative to consider.

HSLA

If you've decided that HSL is the color method for you, then you'll also be able to utilize the Alpha channel for transparency with the hsla() color value function. Like its counterpart rgba(), hsla() simply extends the color scheme with an extra argument in the function:

```
E { color: hsl(hue,saturation,lightness,alpha); }
```

So, for example, if you want an element with a color value of red and 50 percent opacity, you use this rule:

```
E { color: hsl(0,100%,50%,0.5); }
```

The Color Variable: currentColor

In addition to the new color methods I've just described, CSS3 also introduces a new color value keyword: currentColor. This keyword acts as a variable for the current color: the value of currentColor for an element is the value of its own color property. So when an element has a color value of, say, red, the value of currentColor is also red. You can then use that to set a color value on a different property without having to specify red again.

The following example should clarify the usefulness of currentColor. First, I take the following markup:

```
<h2>The Central Intelligence Agency (<abbr>CIA</abbr>).</h2>
<h2 class="ccolor">The Federal Bureau of Investigation (<abbr>FBI</abbr>)</h2>
```

and I apply this CSS to it:

```
h2 { color: black; }
.ccolor {
    background-color: black;
    color: white;
}
h2 abbr { border-bottom: 6px double currentColor; }
```

One h2 displays in black (black) text on the default (white) background, and the other in white text on a black background. Next, I use the currentColor keyword as a value for the border-bottom property on the abbr elements. You can see the result in Figure 10-5.

Figure 10-5: A demonstration of the currentColor color value keyword

Because the first h2 has a color value of black, the color of the border-bottom property of the abbr element is also black. Because the second h2 has a color value of white, the border-bottom property of the abbr element has the same color. These values have taken on the color property of their parent elements.

The currentColor keyword means I don't have to specify the color of the border for every instance of the abbr element. In this example, I don't have to use an extra rule—without it, I have to use something like this:

```
h2 abbr { border-bottom: 6px double black; }
.ccolor abbr { border-bottom-color: white; }
```

Although this may not seem like a big savings, the addition of currentColor means I can update the parent element color and not have to worry about setting the color on any relevant children. On a large site with many different color combinations, you can see that currentColor would be extremely handy.

Summary

The introduction of the opacity property and the Alpha channel to CSS3 may seem minor, but transparency unlocks some significant changes to page designs; overlapping colors have long been a staple of print design, but this style never made serious inroads into web design because of how difficult it was to implement.

And although the HSL color model doesn't impact how visitors experience your website, it allows you as an author to experiment with color more easily during the design process.

In the next chapter, I'll complete the quartet of chapters on element decoration with a look at the gradient background.

Color and Opacity: Browser Support

	Chrome	Firefox	Safari	IE
opacity	Yes	Yes	Yes	Yes
RGBA values	Yes	Yes	Yes	Yes
HSL values	Yes	Yes	Yes	Yes
HSLA values	Yes	Yes	Yes	Yes
currentColor value	Yes	Yes	Yes	Yes

11

GRADIENTS

In this chapter, the last of the quartet about decorative properties, I cover CSS gradients. A *gradient* in this context is the gradual transition between two or more colors—a design standard for many years and one that you might think would be fairly simple to translate into CSS, but which has a long and tortured history on the Web.

CSS gradients were first introduced in WebKit in 2008 and made their way into Safari 4. The syntax they used, however, was completely different from the one you'll see in the rest of this chapter and was deemed too complex by other browser vendors. Various other proposals were put forward (and even implemented) throughout the following years, until a final syntax was agreed on at the end of 2011. This final syntax was rapidly adopted by all browsers, and it's the one I'll cover in this chapter. (Read "Browser Support and Legacy Syntaxes" on page 131 to learn how to support older versions in legacy browsers.)

WARNING *Graphical effects like gradients can be quite computationally taxing and will slow the rendering and performance of pages, especially in mobile browsers. That's not to say you should avoid them, just that you should always evaluate performance against appearance when building your sites.*

Linear Gradients

A *linear gradient* is one that gradually transitions between colors over the length of a straight line connecting two points. At its simplest, a linear gradient changes proportionally between two colors along the full length of the line.

I'll begin by showing the shortest possible syntax for a linear gradient, which is defined using the `linear-gradient()` value function on the `background-image` property:

```
E { background-image: linear-gradient(black, white); }
```

Figure 11-1 shows the result.

Figure 11-1: A simple top-bottom, two-color linear gradient

Each color that you want the gradient to pass through is known as a *color-stop* and is passed into the function in a comma-separated list of arguments. As you can see here, gradients require at least two color-stops: a start and an end. In this example, the gradient begins black and ends white, passing gradually through all the intermediate shades between the two values.

Setting Gradient Direction

The axis between the first and last color-stops is known as the *gradient line*. In the previous example, the gradient line begins at the top of the box and moves to the bottom, vertically. This is the default direction. To set a different gradient line, specify a target side or corner of the box by passing a new argument into the function before the list of color-stops. The argument is a string of keywords, beginning with to and followed by one or two direction keywords. For example, to define a black-to-white gradient running bottom to top, you use this value:

```
E { background-image: linear-gradient(to top, black, white); }
```

To change the same gradient to run diagonally from the top-left corner to the bottom-right one, you use two directional keywords:

```
E { background-image: linear-gradient(to right bottom, black, white); }
```

For finer control over the direction of the gradient line, you can use an angle argument instead of the directional keywords. Angles can be declared using various units—in this chapter, I'll stick with degrees (deg) because they're the most commonly understood, but see "Angle Units" on page 124 for more about alternative units.

The angle value sets the angle of the gradient line: 0deg (or 360deg) goes from bottom to top, 45deg from bottom left to top right, 90deg from left to right, and so on. Negative values make the gradient go counterclockwise: -45deg is the same as 315deg, -315deg is the same as 45deg, and so on. You get the idea.

For example, to create the same top-left to bottom-right gradient as in the previous code example, but using an angle value, you would use this code:

```
E { background-image: linear-gradient(135deg, black, white); }
```

The next code snippet shows three examples of the effects of different direction values: the first from right to left, the second from bottom left to top right, and the last an angle of 120 degrees (roughly, but not quite, top left to bottom right).

```
E { background-image: linear-gradient(to left, black, white); }
E { background-image: linear-gradient(to top right, black, white); }
E { background-image: linear-gradient(120deg, black, white); }
```

Figure 11-2 shows the results.

Figure 11-2: Three different direction values: left to right, bottom left to top right, and 120 degrees

Adding Extra Color-Stop Values

So far I've used a simple gradient with only two color-stops, but you can use more. (Because this book is printed in black and white, I'm limited by the palette that I can choose!) Each color you add is declared by simply adding a new color-stop in the comma-separated list, as in this example where I add a third black color-stop:

```
E { background-image: linear-gradient(black, white, black); }
```

The color-stops are processed in the order listed, so this example creates a gradient that goes from black to white then back to black. Figure 11-3 shows the result.

Figure 11-3: A gradient with three color-stops

Color-stops are evenly distributed along the length of the gradient, so, in this case, the white color-stop is exactly halfway between the two blacks, at the middle point of the gradient. You can alter this distribution by adding a length or percentage value after each color-stop to shift the point along the gradient line where a color-stop is positioned. For example, this code positions the white color-stop at 75 percent of the length of the gradient line:

```
E { background-image: linear-gradient(black, white 75%, black); }
```

Figure 11-4 shows the result. Compare it to Figure 11-3 where no position is defined, and you'll see that the white color-stop has moved further along the gradient line toward the bottom of the element.

Figure 11-4: The second color-stop occurs three-quarters (or 75 percent) of the way down the length of the gradient.

You're not limited to using only percentage values on color-stops; length values are also permitted. This next snippet shows three ways to use length and percentage values, with the result shown in Figure 11-5. I'll walk through each after the code.

```
❶ div { background-image: linear-gradient(to right, black, white 75%); }
❷ div { background-image: linear-gradient(to right, black 50%, white); }
❸ div { background-image: linear-gradient(to right, black, white 50%, black 1px); }
```

Figure 11-5: Using different position values in the color-stops

In ❶, the final color-stop argument has a position of 75 percent so the color-stop begins there and continues as a solid color until the end. In ❷, the first color-stop has the position value, so a solid block of the inherited color (black) is displayed until the 50 percent mark of the gradient line, at which point the gradient begins to transition to the final color-stop value.

Finally, ❸ has three color-stops. The second begins at 50 percent, so the first and second color-stops transition up to that point. The final color-stop is placed just one pixel farther along the gradient line, so there is a sudden shift to that color (with no transition) and the color continues to the end.

Repeating Linear Gradients

Rather than create only a single gradient from one side of an element to another, you can repeat the same gradient until the element is filled using the `repeating-linear-gradient()` function. This function accepts the same fundamental set of values as `linear-gradient` except that a length or percentage value is required for the final color-stop. Here's an example:

```
E { background-image: repeating-linear-gradient(white, black 25%); }
```

This final color-stop value sets the point at which the gradient should end and then start repeating. This code creates a top-bottom gradient (the default) between white and black that covers 25 percent of the height of the box, meaning it repeats four times, as shown in Figure 11-6.

Figure 11-6: A white-to-black repeating gradient

The next code examples use different values; Figure 11-7 shows the result, and I'll explain each, in turn, after you've had a chance to look at the code.

```
❶ .gradient-1 {
      background-image: repeating-linear-gradient(to left, black, white, black 25%);
  }
❷ .gradient-2 {
      background-image: repeating-linear-gradient(45deg, black, white 2px, black 10px);
  }
❸ .gradient-3 {
      background-image: repeating-linear-gradient(315deg, black, black 2px, white 2px, white 4px);
  }
```

Figure 11-7: Different repeating linear gradients

- The first example (❶) uses three color-stops and sets the direction so the gradient goes from right to left. The gradient covers 25 percent of the element, so the black-white-black pattern is repeated four times.
- The second example (❷) uses an angle value of 45deg so the gradient is diagonal and uses pixel units for the color-stops. Again the gradients are black-white-black, but they're distributed unequally so the black-white covers 2px, whereas the white-black covers 8px.
- The last example (❸) uses four color-stops: black-black over 2px and then white-white over 2px. The low length values prevent a gradual change between the two colors, creating the hard diagonal lines you see here.

Radial Gradients

A *radial gradient* is a gradual transition between colors that moves out from a central point in all directions. At its simplest, a radial gradient gradually changes between two colors in a circular or elliptical shape. Radial gradients are defined with the `radial-gradient()` value function, and, as with linear gradients, the simplest way to create one is to pass two color values in as arguments:

```
E { background-image: radial-gradient(white, black); }
```

This results in a simple, two-color, white-black gradient in an ellipse that extends to the farthest corner of its parent element, as shown in Figure 11-8.

Figure 11-8: A simple two-color radial gradient

Using Radial Gradients

You can set the shape of a radial gradient by adding a keyword before the color-stops. The default is `ellipse`, but you can use the alternative `circle` like this:

```
E { background-image: radial-gradient(circle, white, black); }
```

The result shown in Figure 11-9 is more circular than Figure 11-8, although lacking a clearly defined edge. (You'll learn how to set the extent of a radial gradient shortly.)

Figure 11-9: A circular radial gradient

The default center of a radial gradient (from which the gradient radiates) is at the center of the element it's applied to. You can change this point by adding a position argument to the radial-gradient() function. The values used to set this position are exactly the same as those used in background-position—that is, a length, percentage, or keywords. You add the position after the shape keyword (circle, in the example shown here), preceded by the word at. The position is set to the center-right of the element:

```
E { background-image: radial-gradient(circle at 100% 50%, white, black); }
```

You can also set the *extent* of a gradient—that is, the point where the gradient ends—using a length or position value or one of four extent keywords. The extent argument is placed immediately after the shape keyword. For example, this code creates a circular gradient, the extent of which is 50px, meaning it finishes 50px from the center point:

```
E { background-image: radial-gradient(circle 50px, black, white); }
```

The four possible keywords that you can use when setting the extent are closest-corner, closest-side, farthest-corner (the default), and farthest-side. The next listing illustrates the differences among the keywords, with the result of each line shown in Figure 11-10. I'll discuss each rule in turn.

❶ .ext1 { background-image: radial-gradient(closest-corner circle at 10% 60%, white, black); }
❷ .ext2 { background-image: radial-gradient(closest-side circle at 10% 60%, white, black); }
❸ .ext3 { background-image: radial-gradient(farthest-corner circle at 0% 100%, white, black, white, black); }
❹ .ext4 { background-image: radial-gradient(farthest-side circle at 0% 100%, white, black, white, black); }

Figure 11-10: Comparing extent keywords for radial gradients

All four gradients produce the same circular shape. In examples ❶ and ❷, both gradients have the same center position and color-stops, but the extent of ❶ is set by the closest-corner keyword, making the extent of the gradient be the closest corner (the bottom left), whereas the extent of ❷ is the closest side (left, set with closest-side), so this second circle is much smaller than the previous one.

The gradients in examples ❸ and ❹ have the same center position (the bottom-left corner of the element) and each has four color-stop values (alternating black-white). The extent of example ❸ is the farthest corner (top-right, set with farthest-corner), whereas example ❹ has an extent of the farthest side (the right, and you've probably guessed by now that it's set with farthest-side). Although subtle, you should be able to see that the extent of ❹ is more limited than that of ❸.

Using Multiple Color-Stop Values

As with their linear counterparts, radial gradients can accept multiple color-stop values and length or percentage values for positioning control. Any such qualifiers are entered in a comma-separated list. The four examples in the following listing demonstrate some interesting variations. Figure 11-11 shows the results of each line.

```
❶ .gradient-1 { background-image: radial-gradient(farthest-side circle, black, white, black); }
❷ .gradient-2 { background-image: radial-gradient(farthest-side circle, black, white 25%, black); }
❸ .gradient-3 { background-image: radial-gradient(farthest-side circle at left, white, black 25%, white 75%, black); }
❹ .gradient-4 { background-image: radial-gradient(circle closest-side circle at 40% 50%, white, white 25%, black 50%, white 75%, black); }
```

Figure 11-11: Different color-stop values for radial gradients

In example ❶, I've created a gradient with three color-stops (black-white-black) that radiates from the center of the box to its farthest side. The example at ❷ is similar, except that the color-stop begins at 25 percent along the length of the radius.

In example ❸, the gradient begins at the left side of the box and ends at the right side, with color-stops at 25 and 75 percent of the length. The example at ❹ uses five colors, but by specifying both the first and second color-stops to use the same color I've created the solid-white circle in the center.

Repeating Radial Gradients

Just as the linear-gradient() function has repeating-linear-gradient(), a repeating-radial-gradient() can be used to repeat the supplied arguments until the limit specified in the final color-stop is reached. For example, the following code creates a circular gradient that repeats black-white every 20 percent until its extent is reached. The result is displayed in Figure 11-12.

```
E { background-image: repeating-radial-gradient(circle, black, white 20%); }
```

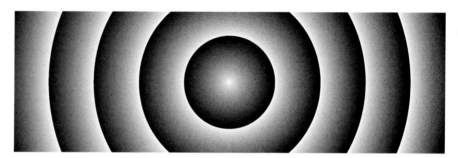

Figure 11-12: A repeating radial gradient

For some further demonstrations of what you can do with repeating radial gradients, see the next block of code. The result is shown in Figure 11-13.

```
❶ .gradient-1 { background-image: repeating-radial-gradient(circle farthest-corner at right top,
  black, white 10%, black 15%); }
❷ .gradient-2 { background-image: repeating-radial-gradient(circle farthest-corner at left,
  white, white 10px, black 15px); }
❸ .gradient-3 { background-image: repeating-radial-gradient(circle farthest-corner, white,
  black 1px, white 2px); }
```

Figure 11-13: Patterns created with repeating radial gradients

The example at ❶ radiates from the top-right corner and passes through three color-stops over 15 percent of the box width, with the limit set by the farthest-corner keyword. In example ❷, I set the center of the gradient to the left side of the box and the limit to the farthest corner, using a white-white (solid) gradient for 10px and then a white-black gradient for 5px. Finally, with example ❸, I seem to have created a work of art! A white-black-white gradient repeats over a very low radius of 2px, creating the interference pattern you see here.

BROWSER SUPPORT AND LEGACY SYNTAXES

Although gradients have a checkered history, the good news is that the final syntax is well implemented by web browsers. Chrome, Firefox, IE10+, Safari 7+ (including Mobile), and Android 4.4+ support all of the properties without a vendor prefix.

Older versions of WebKit (included in Safari 5 to 6.1 and Android 4.0 to 4.3) support a transitional syntax for linear gradients, in which the gradient direction is defined by where it comes *from* instead of where it goes *to*. This rule uses the -webkit- prefix. The following listing compares the old, transitional rule with the final one; the output from both is the same.

```
.old { background-image: -webkit-linear-gradient(left center, black,
white); }
.new { background-image: linear-gradient(to right center, black, white); }
```

If you need to support still older versions of WebKit (Android 3.0 and iOS 4.3 and earlier), you'll meet the original syntax, which was rejected by other browser vendors for being too complex. In this original syntax, both linear and radial gradients are defined with the gradient() value function, with differing arguments. This listing shows the simplest linear and radial gradient possible with this old syntax:

```
E { background-image: -webkit-gradient(linear, 50% 0, 50% 100%,
from(black), to(white)); }
E { background-image: -webkit-gradient(radial, 50% 50%, 0, 50% 50%, 100,
from(black), to(white)); }
```

Honestly, it would take too long to explain what's going on here, especially for the radial syntax. My best advice is to not even consider using this original syntax and instead to provide a graceful fallback to a solid background color or an image instead. You'll save yourself a lot of heartache that way.

Multiple Gradients

Because gradients are applied with the background-image property, you can use CSS3's multiple background values' syntax (see Chapter 8) to apply multiple gradients to an element using comma-separated values. This next listing shows two examples. The first uses linear gradients; the second uses radial gradients. Figure 11-14 shows the results of each example.

```
.linears {
  background-image:
  linear-gradient(to right bottom, black, white 50%, transparent 50%),
  linear-gradient(to left bottom, black, white 50%, black 50%);
}
.radials {
  background-image:
  radial-gradient(closest-side circle at 20% 50%, white, black 95%, transparent),
  radial-gradient(closest-side circle at 50% 50%, white, black 95%, transparent),
  radial-gradient(closest-side circle at 80% 50%, white, black 95%, transparent);
}
```

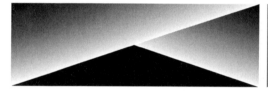 

Figure 11-14: Multiple gradient background values

The example at left shows two linear gradients applied to an element: from top left to bottom right, and from top right to bottom left. The final color-stop has a value of transparent to allow the second gradient to show through below it. (Remember, if you don't set transparency, the gradient will fill the rest of the box and hide the layer below it.) The example at right shows three radial gradients, each of which extends to the closest side, with the center of each at a different point. As with the first example, the last color-stop has a value of transparent to allow the layers below to show through.

Summary

For all the historical problems with CSS gradients, the final syntax is quite elegant and capable of delivering a wide array of beautiful background effects. For a taste of what's possible, see Lea Verou's CSS3 Patterns Gallery at *http://lea.verou.me/css3patterns/* for some effects that really push the envelope—although keep in mind my warning at the beginning of the chapter about performance, as some of these examples can be quite taxing on your mobile browser.

Also, as I write this, plans are afoot to extend the possibilities with a new gradient type, conic, which offers the possibility of even more exciting effects.

Now that we've finished this short run of chapters that look at ways to decorate page elements, we'll move on in the next chapters to cover a whole new field of expertise: transforming and animating page elements.

Gradients: Browser Support

	Chrome	Firefox	Safari	IE
Linear gradients	Yes	Yes	Yes	IE10
Repeating linear gradients	Yes	Yes	Yes	IE10
Radial gradients	Yes	Yes	Yes	IE10
Repeating radial gradients	Yes	Yes	Yes	IE10

12

2D TRANSFORMATIONS

Because of the way HTML works, with each element composed of rectangular blocks and right-angled corners, web pages have traditionally appeared boxy, with lots of straight horizontal and vertical lines, and the only way to provide any variation to this rule was to use images. But back in 2008, the WebKit team proposed a new module that allows elements to be rotated, scaled, skewed, and generally messed around with. This module was adopted for standardization by the W3C and formalized as the 2D Transformations Module (*http://www.w3.org/TR/css3-2d-transforms/*).

Much of the process for transforming elements was adapted from functions in the *Scalable Vector Graphics (SVG)* language, which is used for drawing two-dimensional vector images. SVG is supported by most modern browsers, so Firefox and Opera were quick to implement 2D Transformations in their own products, and IE9 followed along shortly.

The transformation properties for CSS and SVG were so similar, in fact, that the W3C decided to merge them into a single common specification, CSS Transforms (*http://dev.w3.org/csswg/css-transforms/*), which is where work on the module continues today. The long and the short of this story is that, although the CSS Transforms module is still only a Working Draft, the properties within it are well implemented, and you can start using these new features right away.

One thing to note before I introduce the syntax: By the end of this chapter, I'll have introduced some fairly complex functions, so you might want to brush up on your trigonometry. Are you nervous? Don't worry; I'll make it as painless as possible.

The transform Property

A range of different transformations can be applied, but all are declared as functions in the transform property. Here's the basic syntax:

```
E { transform: function(value); }
```

A number of possible functions are available; I'll explore each in turn throughout the rest of this chapter. Each function takes either a single value or a comma-separated list of values. I'll also explain what this means when I discuss each function individually.

You can apply multiple transformations to a single element by simply listing functions, space-separated, in the transform property:

```
E { transform: function(value) function(value); }
```

You need to be aware of one very important caveat when using the transform property, but before I talk about that, I need to introduce the various functions. I urge you, however, to not skip "An Important Note About Transformation Functions" on page 144.

rotate

Probably the simplest of all the functions is rotate(), which does what it sounds like it should do: It rotates the element around a set point. Here's the syntax:

```
E { transform: rotate(value); }
```

The *value* here is a single angle value, just like you used with the CSS gradients introduced in Chapter 11. And, as in that chapter, I'm sticking with the commonly understood degrees (deg) unit for my examples.

To show you rotate() in action, I'll rotate an h2 element by −15 degrees (or 345 degrees) using this rule:

```
h2 { transform: rotate(-15deg); }
```

You can see how this example displays in Figure 12-1. Note that I positioned another h2 element with a light gray background in the same place
as the first one so you can compare the rotated element with the default
(nonrotated) element. I'll do the same for most examples in this chapter.

Figure 12-1: An element rotated by –15 degrees

Position in Document Flow

An important point to make before I move on: Transformed elements
only affect visual rendering of the page, not document layout. The element
itself retains its place in the document flow, so all subsequent elements are
affected by it and its margin and padding. The transformed element does
not affect the page layout but appears as if it were in a new layer above the
rest of the page, which means it can cover subsequent elements.

To illustrate what I mean, I'll rotate another element, but this time flow
some text under it so you can see the effect of the transformation. Here's
the code to rotate the element:

```
h2 { transform: rotate(-10deg); }
```

Figure 12-2 shows the results of this transformation, along with an untransformed reference. Both examples are identical, but for the applied rotate() function. You can clearly see the rotated element covers the text under it, which immediately follows the non-transformed element in the layout. This same rule applies to any element that has the transform property applied to it, so be aware of this going forward.

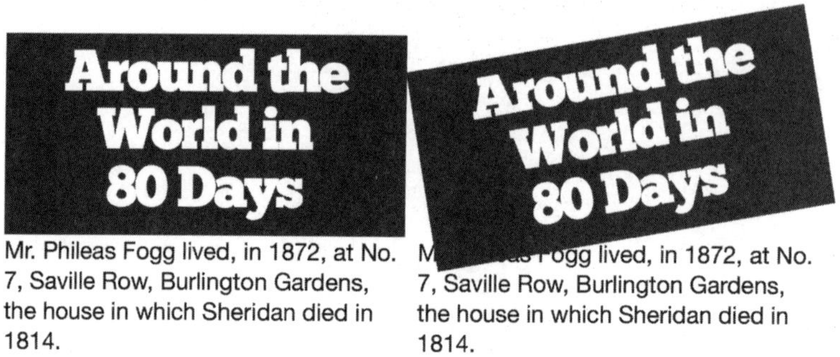

Around the World in 80 Days

Mr. Phileas Fogg lived, in 1872, at No. 7, Saville Row, Burlington Gardens, the house in which Sheridan died in 1814.

Around the World in 80 Days

M̶̶̶̶̶ Fogg lived, in 1872, at No. 7, Saville Row, Burlington Gardens, the house in which Sheridan died in 1814.

Figure 12-2: The effect of a transformed element on the document flow

transform-origin

The *origin* of a transformation is the point on an element about which that transformation happens. This concept is easiest to illustrate using rotate(), although you can apply it to any of the transformation functions introduced throughout the rest of this chapter.

In the case of rotate(), you can visualize the origin by imagining you have a piece of paper (the element) and a pin (the origin of that element). If you use the pin to stick the paper to a flat surface, you can rotate the paper around the pin. By sticking the pin in different places on the paper, you can change how the rotation happens—if the pin is stuck in the center of the paper, the rotation has a short radius, and the paper on either side of the pin moves equally; if the pin is placed at one edge, the whole length of the paper rotates around it. Figure 12-3 illustrates how this might look.

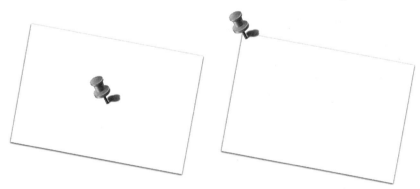

Figure 12-3: Rotating a sheet of paper around a pin: Moving the pin changes the point of rotation.

The default point of origin in the CSS transform property is the element's horizontal and vertical center. You can change this using the transform-origin property:

```
E { transform-origin: value; }
```

The *value* for this property is either one or two length, percentage, or keyword values. Lengths can be any accepted CSS unit (em, px, and so on). The keywords are left, right, top, bottom, and center. If two values are supplied, the first sets the horizontal point and the second sets the vertical; if only one is supplied, that point sets the horizontal, with the vertical presumed to be center (or 50 percent).

So if you want to change the point of origin to the top-left corner, you can use either of the following:

```
E { transform-origin: 0 0; }
E { transform-origin: left top; }
```

And if you want the point of origin to be the bottom-right corner, you can use these values (let's say the element has a height of 50px and a width of 200px):

```
E { transform-origin: 200px 50px; }
E { transform-origin: 100% 100%; }
E { transform-origin: right bottom; }
```

Let me demonstrate the effects of changing the origin of transformation. This example shows three identical elements with the same transform property applied to each but with a different transform-origin value:

```
h2 { transform: rotate(-10deg); }
h2.example-1 { transform-origin: left center; }
h2.example-2 { transform-origin: 100% 50%; }
```

You can see the effects on the three examples in Figure 12-4. The first example uses the default values (center center), so the element rotates around the absolute center. The second example uses values of left center, so the element rotates around the vertical center of the left-hand side. And the third example uses values of 100% 50%, so the element rotates around the vertical center of the right-hand side.

Figure 12-4: Different transform-origin values on a rotated element

translate

The next function we'll look at is translate, which moves the element from its default position along the horizontal or vertical axes (if you need a refresher, refer to "Understanding Axes and Coordinates" on page 64). Movement along the horizontal axis is controlled with the translateX() function and along the vertical axis with translateY():

```
E { transform: translateX(value) translateY(value); }
```

Each of these two functions, translateX() and translateY(), moves the element along the appropriate axis for the length that you specify. You can use any length units or percentage values here, so, for example, you could have:

```
E { transform: translateX(20px) translateY(15%); }
```

This code moves the element 20px to the right (along the *x*-axis) and 15 percent of its own height down (along the *y*-axis). You can see this result in Figure 12-5.

Figure 12-5: An element positively translated along both axes

You can also use negative values in the translate functions, which moves the element in the opposite direction along the axis—that is, up or to the left.

NOTE *You might think translating elements seems similar to using relative positioning and the* left *and* top *properties, but remember that the transformed element retains its position in the document flow and only* appears *to have moved; the visual rendering of the element is transformed, not the element itself.*

The translate() Shorthand Function

A more convenient way to move elements along both axes like this is to use the shorthand function, translate(). This function accepts up to two values in a comma-separated list:

```
E { transform: translate(translateX(),translateY()); }
```

That being the case, you could replicate the transformation shown in Figure 12-5 using the shorthand function with two arguments:

```
E { transform: translate(20px,15%); }
```

And you are allowed to use only one value with the `translate()` shorthand:

```
E { transform: translate(20px); }
```

In this case, the value provided is presumed to be the `translateX()` value, and a value of 0 (zero) is used for `translateY()`. So both of the following declarations are equivalent:

```
E { transform: translate(20px,0); }
E { transform: translate(20px); }
```

Using the translate() Function

To illustrate how the `translate()` shorthand function works, here are two more examples:

```
h2.translate-1 { transform: translate(-20px,20px); }
h2.translate-2 { transform: translate(20px,-20px); }
```

You can see the results of this code displayed in Figure 12-6, again with elements in a lighter gray showing the original position.

Figure 12-6: Elements showing effects of different values in the translate() *function*

In the first example, the `translate()` function has an initial argument of –20px and a second of 20px, so the element is translated 20px negatively on the horizontal axis (to the left) and 20px positively on the vertical axis (to the bottom). The second example has the opposite arguments, so the element is moved positively on the horizontal axis (to the right) and negatively on the vertical axis (to the top).

scale

You can make an element larger or smaller than the original by using scale functions. As with the translate functions, each of the horizontal and vertical values has a function, called scaleX() and scaleY(), respectively:

```
E { transform: scaleX(value) scaleY(value); }
```

The values for scaleX() and scaleY() are unitless numbers, which give a size ratio. The default size is 1; twice the default is 2, half the default is 0.5, and so on. You can also use negative numbers—I'll explain the effect of negative numbers shortly.

To double an element's original size on both axes, you use:

```
E { transform: scaleX(2) scaleY(2); }
```

A shorthand function, scale(), is also available. Note, however, that unlike the translate() shorthand function, if only one value is provided, the other is presumed to be identical. Using the previous example, you could opt instead for the shorthand:

```
E { transform: scale(2); }
```

I'll demonstrate scale in action with a few examples. Here's the code:

```
h2.transform-1 { transform: scale(0.5); }
h2.transform-2 { transform: scaleX(0.5); }
h2.transform-3 { transform: scale(1,-1); }
```

The results are shown in Figure 12-7. The first example has a scale value of 0.5, so the transformed element is half the size of the original—remember I specified only one value in the shorthand, so the other is presumed to be equal. In the second example, I used 0.5 as a value but this time for the scaleX() function, meaning the transformed element is the same height as the original but only half the width.

Figure 12-7: The effects of different values in the scale function

In the final example, I supplied two values to the scale() shorthand: The first is 1 (one), which sets the horizontal size to be the same as the original, but the second is -1 (negative one). Using a negative value has the effect of flipping the element vertically, creating a "reflection" of the original element at the same scale.

skew

To *skew* an element is to alter the angle of its horizontal or vertical axis (or both axes). As with translate() and scale(), each axis has an individual function—this time called skewX() and skewY().

```
E { transform: skewX(value) skewY(value);}
```

The arguments for the skew functions are angle values; I use degrees in my examples. Negative values are permitted. I'll give you three demonstrations, using this code, to show you how they work:

```
h2.transform-1 { transform: skewX(15deg); }
h2.transform-2 { transform: skewY(5deg); }
h2.transform-3 { transform: skewX(15deg) skewY(-15deg); }
```

The results are illustrated in Figure 12-8.

Figure 12-8: Elements transformed by different values in the skew function

In the first example, the element is skewed by 15 degrees along its *x*-axis, causing the vertical edges to slope diagonally. In the second example, the skew is by 5 degrees on the *y*-axis, so the horizontal edges slope diagonally whereas the vertical edges remain unchanged. The final example shows the effect of two values being applied: 15 degrees on the *x*-axis and –15 degrees on the *y*-axis, so the element is sloped on both axes.

Rotating with skew

By looking at the last example in the previous code block, you can see it's possible to replicate the rotate() function using skew. To do this, the angle that you want to rotate the element by is given as a value to skewX() and the inverse value to skewY(); that is, if skewX() is 15 degrees, then skewY() should be –15 degrees, and vice versa. Therefore, the two functions in this code example perform the same job:

```
E {
    transform: rotate(15deg);
    transform: skewX(15deg) skewY(-15deg);
}
```

You'll find this information useful when I introduce the matrix() function later in this chapter.

The skew() Shorthand Function

The CSS Transforms module and various online sources also list a shorthand skew() function that accepts the two individual skew functions as values (in the same way that translate() accepts the translate functions):

```
E { transform: skew(skewX(),skewY()); }
```

I highly recommend, however, you don't use this function, as for some arcane mathematical reasons, which I don't understand, it's considered redundant. It's only defined for legacy purposes; the shorthand function was implemented in some older browsers before the redundancy was noticed. If you require skew on both axes, use skewX() and skewY() instead.

An Important Note About Transformation Functions

When you set the value of the transform property, any functions that you don't list will be presumed to be reset to their default values. To see what I mean, take a look at this CSS snippet where a rule is applied to a div selector to rotate and scale it and another to a *.foo* selector to rotate it with a different value argument:

```
div { transform: rotate(5deg) scale(2); }
.foo { transform: rotate(10deg); }
```

If these rules were applied to a div with a class of *.foo*, the element would be only rotated by 10 degrees and not scaled; as the scale() function is not specified, its value argument is treated as the default, 0deg. To apply both properties, you have to update the code to include the scale() function in the rule applied to *.foo*:

```
div { transform: rotate(5deg) scale(2); }
.foo { transform: rotate(10deg) scale(2); }
```

Transforming Elements with Matrices

Each of the transformation functions used in this chapter so far can also be expressed as a *transformation matrix*. Rather than explaining the theory behind transformation matrices (which is quite complex and could easily be a chapter of its own), I'll just show you how they can be applied to elements in CSS through use of the matrix() function.

I'll keep the explanation as simple as possible and just give you the practical basics. If you really want to dig into the theory, I suggest you read the W3C's explanation in the SVG 1.1 module (*http://www.w3.org/TR/SVG/coords.html#TransformMatrixDefined/*).

The 2D transformation matrices, and the `matrix()` function, accept six values, the combination of which can be used to create the functions introduced already in this chapter. Here's the syntax:

```
E { transform: matrix(a,b,c,d,X,Y); }
```

All of the default values are 0 (zero), and they behave slightly differently depending on which values are supplied—I'll explain what this means as I go along. I said that you can perform all of the functions introduced so far in this chapter with `matrix()`, but the process is not quite that simple—you need to know some trigonometry first.

Before getting to the hard stuff, I'll start with something simple that doesn't require any trig: scaling. If you want to scale an element, you can use *a* and *d* to equate to `scaleX()` and `scaleY()` and set values accordingly, leaving *b* and *c* at 0. Therefore, to double an element's size, you use:

```
E { transform: matrix(2,0,0,2,0,0); }
```

You can also translate an element with `matrix()` by providing horizontal and vertical offset values to *X* and *Y* (respectively). These values are unitless numbers, which represent pixel values (on HTML elements, anyway; in SVG, they are vector point values). That being the case, to double an element's size and offset it by 15px both vertically and horizontally, you use this code:

```
E { transform: matrix(2,0,0,2,15,15); }
```

If you want to skew an element using `matrix()`, well, this is where it becomes a lot more complex—here's where I need to introduce the trigonometric functions. You can read a full explanation of these functions on Wikipedia (*http://en.wikipedia.org/wiki/Trigonometric_functions#Sine.2C_cosine _and_tangent/*), but the following is a quick and dirty summary: The trigonometric functions are ratio values used to calculate angles in a triangle.

The first trigonometric function I'll use is *tan (tangent)*, which is required to skew an element along the *x*- or *y*-axis. Referring to the original `matrix` syntax, the *x*-axis is supplied as a value to *b* and the *y* as a value to *c*. Here's the syntax for each:

```
E { transform: matrix(1,tan(angle),0,1, X,Y); } /* X Axis */
E { transform: matrix(1,0,tan(angle),1, X,Y); } /* Y Axis */
```

The *angle* refers to the degrees (counterclockwise) of the angle you want to skew by. If you want to skew an element by 15 degrees, the value you're looking for is the tangent of 15. So whip out your scientific calculator—if you don't own one, your operating system's calculator should have a scientific mode—and get the result that `tan(15)` = `0.27`. This result is what you provide to the `matrix` function. For example, if you want the skew to be along the *x*-axis, you use this syntax:

```
E { transform: matrix(1,0.27,0,1,0,0); }
```

NOTE *As I'm using degrees in my examples, make sure your calculator's trigonometric type is set to* degrees *if you want to follow along. If you prefer working in gradians or radians, you can update all of these examples accordingly.*

As mentioned, skew functions can also be used to rotate an element—and you can do the same with `matrix()`. This time you have to make use of the *sin (sine)* and *cos (cosine)* trigonometric functions. To rotate an element, the `matrix()` syntax is:

```
E { transform: matrix(cos(angle),sin(angle),-sin(angle),cos(angle),X,Y); }
```

Note that *a* and *d* take the same value, and *b* and *c* take inverse values (if *b* is a positive value, *c* is the negative of the same value, and vice versa). Once again, *angle* refers to the degrees of the angle you want to rotate the element by. To rotate by 60 degrees, you go back to your scientific calculator and calculate the cos and sin of 60. My calculator tells me that `cos(60)` = `0.5` and `sin(60)` = `0.87`, so the required code is

```
E { transform: matrix(0.5,0.87,-0.87,0.5,0,0); }
```

Now let's look at a few examples. Here's the code I'll use:

```
h2.transform-1 { transform: matrix(1,0,0,-1,0,0); }
h2.transform-2 { transform: matrix(1,0,0.268,1,-10,-20); }
h2.transform-3 { transform: matrix(0.98,-0.17,0.17,0.98,0,0); }
```

The output is shown in Figure 12-9.

Figure 12-9: Examples of transformations made with the matrix *function*

In the first example, I've flipped the element vertically, as I did earlier using `scale()` in Figure 12-7. In the next example, I've skewed the element by 15 degrees along the *y*-axis (after calculating that `tan(15)` = `0.268`) and translated it along both axes. The final example shows the element rotated by 10 degrees; the values are the results of the calculations I showed you previously: `cos(10)` = `0.98` and `sin(10)` = `0.17`. As mentioned, the sin value is negative in position *b* and positive in position *c*, which makes the rotation uniform.

I know this is all quite complex, but hopefully I've simplified it enough for you to understand, without making it seem so easy you can't see the scope for great flexibility—as long as you keep your scientific calculator with you at all times! And if this does seem overly complex, and you're having trouble understanding it, remember you can perform all of these transformations using the individual functions, so you can happily forget about matrix and trigonometry, too, if you wish.

Summary

This chapter has introduced the most complex property so far: the matrix() function. Although some might be tempted to say that if you want to perform complex operations, you have to deal with complex syntax, I think the other functions in this chapter do a good job of translating that complexity into something simple. Just remember, easier options are always available if you get fed up with matrix().

This chapter has also introduced some of the most revolutionary properties so far—just a few years ago the notion that you could rotate, skew, and scale elements was just a pipe dream, but today you can do just that. And if you think what you've seen in this chapter is impressive, wait until the next one. I'm going to show you how to add an extra dimension—literally—to your transformation effects.

2D Transformations: Browser Support

	Chrome	Firefox	Safari	IE
2D transformations	Yes	Yes	Yes*	IE9*, IE10

* With vendor prefix

13

3D TRANSFORMATIONS

All of the features and functions I've discussed in this book so far have involved two dimensions; every element has height and width, and all of the calculations have involved only the *x*-axis and *y*-axis. But with the introduction of the *z*-axis in the CSS Transforms Module, CSS3 offers a revolutionary way to transform an element in the third dimension (you can learn more at *http://www.w3.org/TR/css-transforms-1/*).

At the time I wrote the first edition of this book, only Safari (for Mac and iOS) supported 3D transformations, but now just a few years later, stable implementations are in place across all major browsers, including IE10 and above—an incredibly rapid rate of adoption. At the time of this writing, in Safari, you need to apply the -webkit- prefix to all properties, but no other browsers have a requirement for a vendor prefix.

The work of moving objects around in three dimensions can be quite processor-intensive, but most (if not all) browsers have implemented what's known as *hardware acceleration,* performing the required calculations directly on the device's graphics chip rather than in the software of the browser or on the main processor. The result is that 3D-transformed elements usually animate in a way that's smoother and more performant than other elements that are animated using only JavaScript. This being the case, you can go ahead and use 3D transformations in your pages without too much concern.

3D Elements in CSS

Three-dimensional objects in CSS are based on the *Cartesian coordinate system*, which is illustrated in Figure 13-1. You can read about it on Wikipedia (*http://en.wikipedia.org/wiki/Cartesian_coordinate_system/*). I discussed the two-dimensional version of this system in Chapter 6.

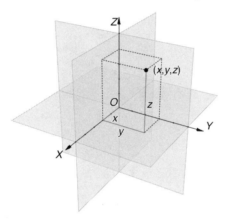

Figure 13-1: The Cartesian coordinate system, with the axes x, y, and z[1]

NOTE   *If you have experience using three-dimensional computer graphics programs, you should be familiar with the calculations and terminology used in this chapter. If not, don't worry; I'll do my best to explain it all as I go along.*

In CSS, the z-axis is based on the viewer: If you think of the x-axis as left to right and the y-axis as up and down, then think of the z-axis as toward and away. When you move an element along the z-axis by a positive value, you move it toward yourself; likewise, moving it by a negative value moves it away from you. You can change this somewhat by using different perspectives, which I'll explain in due course.

I must point out that, although I'll talk a lot about 3D in this chapter, I'm only referring to 3D coordinates. The elements themselves are still two-dimensional; they only have height and width. They are moved around in three-dimensional space, however, like moving a piece of paper around in the air.

---

1. This image is from Wikimedia Commons (*http://commons.wikimedia.org/wiki/File:Coord_system_CA_0.svg*).

Illustrating three-dimensional transformation concepts on the printed page is quite hard, so I strongly suggest you take a look at the examples on the website that accompanies this book (*http://www.thebookofcss3.com/*); I've added transition rules to some of the examples so they animate when you interact with them, showing more clearly the three-dimensional effects that are difficult to convey in a two-dimensional book. These examples should aid your understanding of some of the techniques used in this chapter. I also recommend the test page put together by the team at Westciv (*http://www.westciv.com/tools/3Dtransforms/*). This site allows you to try out different combinations of transformation values to see the effect they have on elements.

Before I introduce the new and extended transformation properties, a quick note about the examples being used in this chapter. Although each example may employ different classes to apply unique style rules, all of the examples use the same basic markup:

```
<div class="d3-parent">
    <div class="d3-child">
        <h2>The Book Of</h2>
        <h1>CSS3</h1>
    </div>
</div>
```

Most of the transformation work is performed on the *.d3-child* element, although a few properties must be applied to a parent, which is why I also have the *.d3-parent* element. I'll be clear about whether properties are applied to parents or children as I go through the chapter.

The Transformation Functions

In Chapter 12, I introduced the transform property and its associated functions, for use in two-dimensional transformations. Three-dimensional transformations use the same property and many of the same functions, but also extend some of those functions and add some entirely new ones. I'll explain each of the transformation functions in turn and note whether they are completely new or extend the existing 2D transformation properties that I have already discussed. Note that the transform property is always applied to the child element (*.d3-child* in the example markup).

Rotation Around an Axis

I'll begin explaining the 3D transformation functions as I did the 2D functions—with rotation. Two-dimensional space has only one axis to rotate around, so the rotate() function requires only a single value. But when you're dealing with three dimensions, you've got three axes to rotate around and, therefore, three properties to control this.

```
E {
        transform: rotateX(angle);
        transform: rotateY(angle);
        transform: rotateZ(angle);
}
```

Like the rotate() function, each of the functions accepts a single angle value (negative values are permitted). I use the deg (degrees) unit in my examples and demonstrate how each of these works by showing the same degree of rotation around each axis using the following code:

```
❶ .trans-x { transform: rotateX(45deg); }
❷ .trans-y { transform: rotateY(45deg); }
❸ .trans-z { transform: rotateZ(45deg); }
```

You can see the results in Figure 13-2. The first example (❶) shows an element rotated around the *x*-axis. To understand what's happening here, imagine a line running horizontally across the center of the element; the half of the element above the line is inclined 45 degrees away from you, and the half below the line is inclined 45 degrees toward you. The next example (❷) applies the rotation on the *y*-axis. Imagine a vertical line running down the center of the box; the half of the element to the left of the line is inclined 45 degrees toward you and the half on the right, 45 degrees away. The final example (❸) shows the same rotation again, but this time around the *z*-axis, which has the same effect as the two-dimensional rotate() function.

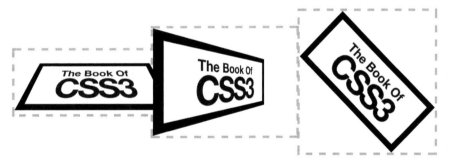

Figure 13-2: A rotation of 45 degrees around each of the three axes

If you want to rotate an element around more than one axis, you can apply multiple functions to an element:

```
E { transform: rotateX(angle) rotateY(angle) rotateZ(angle); }
```

Another new function—rotate3d()—also allows you to rotate an element around multiple axes; however, it's not a shorthand function. Here's the syntax:

```
E { transform: rotate3d(x,y,z,angle); }
```

The *angle* value is straightforward, but the *x*, *y*, and *z* values are not quite so simple. Each takes a number value, which is used to calculate a direction vector (the full explanation of which is beyond the scope of this book; visit *http://mathworld.wolfram.com/CartesianCoordinates.html* for an overview of the topic). The origin of the vector is the point where all the axes meet—by default, the center of the element—represented by the values 0,0,0. A direction vector is a line in three-dimensional space, going from the origin to the coordinates given by the *x*,*y*,*z* values provided to the rotate3d() function. The element will be rotated around this line by the amount specified in the *angle* value.

This subject is quite complex, so I'll explain by showing a few simple examples, once again with the same 45 degrees of rotation, using the following code:

```
❶ .trans-x { transform: rotate3d(1,1,0,45deg); }
❷ .trans-y { transform: rotate3d(1,0,1,45deg); }
❸ .trans-z { transform: rotate3d(0,10,10,45deg); }
```

You can see the output in Figure 13-3. The first (left) example (❶) has the values 1,1,0, meaning the imaginary line goes to a point 1px along the *x*-axis and *y*-axis. (In fact, the "line" continues past that point in the same direction; the values 10,10,0 or 1000,1000,0 would produce the same results.) The element is rotated 45 degrees around that line. The second (middle) example (❷) has the values 1,0,1, creating a point 1px along the *x*-axis and *y*-axis and rotating the element by 45 degrees around that line. The final example (❸), shown on the right, has the values 0,10,10, so the element rotates 15 degrees around a line between the origin and a point 10px along the *y*-axis and *z*-axis. Remember that any two equal values would have the same effect.

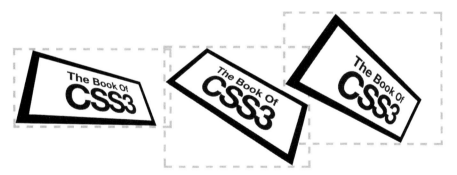

Figure 13-3: Rotation using directional vectors with the rotate3d function

You probably won't use the rotate3d() function often when coding pure CSS transformations as the calculations involved are quite complex. But when combined with the mathematical processing capabilities of JavaScript, the flexibility of this approach could really come into its own.

Perspective

The next function, perspective(), is actually one of the most important as it creates an artificial viewpoint from where you view the object in three-dimensional space, providing the illusion of depth. If not specified, the element will appear "flat" to the viewer, regardless of any other trans-form functions applied (unless perspective is inherited from the parent; see "The perspective and perspective-origin Properties" on page 159 for details). Here's the syntax:

```
E { transform: perspective(depth); }
```

The value *depth* is either a length unit or the default keyword none. This length sets a "viewpoint" at that distance along the z-axis away from the element's origin ($z = 0$). A low depth value—say, 50px—will make the element appear extremely close to the viewer, with exaggerated dimensions; a value of around 1000px can be considered "normal."

The perspective() function is probably easier to show than to describe. In the next example, I use different values for the function to show you how various values change the viewers . . . er, perspective. Here's the code:

```
❶ .trans-1 { transform: perspective(1000px) rotateX(30deg) rotateY(45deg); }
❷ .trans-2 { transform: perspective(250px) rotateX(30deg) rotateY(45deg); }
❸ .trans-3 { transform: perspective(150px) rotateX(30deg) rotateY(45deg); }
```

WARNING *The perspective() function must always be listed first when using multiple functions on the transform property; if listed after other functions, it will be ignored.*

You can see the results of the code in Figure 13-4. In the example on the left (❶), the element is viewed from a perspective() distance of 1000px. This is, as I said, the "normal" distance; the element is rotated around two axes but appears to be correctly proportioned. In the middle example (❷), the perspective() value has decreased to 250px, making the element appear exaggerated in proportion as I placed the viewpoint closer to the element. The final (right) example (❸) shows the element from a perspective() value of 150px, which means you are effectively viewing it from 150px along the z-axis, making the element appear quite exaggerated.

Figure 13-4: The effects of different perspective() function values

Before I move on, I want to make a slight digression. You may be wondering why the code contains so much repetition; why couldn't I have done something like this instead?

```
.d3-child { transform: rotateX(30deg) rotateY(45deg); }
.trans-1 { transform: perspective(20px); }
.trans-2 { transform: perspective(50px); }
.trans-3 { transform: perspective(1000px); }
```

The reason is if I don't specify a function, its value is presumed to be the default, so the values I set in the functions on the h1 element are effectively overwritten by (the absence of) the functions in the subsequent styles. I explained this in Chapter 12 in the section "An Important Note About Transformation Functions."

Translation Along the Axis

The translateX() and translateY() functions (and their shorthand, translate()) are used to move an element along its axis by a specified length in two dimensions, but the move into a third dimension requires a new function: translateZ(). The syntax is identical to its sibling properties:

```
E { transform: translateZ(length); }
```

The *length* value is any number with a unit of length. For example, to move an element 30px along the z-axis (toward the viewer), use this:

```
E { transform: translateZ(30px); }
```

Now that you've met the new functions, let's see them at work. In the following example, I show two elements that are styled identically but for different values for the translateZ() function:

```
❶ .trans-z1 { transform: translateZ(-40px); }
❷ .trans-z2 { transform: translateZ(40px); }
```

You can see the results in Figure 13-5—note that I've angled the parent elements slightly and also made the elements transparent so you can more easily see the effect. In the first example (❶, on the left), the translateZ() function has a value of −40px, moving it negatively along the z-axis and making it appear smaller than its parent. The next (❷, on the right) has a value of 40px for translateZ(), moving it positively by that amount along the z-axis and making it appear larger.

NOTE *This concept is much easier to grasp when you see the elements animated, so I once more encourage you to look at the accompanying example files to get a better feel for the way these functions behave.*

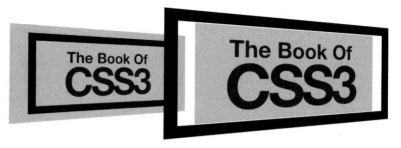

Figure 13-5: Translation in different directions along the z-axis

A shorthand function, `translate3d()`, is also available. This shorthand allows you to set all three values simultaneously. The syntax is a logical extension of the translate() function:

```
E { transform: translate3d(translateX,translateY,translateZ); }
```

Each of the arguments is equivalent to the named function, so each accepts a numerical value, positive or negative, with a CSS length unit or percentage, as shown here:

```
E { transform: translate3d(0,100%,1em); }
```

Scaling

I also introduced the scale() function, along with the subfunctions scaleX() and scaleY(), in Chapter 12. The move to three dimensions adds a new sub-function, scaleZ(), which has this syntax:

```
E { transform: scaleZ(number); }
```

As with its siblings, the *number* value provides a factor to scale the element by, so a value of 2 doubles the element's size along the z-axis. The resulting behavior is probably not what you'd expect, however; the element itself has no depth, if you recall, so an increase in scaleZ() by itself doesn't seem to change the element. What the increase actually does is act as a multiplier to any value that's supplied to translateZ(). For example, consider this code:

```
E { transform: scaleZ(3) translateZ(10px); }
```

The scaleZ() function's value of 3 multiplies the translateZ function's value of 10px, so the element appears 30px (3 × 10px) along the z-axis.

In addition to scaleZ(), a new shorthand function, scale3d(), has also been added. Here is its syntax:

```
E { transform: scale3d(scaleX,scaleY,scaleZ); }
```

As should be fairly clear, this shorthand simply accepts a number for each of the values, acting as a scaling factor on the pertinent axis. Here is a pair of examples to show you 3D scaling in action:

```
❶ .trans-z1 { transform: scaleZ(2.5) translateZ(-10px); }
❷ .trans-z2 { transform: scale3d(1.25,1.25,4) translateZ(10px); }
```

The results appear in Figure 13-6. The first (left) example (❶) shows an element with a translateZ() value of –10px and a scaleZ() value of 2.5; as I mentioned, scaleZ() acts as a multiplier of translateZ(), so the element moves 25px negatively along the z-axis. In the second example (❷), I used the scale3d function to set values of 1.25 on the x-axis and y-axis and 4 on the z-axis. The resulting element, shown on the right, is 25 percent larger on the two-dimensional axes, and the scaleZ() value multiplies the translateZ() value of 10px to move the element 40px along the z-axis.

Figure 13-6: Scaling on different and multiple axes

The Transformation Matrix

One of the more esoteric aspects of 2D transformations that I introduced in Chapter 12 is the matrix() function. This function allows you to apply complex transformations using six values (based around a grid pattern) and some trigonometric calculations. You can also apply 3D transformations using a matrix with the matrix3d() function. But if you thought the 2D matrix was hard to grasp, you might want to skip this one—matrix3d() has a whopping 16 values! Here's the syntax:

```
E { transform: matrix3d(
    m01,m02,m03,m04,
    m05,m06,m07,m08,
    m09,m10,m11,m12,
    m13,m14,m15,m16
); }
```

NOTE *The line breaks are shown here for clarity; you don't need to use them in practice.*

Each of the *m* values is a number, but I can't even begin to explain what each of them does! I suggest you read an introduction to the subject (*http://dev.opera.com/articles/understanding-the-css-transforms-matrix/* is a good place to start) and decide if this is something you want to learn more about.

Here, I provide some simple examples using this code to demonstrate the functionality:

```
❶ .trans-1 { transform: matrix3d(1,0,0,0,0,1,0,0,0,0,1,0,10,10,10,1); }
❷ .trans-2 { transform: matrix3d(1.5,0,0,0,0,1.5,0,0,0,0,2,0,0,0,10,1); }
❸ .trans-3 { transform: matrix3d(0.96,-0.26,0,0,0.26,0.96,0,0,0,0,1,0,-10, 0,20,1); }
```

You can see the results in Figure 13-7. The first (left) example (❶) shows the element moved 10px along each axis with the equivalent of the translate3d() function—the *m13*, *m14*, and *m15* values in the matrix operate as translateX(), translateY(), and translateZ(), respectively. In the second example (❷), I scaled the image by a factor of 1.5 on the *x*-axis and *y*-axis (the *m1* and *m6* values) and by a factor of 2 on the *z*-axis (the *m11* value), which multiplies the translateZ() value (*m15*) to move the element 20px along the *z*-axis, as shown in the middle example. The final example (❸) requires a scientific calculator for some trigonometric functions, as I've rotated the element by 15 degrees on the *z*-axis. To create the rotation, you need to give a value of cos(15)—which is 0.96—to *m1* and *m6* and then sin(15)—that is, 0.26—to *m5* and negative sin(15) to *m2*. I also translated the element by 10px on the *x*-axis with the value in *m13*. You can view the result on the right in the figure.

Figure 13-7: Transformations applied with the matrix3d() function

As I'm sure you can see, this function is quite powerful—and quite complex. Whether you want to learn the full potential of matrix3d() depends largely on you and your projects, but I feel it's beyond the scope of this book. Don't forget you can perform all of these transformations with the individual functions; you'll end up with more code, but it will be easier to understand—not only for yourself but also for anyone tasked with maintaining the website after you!

The perspective and perspective-origin Properties

Earlier in the chapter, I introduced the perspective() transformation function, but a perspective property is also available. The syntax is pretty straightforward:

```
E { perspective: depth; }
```

The property operates in the same way as the function: The *depth* value is a length unit that sets the distance from the element's origin, $z = 0$. In fact, the only difference between the function and the property is that the value supplied to the property applies only to its child elements, not to itself.

The companion property of perspective is perspective-origin. This property sets the point in 3D space from which you view the element. Here's the syntax:

```
E { perspective-origin: x-position y-position; }
```

The *x-position* value can be any one of the keywords—left, right, or center—and the *y-position* value can be top, bottom, or center. Percentage or length values can also be used. You should be familiar with these pairs of values from using other properties, such as background-position or transform-origin.

The default is center center (or 50% 50%), so you are viewing the line of perspective as if it started at the absolute center of the element. Changing the values of perspective-origin changes the origin of that line of perspective.

That may sound a little brain-bending; once again, showing it is easier than explaining it. In this next example, I show the same transformed element from different perspective origins. Here's the code:

```
  .d3-parent { perspective: 200px; }
  .d3-child { transform: rotateX(45deg) rotateZ(90deg); }
❶ .trans-1 { perspective-origin: left center; }
❷ .trans-2 { perspective-origin: 100% 100%; }
❸ .trans-3 { perspective-origin: 75% 25%; }
```

The examples are illustrated in Figure 13-8. A reference example is shown first (at the far left); this is a transformed element viewed from the default origin of center center. The second example (❶) is the same element but with perspective-origin at the center of the left-hand side of the element. The angle you're viewing the element from has changed; the viewpoint appears to be to the left of the element. In the third example (❷), I used length values of 100% 100%, which changes the origin to the bottom of the right-hand side. The viewpoint appears to be to the right of the element, looking up. The last (far right) example (❸) is viewed from a point 75 percent along the *x*-axis and 25 percent along the *y*-axis; this example is similar to the reference example, but the viewpoint has shifted slightly to be just to the right of, and slightly above, the element.

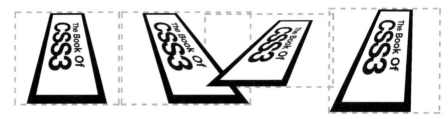

Figure 13-8: Different values for the perspective-origin *property*

The Transformation Origin

When explaining 2D transformations in Chapter 12, I talked about each element's origin point—the point at which all transformations are applied—and how you can set its position using the transform-origin property. The same property is also used for setting the origin point of 3D transformations, but as three dimensional coordinate systems have three axes (*x*-axis, *y*-axis, and *z*-axis), the property also accepts three values:

```
E { transform-origin: x y z; }
```

The first two values, *x* and *y*, act the same as in the transform-origin property for 2D elements; that is, they accept values as either a keyword (left, right, center for *x*, and top, bottom, center for *y*), a length unit, or a percentage. The default value is center center, or 50% 50%. The third value, *z*, is a length value, which sets the distance along the *z*-axis that the transformation will happen. This value can seem quite counterintuitive as it seems to act in reverse; if a negative value is given, the transformation origin is behind the element, which makes it appear in front of its parent; likewise, a positive value places the origin in front of the element, making the element appear behind its parent.

I'll illustrate this with a demonstration showing three elements identical in all values but transform-origin. Here's the relevant code for these examples:

```
  .d3-child { transform: rotateX(45deg) rotateZ(90deg); }
❶ .trans-1 { transform-origin: 50% 0 0; }
❷ .trans-2 { transform-origin: 50% 100% 0; }
❸ .trans-3 { transform-origin: center bottom -50px; }
```

You can see the output in Figure 13-9. From left to right, the first example is, once again, a reference element, with the origin at its default position, dead center. The next (❶) shows the same element with the transform-origin value set to the center of the top side, and in the original (unchanged) position on the *z*-axis. The third example (❷) sets the transformation origin to the center-bottom of the element, and the final (far right) example (❸) has the same transformation origin on the *x*- and *y*-axes (set with keywords rather than percentages) but it's 50px along the *z*-axis—that is, toward the viewer (as it appears).

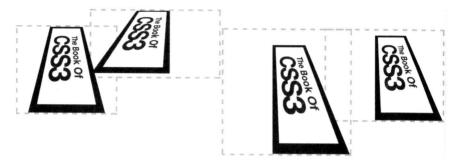

Figure 13-9: Different transform-origin values on a transformed element

As before, you'll see these differences much more clearly if you view the example files, as you can see the elements actually rotate around their transformation origin.

The transform-style Property

When elements transformed in 3D are nested, the default behavior is that all descendant elements are flattened to the plane of the parent—that is, any transformation functions applied to child elements are ignored. You can change this behavior with a property called transform-style; here's the syntax:

```
E { transform-style: keyword; }
```

The keyword value can be either flat (the default) or preserve-3d. Explaining the difference is easier if I start with an example: In this, I have two elements with identical rules applied, except for the value given to transform-style:

```
.trans-1 { transform-style: flat; }
.trans-2 { transform-style: preserve-3d; }
```

The difference, as shown in Figure 13-10, is quite stark: The example on the left has the default value of flat, so the inner element is kept in the same dimensional plane as its parent; you can clearly see the contrast with the second example, which has a transform-style value of preserve-3d, where the inner element sits in a separate plane, further along the *z*-axis from its parent.

WARNING *Internet Explorer 10 and 11 don't support the preserve-3d value of this property.*

Figure 13-10: Comparing the effects of different values for the
transform-style property

Showing or Hiding the Backface

Sometimes you'll encounter a situation where the element has been rotated
to such a degree that it faces away from you and you are seeing the "back"
of it (known as the *backface*). By default, the element behaves as if it were
transparent, so you will see the reverse of what appears on the front. You can
change this by using the backface-visibility property, which has this syntax:

```
E { backface-visibility: state; }
```

The *state* value is one of two keywords: hidden or visible. The default
is visible, which behaves in the way I just described; the alternative, hidden,
shows nothing. These work in the same way as the visibility property,
which you should be familiar with from CSS2.

The following is a quick example illustrating the difference between
the two *state*s by showing two elements that are identical except for their
backface-visibility values. Here's the code:

```
.d3-child {
    backface-visibility: visible;
    transform: rotateY(180deg);
}
.bf-hidden { backface-visibility: hidden; }
```

You can see the result in Figure 13-11. Both example elements are
rotated around the *y*-axis so they are facing away from you. The example on
the left shows the element with a value of visible on the backface-visibility
property, so you can clearly see the back of the element. In the example on
the right, you can see . . . well . . . nothing. The backface-visibility property
has a value of hidden, so nothing is displayed—no border, no background-color,
nothing. To confirm that the element is actually there, visit the website that
accompanies this book and take a look at the animated code examples so
you can better see how they work.

Figure 13-11: Demonstrating the `backface-visibility` property

Summary

The introduction of the third dimension takes CSS into areas that are rich with potential—many demos are available that show clever uses of 3D transformations to build objects or environments. But, for me, the best use of the extra dimension is in smaller, subtle details; adding depth to rollover effects or making two-sided "cards" that flip to reveal information on the reverse.

As with everything, CSS 3D transformations are best used appropriately, so they add to the user experience of your websites rather than detract from it with unnecessary tricks.

3D Transformations: Browser Support

	Chrome	Firefox	Safari	IE
3D transformations	Yes	Yes	Yes[*]	IE10[†]

[*] With vendor prefix
[†] No support for the preserve-3d value for `transform-style`

14

TRANSITIONS AND ANIMATIONS

We often think of web pages as having three layers: content (HTML), presentation (CSS), and behavior (JavaScript), and the general understanding is that these layers should all be kept absolutely separate—don't use presentational or behavioral rules in the content layer (in other words, no CSS or JavaScript inline in the markup). This separation is not quite as clear cut as it seems, however—for a start, CSS has always included some behavioral aspects (the :hover pseudo-class being a prime example).

This line between presentation and behavior was blurred even further when the WebKit developers introduced two new behavioral modules that have been adopted as CSS3 components: Transitions and Animations. These modules allow for the animation of element properties, adding movement to otherwise static pages even when JavaScript is not available.

Some have argued—and perhaps still do—about whether the Transitions and Animations Modules should be included in CSS, as they fall firmly in the behavioral layer. But, as the W3C has decided to offer them for discussion as an "official" part of CSS3, we no longer need to debate the ethics of them—we can just have fun with them, instead!

The difference between transitions and animations is that the former are *implicit* and the latter are *declared*. That means transitions only take effect when the property they are applied to changes value, whereas animations are explicitly executed when applied to an element.

I'll start this chapter with a look at the Transitions Module, as it is the simpler of the two modules; however, both modules have a lot of syntax in common, so much of what you learn from one can be directly applied to the other.

Transitions

CSS2.1 has no in-between states: When the value of a property changes, the change is abrupt. Consider an element with a width of 10em, which changes to a width of 20em when you hover your mouse over it. You'll notice the element does not progress smoothly between the two states but jumps instantly between them. CSS3 changes this behavior with the introduction of the Transitions Module (*http://www.w3.org/TR/css3-transitions/*). In CSS, a *transition* is an animation that moves a property between two states.

As I mentioned in the introduction to this chapter, transitions are an *implicit* animation, which means they are triggered only when a new value is set for a CSS property—this could be when new values are applied on hover or through JavaScript manipulation. For a transition to occur, four conditions must be in place: an initial value, an end value, the transition itself, and a trigger.

Here's an example of those four conditions in a simple transition (don't worry about the properties I've used just yet; I'll explain everything in due course):

```
div {
    background-color: black;
    transition: background-color 2s;
}
div:hover { background-color: silver; }
```

The div element provides the initial value (background-color: black) and the transition (background-color 2s). The trigger is the :hover pseudo-class, which sets the end value (silver) for the background-color property.

So here we have a div element with a black background that, when the mouse is passed over it, transitions smoothly to silver. All transitions act in reverse when the trigger is no longer active, so when the mouse is moved off of the div, the background smoothly transitions back to black.

Now that you have a general idea of how transitions work, I'll explore each of the transition properties in turn.

NOTE   *The transition properties are implemented in all modern browsers, including mobile, without vendor prefix. To cater to older versions of WebKit-based browsers, however— especially Safari and versions previous to 4.4 of Android—you should also duplicate your rules with the -webkit- prefix.*

transition-property

The first new property, transition-property, specifies which property (or properties) of an element will be animated (that's the most number of times I've ever said *property* in a single sentence). Here's the syntax:

```
E { transition-property: keyword; }
```

An acceptable keyword value is either all or none or a valid CSS property. The default value is all, which means every valid property will be animated. I stress *valid* CSS property because not every property can be transitioned; the specification has a full list of the ones that can at *http://www.w3.org/TR/css3-transitions/#properties-from-css-/*.

Here's an example of transition-property:

```
h1 {
    font-size: 150%;
    transition-property: font-size;
}
```

This code sets an initial value of 150% on the font-size property and declares this is the property that will be transitioned when the (not yet specified) trigger is activated. Note that I will add properties to this example throughout the rest of this section before showing the completed example in action in "The Complete Transition Example" on page 173.

transition-duration

The next property is transition-duration, which defines the length of time that the transition takes to complete. Here's the syntax:

```
E { transition-duration: time; }
```

The *time* value is a number with a unit of *ms* (*milliseconds*) or *s* (*seconds*). Because 1000 milliseconds equals 1 second, a value of 1.25s is the same as 1250ms. The default value is 0 (zero), meaning this property is the only one required to create a transition. A transition can occur if you declare a transition-duration without a transition-property (as that defaults to all, so all valid properties will animate) but not vice versa.

To make the example transition from the previous section happen over a period of two seconds, you add this code:

```
h1 {
    font-size: 150%;
    transition-property: font-size;
    transition-duration: 2s;
}
```

Although you can supply negative values to this property, they will be interpreted as the default 0.

transition-timing-function

To control the manner in which an element transitions between states, you use the transition-timing-function property. This property allows for variations in speed along the duration of the transition, which gives you control over the animation's pace. This property has three different value types: a keyword, the cubic-bezier() function, or the steps() function. I'll discuss those two functions in detail, but to begin, I'll focus on the keywords.

Timing Function Keywords

The syntax of the transition-timing-function property when used with a keyword is quite straightforward:

```
E { transition-timing-function: keyword; }
```

The possible keyword values are ease, linear, ease-in, ease-out, and ease-in-out. The default value is ease, which starts slowly, accelerates quickly, and slows down again at the end. The linear value progresses steadily from the start of the transition to the end, with no variation in speed. With the ease-in value, the animation begins slowly and then speeds up toward the end, and the ease-out value acts in reverse. Finally, ease-in-out starts slowly, speeds up through the middle, and then slows down again at the end, similar to—but less dramatic than—the ease value.

With that explained, let's add a simple timing function to the example transition:

```
h1 {
    font-size: 150%;
    transition-property: font-size;
    transition-duration: 2s;
    transition-timing-function: ease-out;
}
```

The Cubic Bézier Curve

If you want finer control over the transition-timing-function property, you should use the cubic-bezier() function. In case you're not familiar with cubic Bézier curves—and indeed, why would you be?—allow me to explain. First, here's the syntax:

```
E { transition-timing-function: cubic-bezier(x1, y1, x2, y2); }
```

A cubic Bézier curve is a smooth, continuous curve that passes through four points plotted on a grid that goes from 0 to 1 along both axes. The four points are known as P_0, P_1, P_2, and P_3. They define curvature and are plotted with pairs of (x, y) coordinates, where the first (P_0) is always at $(0, 0)$ and the last (P_3) is always at $(1, 1)$. The other two points are defined in the function: $(x1, y1)$ and $(x2, y2)$. An example, shown in Figure 14-1, illustrates this best.

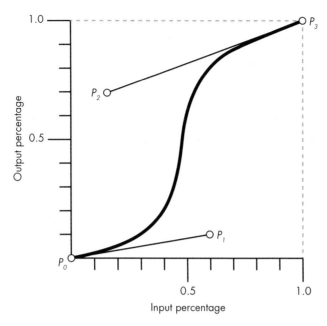

Figure 14-1: An example of a cubic Bézier curve

Figure 14-1 shows the four points mapped onto the grid to create a Bézier curve. The coordinates of each point are shown in Table 14-1.

Table 14-1: The Coordinate Points
Used to Plot a Bézier Curve

Point	Coordinates (x, y)
P_0	(0, 0)
P_1	(0.6, 0.1)
P_2	(0.15, 0.7)
P_3	(1.0, 1.0)

You would use the following CSS to represent this curve (remember, you don't need to define P_0 and P_3 because they always have the same values):

```
E { transition-timing-function: cubic-bezier(0.6, 0.1, 0.15, 0.7); }
```

A linear animation progresses in a straight line from (0, 0) to (1, 1), but this example animation follows the progression of the curve toward the final point over the set duration. If you imagine the duration to be 1 second, you can see the speed gradually increases at the start, between 0 and (roughly) 0.5 seconds, and then increases sharply to about 0.7 seconds, and then assumes a slower rate until the end of the animation.

All of the transition-timing-function keywords described earlier are produced with cubic Bézier curves. Table 14-2 shows each of the keywords and their corresponding values for the cubic-bezier() function.

Table 14-2: Comparing `transition-timing-function` Keywords with Their Equivalent Cubic Bézier Values

Keyword Value	Cubic Bézier Value
ease	0.25, 0.1, 0.25, 1
linear	0, 0, 1, 1
ease-in	0.42, 0, 1, 1
ease-out	0, 0, 0.58, 1
ease-in-out	0.42, 0, 0.58, 1

As with the transformation matrices I introduced in Chapter 13, `cubic-bezier()` functions can be quite daunting if you're not used to math. But don't worry—you can always use the keyword values, which will be more than sufficient in most cases.

A great tool to make cubic Bézier curves a little easier is Lea Verou's *http://cubic-bezier.com/*. This tool allows you to create your own curves using a visual interface, see them run in real time compared to the keyword aliases, and export them as `cubic-bezier()` functions—a really useful aid to understanding.

The steps() Function

An alternative to smooth, eased transitions is to use the `steps()` function, which runs the animation in a series of staggered intervals. The syntax of the function looks like this:

```
E { transition-timing-function: steps(count, direction); }
```

The *count* value is an integer that states how many intervals the animation should run through, and the optional *direction* is one of two keywords—start or end (the default)—that sets the point at which the change happens in each interval. That probably doesn't make a lot of sense right now, but bear with me.

Let's see a very simple example of how the `steps()` works. Take a look at the following rule, in which the `steps()` function has a step count argument of 4 and uses the simple form of the function by omitting the optional direction keyword:

```
E { transition-timing-function: steps(4); }
```

Visualized on the timing function grid used for the `cubic-bezier()` function, it would look like Figure 14-2. So rather than a single line of transition, steps are like seeing snapshots of the animation in action.

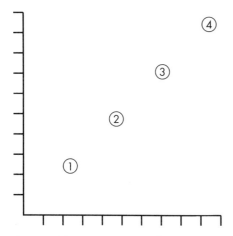

Figure 14-2: A transition over four stepped intervals

When an animation is displayed in steps, use the *direction* keyword to select when the change of each step occurs: the default end keyword means the change happens at the end of the step (pause, then change), and the alternative start means the change happens at the start of the step (change, then pause).

This process is also easier to visualize on the timing function grid; in the following code, the same step count is shown with differing direction keywords:

```
E { transition-timing-function: steps(4, start); }
E { transition-timing-function: steps(4, end); }
```

You can see the difference in Figure 14-3, and I strongly urge you to take a look, if you can, at the accompanying example file (available from *http://thebookofcss3.com/*)—seeing the two in action is the best way to understand the difference.

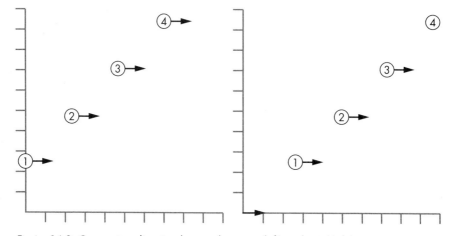

Figure 14-3: Comparing direction keywords: start (left) and end (right)

transition-delay

The final property in the transition-* family is transition-delay, which sets the time when the transition starts. Here's the syntax:

```
E { transition-delay: time; }
```

As with transition-duration, the *time* value is a number with a unit of either milliseconds (ms) or seconds (s). The default value is 0 (zero), meaning the transition happens as soon as the trigger is . . . well, triggered. Any other positive value starts the transition after the specified length of time has passed.

For example, if you wanted to set a delay of a quarter of a second at the start of the example transition, here's the code you would use:

```
h1 {
    font-size: 150%;
    transition-property: font-size;
    transition-duration: 2s;
    transition-timing-function: ease-out;
    transition-delay: 250ms;
}
```

You can also use negative values for transition-delay, which has an interesting effect: The transition begins immediately but skips ahead by the amount of the negative value. To illustrate what I mean, let's consider a transition with a duration of 4s but a delay of -2s:

```
E {
    transition-duration: 4s;
    transition-delay: -2s;
}
```

When triggered, the transition starts immediately, but as if two seconds had already passed (two seconds being the duration minus the delay). In this case, the animation would start halfway through the transition.

The transition Shorthand Property

Throughout this section, I've built an example transition property by property. So far, the code looks like this:

```
h1 {
    transition-property: font-size;
    transition-duration: 2s;
    transition-timing-function: ease-out;
    transition-delay: 250ms;
}
```

This code seems like quite a lot to write for each transition. But, as with all of the other CSS properties that are part of a "family" (background-*, border-*, and so on), the transition-* family has a shorthand. Here's the syntax:

```
E { transition: property duration timing-function delay; }
```

One important thing to be aware of here is that there are two time values: transition-duration and transition-delay, which must be declared in that order. If only one is declared, the syntax presumes it is transition-duration, and the transition-delay will be set at the default (or inherited) value.

If you use the values from the example transition with the shorthand property, here's the result:

```
h1 { transition: font-size 2s ease-out 250ms; }
```

It's quite apparent that this is a lot less code to write.

The Complete Transition Example

Now that I've explained all of the component properties, let's take a look at the example transition in action. The full code is shown here:

```
h1 {
    font-size: 150%;
    transition: font-size 2s ease-out 250ms;
}
h1:hover { font-size: 600%; }
```

Figure 14-4 shows what happens when I pass my mouse over the h1 element.

Figure 14-4: Three stages of an animated transition on the font-size property

Obviously, I can't show the full animation on the printed page, but the illustration shows three stages of the transition: the initial, pre-transition stage (left) with a font size of 150 percent; an intermediate, mid-transition stage (center), which is just under two seconds into the animation when the font size has increased; and the final, post-transition stage (right) where the font size is 600 percent.

As I've already mentioned, transitions act in reverse when the condition that acts as a trigger is no longer being met, so when you remove your mouse from over the h1 element, you can read this example from right to left to see what will happen.

Multiple Transitions

You can easily add multiple transitions to an element by providing a list of comma-separated values to the individual or shorthand properties. That being the case, both of the following code examples are valid:

```
E {
    transition-property: border-width, height, padding;
    transition-duration: 4s, 500ms, 4s;
}
E { transition: border-width 4s, height 500ms, padding 4s; }
```

Note that if a property has fewer values than the others, that list of values will be looped. With that in mind, you could rewrite this code example slightly:

```
E {
    transition-property: border-width, height, padding;
    transition-duration: 4s, 500ms;
}
```

Here, transition-property has three values, whereas transition-duration has only two. This means the third value of the former (padding) is matched with the first value of the latter (4s), matching what was supplied in the first example.

Here's a practical example:

```
.widget {
    background-color: black;
    left: 10%;
    top: 60%;
    transition: background-color 4s linear, left 2s ease-in-out, top 2s ease-in-out;
}
div:hover .widget {
    background-color: silver;
    left: 75%;
    top: 10%;
}
```

Here, I've used the transition shorthand to apply three transitions. The first transition changes the background-color from black to silver in a linear timing function, and the next two change the left and top properties with ease-in-out timing functions. The background-color transition takes place over four seconds, and the others, over two.

Figure 14-5 shows three stages of the transition: The first stage (left) shows the element pre-transition, with a black background and positioned at the bottom left of its parent element; the next stage (center) is mid-transition, as the element is changing color and moving to the top right of its parent; and the final stage (right) shows the element post-transition, with a silver background and in its final position.

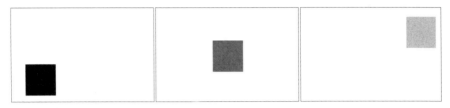

Figure 14-5: Three stages of an animated transition on the background-color, left, and top properties

Animations

Transitions are good but naturally limited; they are only applied when a property value changes. The CSS3 Animations Module (*http://www.w3.org/TR/css3-animations/*) goes beyond what is possible with transitions, allowing animations to be applied directly to elements with a syntax that is more flexible and permits more granular control. Animations and transitions have quite a lot of syntax in common, but the process for creating animations is very different: First, you define the properties and timings, and then you add the animation controls to the elements that will be animated.

NOTE   *CSS animations are implemented in IE10+ and all other modern browsers, but, as of the time of writing, you'll still need to use the -webkit- vendor prefix for Chrome and Safari, on both desktop and mobile.*

Keyframes

You can think of CSS animations as a series of transitions, chained into a sequence. The first step in creating your own animations is to define your *keyframes*, which are the points that set the start and end of a transition. The most simple animation has two keyframes—one at the start and one at the end—whereas more complex ones have multiple keyframes in between. Figure 14-6 illustrates how an animation with three keyframes would appear.

In CSS, keyframes are declared in the @keyframes rule, which has the following syntax:

```
@keyframes name {
    selector { property : value;  }
}
```

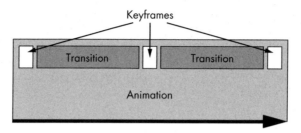

Figure 14-6: An animation with three keyframes and transitions between each

Remember you'll also have to duplicate your keyframe ruleset to accommodate WebKit-based browsers. Use the WebKit prefix: @-webkit-keyframes.

The first value for the @keyframes rule is *name*; this unique identifier is used to call the animation, which I'll discuss later. You can use pretty much any value here (use hyphen separation, not spaces, if you want a name with multiple words), although I suggest using a word or term that is relevant to the animation it describes—your stylesheets will be much easier to follow if you do.

The next value, `selector`, sets the position along the duration of the animation that the keyframe will occur. The usual value here is a percentage value; for example, if you want the keyframe to occur halfway through your animation, use 50%. You can also use one of the keywords, `from` or `to`, which are analogous to 0 percent and 100 percent, respectively.

Within each keyframe selector is a CSS declaration or series of declarations that are applied to a selected element at the specified stage of the animation. If this is all blowing your mind, let me clarify with an example. The following code describes a simple animation, which I've named *expand*, with three keyframes:

```
@keyframes expand {
❶ from { border-width: 4px; }
❷ 50% { border-width: 12px; }
❸ to {
❹     border-width: 4px;
        height: 100%;
        width: 100%;
    }
}
```

At the beginning of the animation (❶), the selected element has a border that is 4px wide; halfway through the animation (❷), the border is increased to a width of 12px; and at the end of the animation(❸), the border is back to 4px wide, and the height and width are both 100%. Between each of the keyframes, the elements are animated gradually, so between the start and halfway through the animation, the border is animated to change width smoothly from 4px to 12px.

Note that inheritance operates on individual keyframes, so if you want a change to persist between frames, you need to specify it in each frame. If

I hadn't specified border-width again in the to keyframe (❹), it would default to the inherited value of the element the animation was applied to, meaning the animation would be quite different.

Keyframe selectors can be chained just like other CSS selectors, so I could write the previous code example like this:

```
@keyframes expand {
    from, to { border-width: 4px; }
    50% { border-width: 12px; }
    to {
        height: 100%;
        width: 100%;
    }
}
```

Likewise, you are not required to list the keyframe selectors in time order; putting to before from is perfectly acceptable (although harder to maintain, I bet), and any declaration conflicts are resolved by using the cascade: Rules declared later take preference. For example, take a look at the following keyframe ruleset where two keyframes have been defined at the same point:

```
@keyframes example {
    10% { background-color: red; }
    10% { background: green; }
}
```

When the animation is applied, the element's background color will be green at the 10% point, as the rule declared later would apply.

Once you've defined the keyframes, the next step is to apply animation control properties to the elements you want to animate. As I mentioned in the introduction to this section, many of the animation properties share syntax with their counterparts in the transition-* family, so you should already be pretty familiar with them.

animation-name

The animation-name property refers to an animation that's been defined with the @keyframes rule, and, as such, the syntax is quite straightforward:

```
E { animation-name: name; }
```

You can see it requires only a single value, which is the name of an already defined animation. To call the animation created in the previous section, you use this:

```
div { animation-name: expand; }
```

The only other permissible value (and the default) is none, which prevents any animations from occurring on this element.

animation-duration

The duration of an animation is set by the animation-duration property, which is functionally identical to the transition-duration property introduced earlier in this chapter:

```
E { animation-duration: time; }
```

As with transition-duration, the time value is a number with a unit of either ms or s, or a 0 (zero), which prevents the animation from running. (Negative values are also implemented as 0.) To extend the example animation so it's six seconds in duration, you add this line:

```
div { animation-duration: 6s; }
```

animation-timing-function

Another property that should be familiar is animation-timing-function, which again is functionally identical to its counterpart transition-timing-function:

```
E { animation-timing-function: value; }
```

Permitted values are the timing function keywords (ease, linear, ease-in, ease-out, and ease-in-out), the cubic-bezier() function (explained in "The Cubic Bézier Curve" on page 168), or the steps() function (explained in "The steps() Function" on page 170). Therefore, if you want to make your animation "ease in" at the start, you add this code:

```
div { animation-timing-function: ease-in; }
```

animation-delay

Yet another familiar property is animation-delay, which is identical in function to its counterpart, the transition-delay property:

```
E { animation-delay: time; }
```

Like animation-duration (and the two corresponding transition-* properties), the time value is a number with a unit of either ms or s, which sets the delay before an animation begins. A 0 (zero) means no delay. As with transition-duration, negative values cause the animation to "skip" by that amount.

To delay the example animation by two seconds, you include this code:

```
div { animation-delay: 2s; }
```

animation-iteration-count

Unlike a transition, which only happens once (or twice, if you want to count the reverse), an animation can be repeated any number of times. The number of repetitions is set by the animation-iteration-count property, which has this syntax:

```
E { animation-iteration-count: count; }
```

The *count* value in this syntax is either a whole number or the keyword infinite. A number value sets how many times the animation repeats. The default value is 1 (one), meaning the animation plays from start to end once and then stops. The infinite value means the animation loops indefinitely or at least until another condition is met that changes this value. A value of 0 (zero) or any negative number prevents the animation from playing.

To continue with the example I've built throughout this section, if I want the animation to repeat 10 times, I need to add the following declaration:

```
div { animation-iteration-count: 10; }
```

animation-direction

Animations play from start to finish, but they can also play in reverse. You can set whether your animation always plays in one direction or alternates playing forward and backward. To do this, use the animation-direction property:

```
E { animation-direction: keyword; }
```

The keyword value has two options: normal or alternate. The default is normal, which always plays the animation forward: The animation plays through from start to finish, and then, if it is set to repeat, it plays again from the start. If the alternate value is used, the animation plays from start to finish and then plays in reverse before starting over again. If you consider each iteration of the animation as a "cycle," the odd-numbered cycles play forward and the even-numbered play backward. You can see the difference in Figure 14-7.

To complete the example animation, let's set the animation to alternate forward and backward:

```
div { animation-direction: alternate; }
```

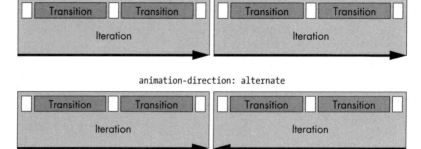

Figure 14-7: An animation played in the normal direction repeats itself from start to finish; when played using alternate, each second cycle plays finish to start.

animation-fill-mode

If your animation is finite—that is, if it doesn't have an infinite value for the animation-iteration-count property—then you use the animation-fill-mode property to set how the element appears outside of the animation cycle. To show you what I mean by that, let's consider the following style rules:

```
@keyframes example {
    from { background-color: red; }
    to { background-color: blue; }
}
E {
    animation-delay: 1s;
    animation-duration: 1s;
    animation-iteration-count: 2;
    animation-name: example;
    background-color: green;
}
```

In this rule, element *E* will be green for the 1s delay before the animation is triggered, then instantly change to red, then transition to blue, iterating twice (2), and then at the end revert back to the initial green.

You can change this behavior with animation-fill-mode. The syntax looks like this:

```
E { animation-fill-mode: keyword; }
```

The permitted keywords are none (the default), backwards, forwards, or both. If you use backwards, the declarations specified in the 0% (or from) keyframe will be applied to the element before the animation begins; if you use forwards, the declarations in the 100% (or to) keyframe will be applied when the animation ends; or if you use both, the 0% declarations will apply before the animation and the 100%, after.

So returning to the previous example code, if you add the following rule:

```
E { animation-fill-mode: both ; }
```

then element *E* would begin red, before transitioning to blue and staying that color at the end of the animation; its original green wouldn't be applied at any point.

animation-play-state

The `animation-play-state` property sets whether an animation is active. Here's the syntax:

```
E { animation-play-state: keyword; }
```

The keyword value has two options: `running` means the animation is playing, and `paused` means it isn't. You can use this property to perform a play/pause action:

```
E:hover { animation-play-state: paused; }
```

In this example, if you presume that element *E* has an animation applied, passing the mouse over the element pauses the animation until the mouse is moved off, at which time the animation continues.

The animation Shorthand

Throughout this section, I've assembled an example animation one property at a time. Here's how all the properties combined appear:

```
div {
    animation-name: expand;
    animation-duration: 6s;
    animation-timing-function: ease-in;
    animation-delay: 2s;
    animation-iteration-count: 10;
    animation-direction: alternate;
    animation-fill-mode: forwards;
    animation-play-state: running;
}
```

That's a lot of properties to declare for each animation. Once again, however, you can take advantage of a shorthand property called `animation`, and here's the syntax:

```
E { animation: name duration timing-function delay iteration-count direction
fill-mode play-state; }
```

As with the `transition` shorthand, `animation-duration` and `animation-delay` must be specified in order. If either is left out, the syntax presumes it is `animation-delay`, which receives a default value of `0`.

To make the example I've been building in this chapter somewhat more compact, I can use this shorthand code:

```
div { animation: expand 6s ease-in 2s 10 alternate both running; }
```

That may still seem verbose, but at its most simple, only two values are required for the animation property to function: the name of the keyframe and a duration:

```
div { animation: expand 6s; }
```

The Complete Animations Example

With all of the properties explained, let's take a look at the full example animation in action. Here's the CSS (some rules have been omitted for brevity; see the example files for the complete code):

```
@keyframes expand {
❶ 0% { border-width: 4px; }
❷ 50% { border-width: 12px; }
❸ 100% {
        border-width: 4px;
        height: 100%;
        width: 100%;
    }
}
div {
    ...
    animation: expand 6s ease 0 infinite alternate;
}
```

Unfortunately, I can't show animation in this book, so I'll settle for describing it. Figure 14-8 shows the state of the element at three of the animation's keyframes: The keyframe at 0% (❶) shows the element with a border-width of 4px and the inherited height and width (100px each, not shown here); in the 50% keyframe (❷), the border-width is increased to 12px; and in the final, 100% keyframe (❸), the border-width returns to 4px and both height and width have changed to 100%.

Figure 14-8: Three stages of an animation affecting the border-width, height, and width properties

Because my `animation-direction` value is alternate, the animation would then play in reverse, shrinking back to its original dimensions, and then continue growing and shrinking infinitely because of the value of `animation-iteration-count`.

Multiple Animations

You can add multiple animations to an element using a comma-separated list. This method works for each of the subproperties and the shorthand property, so both of these examples are valid:

```
E {
    animation-name: first-anim, second-anim;
    animation-duration: 6s, 1.25ms;
    animation-delay: 0, 750ms;
}
E { animation: first-anim 6s, second-anim 1.25ms 750ms; }
```

Here, lists of values are looped through to ensure that all properties have the same number of values applied, in exactly the same way as described in "Multiple Transitions" on page 174.

Summary

Adding animations to CSS was originally considered a contentious move, but I think the syntax used by the writers of these modules is pretty graceful and adds a lot of flexibility without being overwhelmingly complicated.

Developers expressed concern that transitions and animations would be misused and that we'd end up with a lot of garish, unusable websites. Although a genuine concern, one really can't stop people from doing that now with the existing CSS properties (and, indeed, many do!). But used sparingly and appropriately, these powerful new tools can add vibrancy to web pages.

Transitions and Animations: Browser Support

	Chrome	Firefox	Safari	IE
Transitions	Yes	Yes	Yes	IE10
Animations	Yes*	Yes	Yes*	IE10

* With vendor prefix

15

FLEXIBLE BOX LAYOUT

That web pages look as good as they do is a minor miracle (comparatively speaking, of course!). Since the move away from table-based layouts to pure CSS, developers have often had to create complex page structures using simple tools such as float, margin, and position—tools perhaps not even intended for that purpose when they were first created. As CSS has matured and browsers have grown more powerful, a new range of alternative layout approaches has been proposed.

The one most widely implemented is called Flexible Box Layout (or *Flexbox*). This approach is defined in the Flexible Box Layout Module (*http://www.w3.org/TR/css-flexbox-1/*), and it makes elements resize flexibly to better fit their available space, without the need for floats, positioning, or complex calculations.

Although you can certainly create entire page layouts with Flexbox, it is most suitable for working with interface elements and smaller components. When working with whole page layouts, consider using the Grid Layout Module, which I'll introduce in Chapter 17. But if you're building a user interface or an app (especially an app with a lot of buttons, form elements, or interactive regions), you'll find Flexbox extremely useful.

Declaring the Flexible Box Model

The first step in using Flexbox is to create the *flex container*—the parent element that will create a new formatting context for its contents. To declare a flex container, you simply use a new value for the display property:

```
E { display: flex; }
```

This creates a block-level flex container; you can use the alternate inline-flex value if you prefer an inline-level container.

Now you can add *flex items* to the flex container. A flex item is any child of the flex container, which is subject to the formatting context created by the container. For example, in the following code if #container is set as the flex container, the two child items will become flex items:

```
<div id="container">
  <div id="a">...</div>
  <div id="b">...</div>
</div>
```

This combination of markup and CSS is shown in Figure 15-1. Notice that the two elements are of equal width and laid out next to each other, without needing to use floats or positioning properties. By default, flex items are laid out in the direction of the document text—that is, from left to right for languages such as English, from right to left for languages such as Arabic (specified with the dir HTML attribute or direction CSS property), and from top to bottom for languages such as Japanese (set with the text-direction CSS property, but not yet broadly supported).

Figure 15-1: Child items of a flex container are laid out horizontally by default.

NOTE   *All of the examples throughout the rest of this chapter use the left-to-right direction, unless otherwise stated.*

To alter the default layout direction, you can use the flex-direction property on the container. The default value row lays items out in a row, whereas a value of column lays them out from top to bottom in a column.

```
E {
  display: flex;
  flex-direction: column;
}
```

Flexbox Alignment

Flexbox uses two axes for alignment. As shown in Figure 15-2, the *main axis* goes in the direction that items are placed, from left to right or top to bottom. When the value of flex-direction is row, the main axis is horizontal; when it is column, the main axis is vertical. The *cross axis* is the line that runs perpendicular to the main axis: it's vertical when the direction is row and horizontal when it's column.

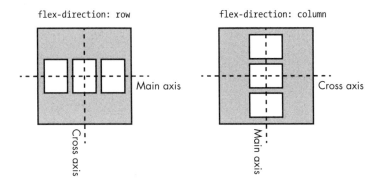

Figure 15-2: The main and cross axes depend on the direction of the layout of the flex children.

When dealing with flex containers and items, you'll often see points referred to as the start and end of axes. Because flex axes can be reversed (from top to bottom or bottom to top, and left to right or right to left), you use start and end rather than relative directions to prevent confusion. For example, when the main axis is horizontal and the direction is from left to right, the start of the main axis is the left and the end is the right; but if the main axis is vertical, the start of the main axis is at the top and the end is at the bottom (or vice versa if reversed).

Reversing the Content Order

One of Flexbox's great capabilities is that you can quickly change the order in which items are displayed, regardless of their order in the DOM. For example, Figure 15-1 shows two items laid out in a row, in the order in which they're declared in the DOM. What if you want to change their order so #b comes before #a?

You can do this quickly with the flex-direction property, using the value row-reverse to reverse the order in which the flex items are displayed, as shown here. (The column-reverse property value reverses the order of flex items vertically displayed in columns.)

```
E { flex-direction: row-reverse; }
```

The result is shown in Figure 15-3.

Figure 15-3: The row-reverse value quickly reverses the order of flex items.

Because reversing directions like this also reverses the axis direction, in the case of row-reverse, the start of the axis is on the left, and the end is on the right. In the case of column-reverse, the start is at the bottom, and the end is at the top.

Fully Reordering Content

You can create custom ordering patterns with the order property. The order property is applied to the flex items (not their container). The value of the property is a number that creates an *ordinal group* that groups together items with the same value and orders them by their ordinal group: All items in the lowest numbered group come first, then all items in the second-lowest numbered group, and so on. Any items without a declared value are shown first because they have the default value of 0.

Items with the same ordinal group number are grouped in the order in which they appear in the DOM. For example, consider four flex items, #a through #d:

```
<div id="container">
  <div id="a">...</div>
  <div id="b">...</div>
  <div id="c">...</div>
  <div id="d">...</div>
</div>
```

If no explicit values are set, and if flex-direction isn't reversed, the children are displayed in the order in which they appear in the DOM: #a, #b, #c, #d. But let's reorder them by using different values on the order property:

```
#a { order: 2; }
#b, #d { order: 3; }
#c { order: 1; }
```

With these rules applied, the order in which the items are laid out becomes: #c, #a, #b, #d. Item #c comes first because it has the lowest ordinal group number, followed by #a with the next highest number, then #b and #d—both of which are in ordinal group 3. Item #d comes last because it comes later in the DOM order.

Figure 15-4 shows the result.

Figure 15-4: The flex items reordered using ordinal groups

Notice that items #c and #a share the same background colors, as do #b and #d. The background colors should alternate because I'm using the :nth-child() pseudo-class discussed in Chapter 4:

```
.flex-item:nth-child(even) { background-color: gray; }
```

But remember that the items have only changed order visually; they retain the same order in the markup, which is why :nth-child() applies the gray background to the elements that should be even numbered—namely, #b and #d.

Adding Flexibility

When using Flexbox, you will almost certainly encounter situations where the combined lengths of flex items along the main axis are greater or less than the width of the flex container. When this happens, the "flexible" part of Flexbox comes into play. Several properties allow flex items to grow or shrink to fill their container. I'll walk you through them in this section.

The flex-grow Property

Let's say you have a flex container 600px wide that contains three flex items. Each one is 150px wide, making a combined width of 450px. The difference between the width of the container and the combined width of the items leaves an empty space of 150px (that's 600 – 450) at the end of the items, as shown in Figure 15-5.

Figure 15-5: Three flex items with a combined width narrower than the width of their container leaves empty space on the right.

To expand the items to fill the container, you can use the `flex-grow` property:

```
.flex-item { flex-grow: 1; }
```

The value of the `flex-grow` property is basically a ratio that's used to distribute the empty space between the flex items so they expand. In this case, I used a 1:1:1 ratio to divide the empty 150px equally between the three flex items. Because 150 divided by 3 is 50, each item is expanded by 50px, making their total width equal to the width of the container, as shown in Figure 15-6.

Figure 15-6: The three flex items now fill the width of their container.

You can also provide different values to adjust the distribution ratio. For example, to make #b take up more of the width of the container than the other two items, you could set a value of 3 for #b:

```
#b { flex-grow: 3; }
```

Now the 150px will be redistributed using the ratio 1:3:1, so for every one pixel distributed to #a and #c, #b will receive three. As a result #a and #c will each be expanded to 180px wide, whereas #b will be 240px wide as shown in Figure 15-7.

Figure 15-7: Because #b has a higher flex-grow value, when resized, it's wider than its siblings.

Because the default value for flex-grow is 0 (zero), flex items will keep their width and not expand to fill the container unless explicitly instructed to do so.

The flex-shrink Property

Just as flex-grow is used to expand flex items to fill their container, flex-shrink is used to shrink items. For example, let's revisit our flex container from the previous section with items #a, #b, and #c; only in this case, we'll make each item 300px wide. Now the total width of the three items is 900px, which exceeds the 600px width of the parent by 300px.

To shrink these elements to fit within the container width, you could use the flex-shrink property:

```
.flex-item { flex-shrink: 1; }
```

The flex-shrink property works like flex-grow but in the opposite direction. For example, a value of 1 (the default) reduces each item by the same proportion—each by 100px (300 divided by 3). The resulting items will be 200px each, for a total of 600px, which matches the width of the container.

Like flex-grow, different values change the distribution ratio. For example, if you use a value of 3 for item #b, its width is reduced by three pixels for every one-pixel reduction of the other two items.

```
#b { flex-shrink: 3; }
```

Higher numbers reduce the elements by a greater factor. In this example, for each pixel removed from the width of #a and #c, three are removed from #b. As you can see in Figure 15-8, #a and #c are 240px in width, whereas #b is only 120px, which is narrower than its original width.

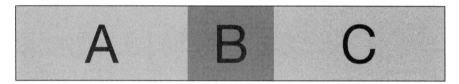

Figure 15-8: Flex item #b has a higher flex-shrink value than its siblings, so it's shrunk proportionally more to fit its container.

The flex-basis Property

The width of flex items can be set either by the content they contain or by an explicit width value, and any growth or shrinkage is calculated from that base width. To change how the width adjustment is calculated, you can set a flex-basis value on an element. This property takes as a value a length unit. Here's an example:

```
.flex-item { flex-basis: 100px; }
```

When flex-basis is applied, any existing width value is ignored, and the value that you specify for the flex-basis is used to calculate the adjustment. For example, in the previous two sections, the width value of 150px is ignored and all growth or shrinking is based on the flex-basis value of 100px. You could add the flex-basis value of 100px to #b in Figure 15-7, like this:

```
.child-item {
    flex-grow: 1;
    width: 150px;
}
#b {
    flex-basis: 100px;
    flex-grow: 3;
}
```

Now the empty space in the container will be redistributed using the ratio 1:3:1, which means that, based on the width values, #a and #c would expand by 30px each and #b by 90px. Because of the flex-basis value, however, that space distribution is performed as if #b had a width of 100px, not the specified width value of 150px.

At first, it seems illogical that #b ends up wider than its siblings despite having a lower width set by its flex-basis value. The reason is that there is now a spare width of 200px (the combined widths of the flex items is 400px; the parent is 600px). This 200 is redistributed between the three boxes using the ratio 1:3:1. Although #b begins at 100px wide, it receives 120px of the spare space whereas #a and #c receive 40px.

As a result, #a and #c end up 190px wide, and #b is 220px wide. Compare the result shown in Figure 15-9 with Figure 15-7 to see the difference.

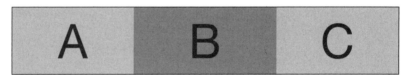

Figure 15-9: Because #b has a flex-basis value applied, it's resized to be larger than its siblings.

The flex Shorthand

As with many properties, the flex-* family has a shorthand property called flex. The values it takes are, in order, flex-grow, flex-shrink, and flex-basis. Consider this example:

```
E { flex: 1 2 150px; }
```

Here, element *E* has a flex-grow value of 1 and a flex-shrink value of 2. The value used is chosen based on the width of the flex items in comparison with their flex container; where flex items don't fill their container, the flex-grow value is used, and where flex items exceed their container, the flex-shrink value comes into play. The final value, 150px, is the flex-basis value.

Alignment Inside the Container

When you have items with fixed dimensions inside a flex container, you'll likely have empty space along one or both of the axes. For example, in Figure 15-5, three flex items that are each 150px wide didn't fill the width of their 600px container. When this is the case, you can align the items inside the container to make better use of the available space.

Horizontal Alignment with justify-content

Thankfully, Flexbox offers tight control over alignment and placement, allowing you to redistribute unused space with the justify-content property. This property is applied to the flex container and accepts a series of keyword values that are applied differently depending on the direction of the flex parent (row, column, reversed row, and so on):

```
.flex-container { justify-content: keyword; }
```

The default value is flex-start, which (as shown in Figure 15-5) aligns all flex items to the left of the parent with the unused space occupying the remaining width to the right. The alternative values are the following:

- flex-end, which aligns items to the right of the container with the unused space to the left
- center, which distributes the unused space to either side of all items, centering the items in the container
- space-between, which adds an equal amount of space between each item but none before the first or after the last item
- space-around, which puts an equal amount of space on both sides of each item

The following code shows a few different values for the sake of comparison, with the results shown in Figure 15-10.

```
.container-a { justify-content: flex-start; }
.container-b { justify-content: center; }
.container-c { justify-content: space-around; }
```

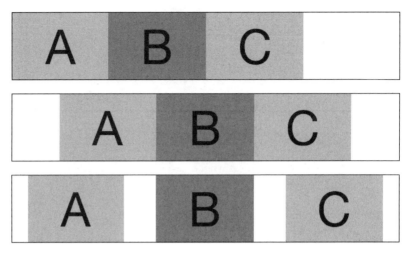

Figure 15-10: Different values for the justify-content *property:* flex-start *(top),* center *(middle), and* space-around *(bottom)*

Vertical Alignment with align-items

When the height of your flex items is less than the height of the flex container, you can use the property align-items to adjust the items within the container:

```
.flex-container { align-items: keyword; }
```

The principal keyword values for this property are:

- stretch, which makes items the same height as the parent
- flex-start, which aligns items to the top of the container
- flex-end, which aligns items to the bottom of the container
- center, which aligns items to the vertical center of the container, with equal space above and below

The default value is stretch if the items have no height explicitly specified, or flex-start if they do.

In the following listing, I've set the flex container to have a flex-direction value of column, so the main axis is vertical and the cross axis is horizontal. Figure 15-11 shows the results.

```
.container-a { align-items: stretch; }
.container-b { align-items: flex-end; }
.container-c { align-items: center; }
```

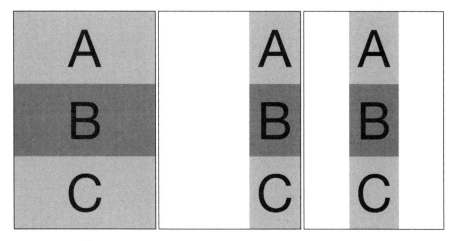

Figure 15-11: Alignment on the cross axis is controlled with different values for align-items: stretch (left), flex-end (middle), and center (right).

Notice that with no explicit width set, the flex items in the second and third columns are sized only to the width of their content, and then aligned within the container based on its align-items value.

Cross-Axis Alignment with align-self

To control the cross-axis alignment of individual items, use the align-self property. This property applies to the item, not the container. The values are the same as for align-items, and they have the same effects on the selected item only; sibling items are unaffected.

For example, in the following listing, element #c has a different value than its siblings:

```
.container { align-items: flex-end; }
#c { align-self: flex-start; }
```

The effect (using the default row direction) is shown in Figure 15-12.

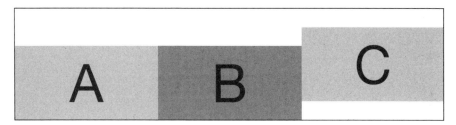

Figure 15-12: Flex item #c is aligned differently from its siblings because of the align-self property.

Wrap and Flow

When you have too many items to fit comfortably into one row (or column) of a container, you can break them onto multiple lines using the flex-wrap property. The default value of nowrap preserves all the items on the same line, whereas a value of wrap breaks them onto extra lines below the first (or to the right in column view), if required.

```
.flex-container { flex-wrap: wrap; }
```

The value wrap-reverse changes the direction of the cross axis so new lines appear above (or to the left). Figure 15-13 compares the effect of the two different values.

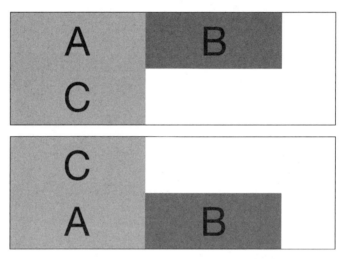

Figure 15-13: Comparing the effects of different values for the flex-wrap property. The top example has a value of wrap, so element #c appears on a new line below, whereas in the bottom example, the value is wrap-reverse, so element #c is on a new line above.

The flex-flow Shorthand

You can combine flex-wrap with flex-direction in the shorthand flex-flow property. For example, to set a column with multiple lines and a reversed cross axis, use this:

```
E { flex-flow: column wrap-reverse; }
```

Aligning Multiple Lines with align-content

When items wrap over multiple lines, you can control their alignment with the align-content property. This property works like justify-content but on the cross axis. It has the same possible values—flex-start, flex-end, center, space-between, and space-around—and also adds stretch, which resizes the items to fill all unused space. Figure 15-14 compares the effects of the values center and space-between.

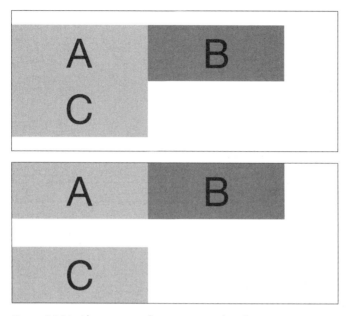

Figure 15-14: Alignment on the cross axis when flex items are wrapped is controlled with align-content: center (top) and space-between (bottom).

Browser Support and Legacy Syntaxes

As I write this, Flexbox is well implemented across all major modern browsers, but it has a long history of syntax changes, and supporting a handful of older browsers can be troublesome. For example, Internet Explorer 10 implements an earlier version of the spec, which uses the -ms- prefix for all properties. The IE10 implementation and the modern spec have a few key differences: IE10 uses -ms-flexbox as the name of the value for the display property, rather than flex; and -ms-flex-align and -ms-flex-pack are used rather than align-items and justify-content (their values differ a little, too). IE10 also lacks any implementation of flex-wrap or the flex-flow shorthand. If you need to support IE10, I suggest reading all about the differences from the spec in the IE10 Developer Guide (*http://msdn.microsoft.com/en-us/library/ie/hh673531%28v=vs.85%29.aspx*).

Older versions of WebKit-based browsers, especially Safari 6 and below, use an even more outdated syntax. If you really need to support these older browsers fully, see Stephen Hay's introductory article from 2009 (*http://www.the-haystack.com/2010/01/23/css3-flexbox-part-1/*).

But don't let these concerns put you off from using Flexbox. Only a handful of browsers require these older properties, and with a little extra work, you can take advantage of the layout gains that Flexbox brings.

Summary

Although it introduces a number of unfamiliar new terms and concepts to CSS, Flexbox is an elegant and logical proposal that solves several common problems with website layouts. Flexbox is harder to describe in writing than it is to learn by doing!

Taking the time to understand Flexbox fully is certainly worthwhile, as many of the new concepts and keywords it introduces are essential to other layout modules now being produced, making it essential to the future of rich layouts on the Web.

Flexbox: Browser Support

	Chrome	Firefox	Safari	IE
Flexible box layout	Yes	Yes	Yes[*]	IE10[†], IE11

[*] With vendor prefix
[†] Supports an older syntax, with vendor prefix

16

VALUES AND SIZING

Much of CSS3, from its many new selectors to layout and font properties, is designed to give you more granular control over presentation than was available in CSS2.1. That control will be even more evident in this chapter, as I introduce new value functions and units, as well as methods to calculate dimensions automatically.

Relative Length Units

In CSS a *relative length unit* is one whose value is relative to another property. The two relative units in CSS2.1 are em, which is calculated from the font-size property of an element, and ex, which is calculated from the x-height of the element's font (see "font-size-adjust" on page 56).

CSS3 expands the range of relative units, which are no longer relative solely to an element's font size. The new units are defined in the Values and Units Module (*http://www.w3.org/TR/css-values/*).

Root-Relative Units

The first new unit introduced in CSS3 is the rem, or *root em*. It behaves like the em unit from CSS2.1, but instead of being relative to the font-size value of the current element, it's relative to the font-size value of the document root (the html element).

Although em is quite useful, it's not without its drawbacks, which become most apparent when nesting elements. To illustrate the problem, I'll use this markup:

```
<ul>
    <li>Western gorilla
        <ul>
            <li>Western lowland gorilla</li>
            <li>Cross River gorilla</li>
        </ul>
    </li>
</ul>
```

and this simple style rule:

```
li { font-size: 2em; }
```

If you presume that the root font-size of the document is the common browser default of 16px, the first li element will have a calculated font-size of 32px (16 multiplied by 2). But the font-size of the li elements nested inside the first would be calculated relative to the inherited value, making them 64px (32 multiplied by 2).

This is where the rem unit becomes essential. Here's the same code as the previous example, only now using the rem in place of the em unit:

```
li { font-size: 2rem; }
```

Again, presuming a root font-size of 16px, the first li has a calculated font-size of 32px. This time, however, the font-size of the nested li elements is also relative to the root value, the same as their parent. And no matter how many nested layers down you go, that value is always relative to the root.

Viewport-Relative Units

When building responsively, developers tend to use percentage values for layout elements, as they scale fluidly across the range of different screen sizes that websites need to cater to. Percentages are useful at a top level, but—as you just saw with em units—you can run into difficulties when using percentages with nested elements.

This code illustrates the problem:

```
<div class="parent">
    <div class="child">...</div>
</div>
```

Now, imagine that .parent is 75 percent of the viewport width, and you want .child to be 65 percent of the viewport width—not the width of its parent. To do this, you have to divide 65 by 75, giving you a result of 86.666 (percent). This calculation is simple enough, but the deeper the nesting goes, the more complex the calculations become.

A better solution is to use CSS3's viewport-relative units—vh and vw—which represent viewport height and width, respectively. Each unit of value represents 1 percent of the appropriate viewport dimension: 1vh is 1 percent of the viewport height, and 1vw is 1 percent of the viewport width. For example, the following code makes an element 75 percent of the viewport width and 50 percent of its height:

```
E {
    height: 50vh;
    width: 75vw;
}
```

The advantage of using these units is that when elements are nested, the units remain relative to the viewport. So, in the case of my previous example, to make .child 65 percent of the total viewport width, you simply do this:

```
.child { width: 65vw; }
```

No calculation required!

Another pair of supplemental units is available, too: vmax is equivalent to whichever is the greater value of vh and vw, and vmin is equivalent to the lesser value. For instance, if the viewport were 480×640, the height would be greater, so vmax would be equivalent to vh, and vmin would be equal to vw. Swap the viewport dimensions (640×480), and vmax and vmin reverse their values.

So if you presume a viewport of 480×640, in the following code snippet, element E is 640px wide, and element F is 480px wide:

```
E { width: 100vmax; }
F { width: 100vmin; }
```

The utility of vmax and vmin is in ensuring an element remains proportional to the viewport regardless of orientation—useful when that orientation can easily change, such as on a mobile or tablet device.

Internet Explorer 9 implemented vmin as the vm unit, but neither it nor IE10 supports vmax (support was added in IE11). Many older smartphone browsers don't support these properties, although newer versions (such as iOS 6.0 and Android 4.4 and above) do (though often without support for vmax, most notably in iOS as of this writing).

Calculated Values

One of the biggest changes in CSS3 lies in the way that lengths can be declared. In CSS2.1, lengths are always a single value plus a unit, and if calculations are required (say, subtracting the width of a border from a total width), the developer has to do the calculation. But in CSS3, the browser performs the calculations.

CSS calculations are performed with the calc() function. You can use this function anywhere you use the common value units—length, angle, number, and so on. It takes as an argument any mathematical expression using those common value units and four basic operands: + (addition), - (subtraction), * (multiplication), and / (division).

The calc() function is especially useful when mixing units. For example, you could create an expression to calculate the width of an element (as a percentage) minus its border (as an em) like this:

```
E {
    border: 10px;
    width: calc(75% - 2em);
}
```

Addition and subtraction can be performed with any units, but when using multiplication, at least one argument on either side of the operand must be a unitless number. In the case of division, the argument *after* the operand must be a unitless number. Here are examples of how to perform both multiplication and division:

```
E {
    left: calc(5 * 10em);
    width: (80% / 4);
}
```

You can use parentheses in expressions to show computational order. For example, the following code shows an expression that performs three calculations:

```
E { height: calc(10% * 5 + 15% * 2); }
```

The expression first multiplies 10 percent by 5, and then adds it to the result of 15 percent multiplied by 2. This setup works fine, but it's is not immediately apparent when you look at it, and given a quite complex calculation could be difficult indeed to immediately understand. The expression becomes easier when written with parentheses:

```
E { height: calc((10% * 5) + (15% * 2)); }
```

You can also use nested calc() functions to achieve the same result.

When using multiplication or division in an expression, you must insert a single whitespace character around the operand—failing to do this means the expression is invalid and the property will be ignored. The following code shows an expression written twice: the first one is invalid because it has no space around the operand; the second is correctly formatted and, therefore, valid.

```
E { border-width: calc(1em*10); } /* Invalid */
E { border-width: calc(1em * 10); } /* Valid */
```

Sizing Elements

The size of an element is generally set using the width or height properties or their max- and min- variants, together with either an absolute (px), relative (em), or percentage value. Although these options are good enough for most day-to-day use, I often find times when I wish the box model were a little more flexible or aware of the elements around it. CSS3 introduces new properties and values aimed at providing this extra flexibility through a box-model toggle and new content-aware sizing methods.

Box Sizing

For many years, Internet Explorer implemented its box model in contravention of the W3C spec. The W3C model dictated that the width value was the width of the content box and that any padding and borders were extra. In IE's model, on the other hand, the width value was equal to the total width of the element including any padding and borders. Consider these style rules:

```
E {
    border: 5px;
    padding: 10px;
    width: 100px;
}
```

In the IE model, the content box would be 70px wide, whereas in the W3C model, it would be the full 100px.

Although the standard model is more logical, at times the IE model is more convenient to use. In CSS3, you can opt to use the IE model with the box-sizing property, which is described in the CSS3 Basic User Interface Module (*http://www.w3.org/TR/css3-ui/*). The syntax is as follows:

```
E { box-sizing: keyword; }
```

The default keyword is content-box, which means apply the specified width or height to the content box only, as in the W3C model. In contrast, the alternative value border-box means any specified length should also include any padding and border boxes.

Figure 16-1 shows the difference. The top example uses the W3C box model, whereas the bottom one has the border-box value applied. As you can see, the total width of the lower example is equal to the content box of the upper.

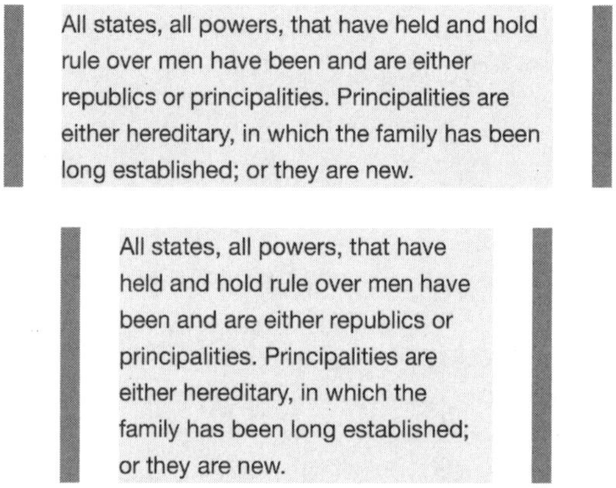

All states, all powers, that have held and hold rule over men have been and are either republics or principalities. Principalities are either hereditary, in which the family has been long established; or they are new.

All states, all powers, that have held and hold rule over men have been and are either republics or principalities. Principalities are either hereditary, in which the family has been long established; or they are new.

Figure 16-1: Comparing values for box-sizing: the default content-box (top) and border-box (bottom)

NOTE *Some people prefer to set a global style rule to apply border-box to all elements. I prefer to apply the rule only as required.*

Intrinsic and Extrinsic Sizing

One challenge in web layout is that elements are ignorant of their content and the context in which they're used—in other words, without JavaScript, an element is not aware of the dimensions of its child or parent elements. CSS3 introduces a new concept that changes that equation a bit with the addition of *intrinsic* and *extrinsic* sizing. Intrinsic sizing is based on an element's children, and extrinsic sizing is based on the size of the parent element. These sizing models are defined in the CSS3 Intrinsic & Extrinsic Sizing Module (*http://dev.w3.org/csswg/css-sizing/*).

All of the intrinsic and extrinsic sizing models are applied using a keyword value on the width or height properties (and their min- and max-variants). For example, this listing shows how a new sizing model would be applied to width:

```
E { width: keyword; }
```

max-content and min-content

The first new keyword values, max-content and min-content, are intrinsic values that make an element as wide or as high as the largest (max-content) or smallest (min-content) item of content (in text, the width of the longest word) it contains. Consider this markup of an img and p element inside a containing div:

```
<div>
    <img src="foo.png">
    <p>...</p>
</div>
```

Say the img element has a width of 200px and the width of the p is 300px. If the div element had a width value of max-content, it would be just wide enough to contain the p, and if it had a value of min-content, it would be just wide enough to fit the img and the text in the p would wrap.

Compare the results shown in Figure 16-2. The container element on the left has the max-content value applied, which makes it as wide as the widest child (the p), whereas the one on the right has min-content applied, which makes it as wide as the narrowest child (the img).

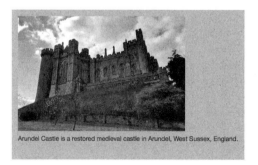
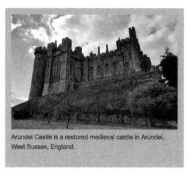

Figure 16-2: The max-content value (left) makes the element as wide as its widest child, whereas min-content (right) makes the element as wide as its narrowest child.

NOTE *As of this writing, the current desktop and mobile versions of Chrome, Firefox, and Safari support these keywords, although each requires vendor prefixes (namely -moz-min-content and -webkit-min-content). Support is not currently present in Internet Explorer or older smartphones.*

fit-content

The next intrinsic keyword value is potentially the most useful. Called fit-content, it sizes an element just as floated elements or table cells do: An element will expand to be just wide enough to contain its content, unless the maximum width of the element is reached, in which case, the content will wrap.

Figure 16-3 compares the effect of fit-content to max-content and min-content. The box at the top left has fit-content applied, and the content wraps when it reaches the limit of the parent container. In contrast, the box at the top right has max-content applied, so it should expand to fit its content—however, the box now exceeds the width of its parent container, which has an overflow value of hidden, meaning the box is clipped.

The box at bottom left also has fit-content applied, so the container resizes to fit the width of the content; the box at the bottom right has min-content applied, so the container is only as wide as the img element and the text content wraps.

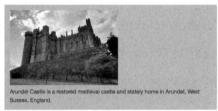 

Figure 16-3: The fit-content value, compared to max-content and min-content

fill

The final keyword in the spec is named fill. (But in Firefox it's available and in Chrome it's fill-available!) This extrinsic value makes an element fill all available space along the height or width of its parent.

Say you want to make an inline-block p element, with border and padding, expand to be as wide as its parent. Generally, you would apply these rules:

```
p {
    border-width: 0 0.5em;
    display: inline-block;
    padding: 0 1em;
    width: 100%;
}
```

As you know, however, an element's "real" width also includes padding and border, so, in this case, the p element would overflow its parent. One solution is to use the `box-sizing` property (see "Box Sizing" on page 203), but you may have good reasons for keeping the standard box model, so a better alternative is to use intrinsic sizing:

```
p { width: fill; }
```

The result is shown in Figure 16-4; the inline-block element, with border and padding, is resized to fill the available space in its parent.

Arundel Castle.

Figure 16-4: Using the `fill` value for `width` makes the inline-block caption shown here fill the available width of its parent.

Summary

In this chapter, I've discussed value units that are relative to a root font size and the viewport, dynamic calculations of values, and CSS3 ways to size elements based on their content and context. I've also discussed the CSS3 switch to a different box model.

Although units and sizing methods may seem like an unglamorous aspect of CSS, they offer you fine-grained control over your layouts, which is always welcome. Because websites are viewed on such a variety of different devices, for an element to be aware of its viewport, content, and context, so it presents content in the most appropriate way, is extremely valuable.

Values and Sizing: Browser Support

	Chrome	Firefox	Safari	IE
Root-relative units	Yes	Yes	Yes	Yes
Viewport-relative units	Yes	Yes	Yes[*]	IE9[†], IE10[‡]
Calculated values	Yes	Yes	Yes	Yes
Box sizing	Yes	Yes	Yes	Yes
Intrinsic/extrinsic sizing	Yes[§]	Yes[§]	Yes[§]	No

[*] Buggy support for vh in iOS
[†] Supports vm instead of vmin, no support for vmax
[‡] No support for vmax
[§] With vendor prefix

17

GRID LAYOUT

Grids are a fundamental design technique. Simple grids have been used by calligraphers since medieval times, and the modern typographic grid has been in use since the second half of the 20th century. For a few years now, efforts have been made to bring grid-based design to the Web, with a number of frameworks using floats, padding, and margins to emulate the possibilities of print, although these efforts have always felt like somewhat of a fragile hack.

Recently, however, browsers have begun to implement a native CSS grid layout system, as detailed in the Grid Layout Module (*http://www.w3.org/TR/css-grid-1/*). This module provides a series of properties designed specifically to create grids on screen, meaning the developer no longer has to hack them together from existing properties and behaviors.

The full range of properties in the Grid Layout Module is quite extensive, so I'll focus on the most immediately useful aspects and not get too bogged down in detail that could be potentially confusing. When appropriate, I'll flag spots where I've omitted some detail.

Grid Terminology

Before introducing the new CSS grid syntax, I'll explain some of the terminology used in the Grid Layout Module. Even if you think you're familiar with typographic grids, take time to read through these definitions as the terminology used in CSS grids is quite distinct.

The following are the key terms used in the Grid Layout Module:

Grid container   The container element that acts as the boundary and sets the dimensions of the grid.

Grid lines   The dividing lines between rows and columns. These lines are notional, not actual.

Grid tracks   A shorthand name for both rows and columns. Each column or row created in the grid is referred to as a *track*. Tracks are the spaces between lines.

Grid cells   Each intersection of a column and a row creates a *cell*. These are like cells in a table.

Grid areas   A cell or multiple cells that mark the space in which a *grid item* will be placed.

Grid items   Each child element placed in the grid.

A grid is created by first setting a number of lines on the grid container to create a series of tracks. Grid items are then positioned on the tracks using lines as coordinates to create areas, as shown in Figure 17-1.

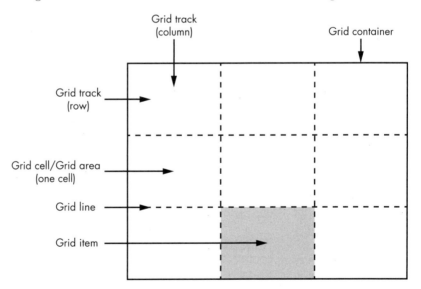

Figure 17-1: A simple 3×3 grid showing the core terms used in the CSS Grid Layout syntax

The grid lines are the lines between cells. They define a series of rows and columns, which are numbered for coordinate placement. (I'll explain this concept in stages as I proceed through this chapter.)

Declaring and Defining the Grid

The first step in creating a grid is to declare the *grid container,* the element used as the grid's foundation. The dimensions of the grid container are the limits of the grid, and all of the grid's properties are applied to it. To declare the grid container, use the display property with the new value grid like this:

```
E { display: grid; }
```

This declaration creates a block-level grid container. The next step is to define its tracks (rows and columns). You can define tracks on an *explicit grid,* with a precise number of columns and rows, or on an *implicit grid,* which is created relative to its content. You can also combine both explicit and implicit grids, and I'll explain each in turn.

Creating Explicit Grids by Setting Track Size

In an explicit grid, you can define a specific number of grid tracks by setting their size using a pair of properties: grid-template-columns and grid-template-rows. The value for each property is a space-separated list of lengths, which sets the width of the column or the height of the row. For example, the following code snippet creates a three-column grid, where the first and last columns are set to 20 percent of the width of the grid container and the second to 60 percent of the width:

```
E { grid-template-columns: 20% 60% 20%; }
```

You can use percentages or any unit of length, including the specialized grid unit of length called a *fraction (fr).* One fr is equivalent to one equal share of any unassigned length in a grid. I'll explain what I mean. Take a look at this code, where the grid container has a width value of 600px, and three columns each have a defined width:

```
E {
    display: grid;
    grid-template-columns: 100px 100px 200px;
    width: 600px;
}
```

The total width of the columns is 400px, which is 200px less than the width of the container. In this case, adding an extra column of 1fr width makes that column as wide as all of the remaining space, or 200px:

```
E { grid-template-columns: 100px 100px 200px 1fr; }
```

Adding another column of the same width makes both columns 100px in width:

```
E { grid-template-columns: 100px 100px 200px 1fr 1fr; }
```

And making one of those columns 3fr in width means the remaining width is divided into four equal portions of 50px each, making 1fr equal to 50px and 3fr equal 150px:

```
E { grid-template-columns: 100px 100px 200px 1fr 3fr; }
```

Returning to the first example in this section, you could replace the percentages with the fr unit to achieve the same result:

```
E { grid-template-columns: 1fr 3fr 1fr; }
```

NOTE *See "Fractions vs. Percentages" on page 213 for an explanation of the advantages of using fractions for laying out grids.*

This code actually defines three grid lines, with an additional one automatically created at the start of the writing direction (which is left, in languages written from left to right). These lines create three vertical grid tracks, or columns, as shown in Figure 17-2.

Figure 17-2: A simple three-column grid in the ratio 1:3:1 (grid lines and numbers added for clarity)

You add rows in the same way. For example, to create three rows with the first one 60px high, the second with the value of auto so it's as high as its content, and the third 5em high, you could use this code:

```
E { grid-template-rows: 60px auto 5em; }
```

Combining these properties lets you fully define your grid. For example, this code creates a basic grid of three columns and three rows, for a total of nine cells:

```
E {
  display: grid;
  grid-template-columns: 1fr 3fr 1fr;
  grid-template-rows: 60px auto 5em;
}
```

The columns of this grid are distributed in the ratio 1:3:1, and the rows are 60px at the top, 5em at the bottom, with a central row set to automatic height to accommodate its content. The resulting grid looks something like Figure 17-3.

Figure 17-3: A 3×3 explicit grid (lines and numbers added for clarity)

FRACTIONS VS. PERCENTAGES

When used on their own, percentages and fractions are interchangeable. For example, in this code, the two rules have the same result:

```
E { width: 50% 50%; }
F { width: 1fr 1fr; }
```

Where they differ is when they are mixed with length units such as px or em. Say you have a grid with one 15em column and you want to fill the remaining space with two equally sized columns. With percentages, you can't really do this, unless you know the width of the container and are happy to perform some complex calculations. You might think you could use calc() (see Chapter 16) to do this:

```
E { grid-template-columns: 15em calc(50% - 7.5em) calc(50% - 7.5em); }
```

But the spec isn't clear if calc() is permitted, and no current grid implementations (at the time of writing) allow you to do this.

In these cases, fractions prove more useful than percentages. When you recall that a grid fraction, or fr, sets aside an equal share of any space yet to be distributed, the fraction-based code you would use for this example becomes clear:

```
E { grid-template-columns: 15em 1fr 1fr; }
```

Here, any undistributed width in the grid will be divided into two equally sized columns.

Although, at times, you may be able to use percentages easily in your grids, fractions keep things simple.

Placing Items in an Explicit Grid

Every immediate child of a grid container becomes a grid item and should be placed in the grid. To do so, you assign the item a cell coordinate using a set of placement properties. The first of these are grid-column-start and grid-row-start, and each takes a single whole number as a value. This number refers to the line at the start of a grid track (whether a column or a row), and the combined track references create the coordinate of a cell.

For example, to place an item in the cell in the second row of the second column, you use this code (Figure 17-4 shows the result):

```
F {
  grid-column-start: 2;
  grid-row-start: 2;
}
```

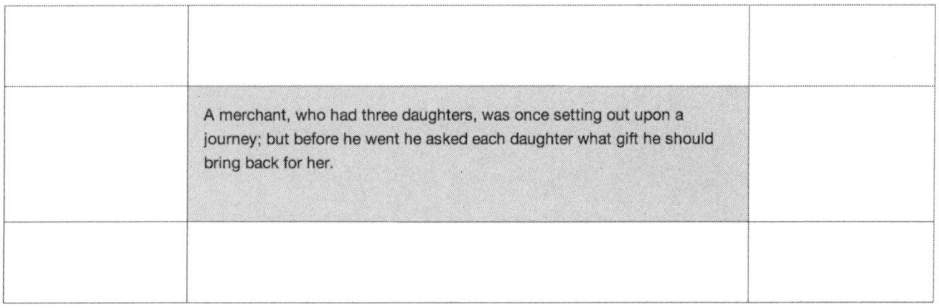

	A merchant, who had three daughters, was once setting out upon a journey; but before he went he asked each daughter what gift he should bring back for her.	

Figure 17-4: An item placed on the grid in the second row of the second column (lines added for clarity)

The default value of both the grid-column-start and grid-row-start properties is 1, so omitting either value places the item in the first row or column. For example, the following code places the item in the cell in the second column of the first row, as shown in Figure 17-5:

```
G { grid-column-start: 2; }
```

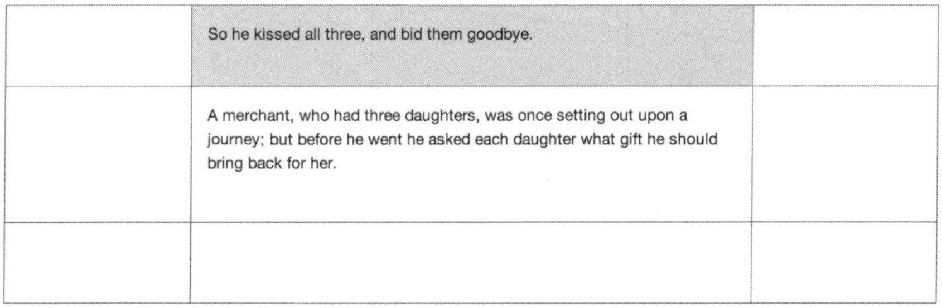

	So he kissed all three, and bid them goodbye.	
	A merchant, who had three daughters, was once setting out upon a journey; but before he went he asked each daughter what gift he should bring back for her.	

Figure 17-5: A second item placed on the grid in the second column, first row (lines added for clarity)

By default, the item is fitted into the designated cell only, with any content that doesn't fit overflowing the cell vertically. You can make an item expand in size to create an area that covers multiple cells in rows or columns by using the grid-column-end and grid-row-end properties. Just like their counterparts, these properties take a single whole number value, which designates the line that the cell should end in. For example, to have an item span three rows, starting at line 1 and ending at 4, here's the code you use:

```
F {
    grid-row-start: 1;
    grid-row-end: 4;
}
```

The item is placed in the first column by default; it starts at line 1 and ends at line 4, meaning it spans three rows, as shown in Figure 17-6.

A merchant, who had three daughters, was once setting out upon a journey; but before he went he asked each daughter what gift he should bring back for her.

Figure 17-6: An item on the grid spanning three rows of the first column (lines added for clarity)

As an alternative to the method just shown, you can, instead, use the span keyword, followed by the number of tracks the item spans. The rewritten rule looks like this:

```
F { grid-row-end: span 3; }
```

The span keyword becomes quite useful when you want to remain agnostic about the line at which a grid item will start, but you always want it to span the same number of columns.

Grid Placement Shorthand Properties

Writing four individual properties to place an element in a grid seems somewhat verbose, and, indeed, shorthand properties will make your code more terse. The properties in question are grid-column and grid-row, and each has the same syntax. The first, grid-column, is short for grid-column-start and grid-column-end, divided by a slash; and the same goes for grid-row being short for grid-row-start and grid-row-end.

I'll illustrate how to use them. Take a look at all of the individual properties applied to the same element:

```
F {
    grid-column-start: 2;
    grid-column-end: 3;
    grid-row-start: 1;
    grid-row-end: span 3;
}
```

Using the shorthand properties, you can write these in a much more manageable way:

```
F {
    grid-column: 2 / 3;
    grid-row: 1 / span 3;
}
```

If even two properties are too much for you, you can actually combine all of these instructions in a single shorthand rule, grid-area, which covers all four properties. Here's the basic syntax:

```
F { grid-area: row-start / column-start / row-end / column-end; }
```

Inserting the appropriate values gives us this very terse—although, arguably, harder to read—rule:

```
F { grid-area: 1 / 2 / span 3 / 3; }
```

Repeating Grid Lines

Although simple grids are fine for some real-world situations, more complex grids give you finer control over content. Having upward of 12 columns in large typographic grids is quite common, and each column usually has a *gutter* (empty space) between it and its neighbor. Defining a grid of 12 columns could be repetitive using the Grid Layout syntax, as you can see in this example code where I've mapped out 12 columns of 1fr each, with a gutter of 10px between them:

```
E { grid-template-columns: 1fr 10px 1fr 10px 1fr 10px 1fr 10px 1fr 10px 1fr 10px 1fr 10px 1fr 10px 1fr 10px 1fr 10px 1fr; }
```

You can use the repeat() function to avoid this type of repetition when using larger grids. This function takes two arguments: an integer that sets the number of repetitions, followed by a comma separator, and the grid line values to be repeated. For example, the following rule creates the same grid as in the previous example, but much more concisely; it defines one track that is 1fr wide and then uses repeat() to create a pattern of a 10px gutter followed by a 1fr column eleven times, for a total of 12 columns of 1fr each.

```
E { grid-template-columns: 1fr repeat(11, 10px 1fr); }
```

Named Grid Areas

In addition to placing items in a grid based on coordinates, you can also place items in *named areas* with the grid-template-areas property. With this property, you can give grid areas specific names using a series of unique identifiers in strings of text. Here, I'll show you what I mean:

```
E {
❶    display: grid;
❷    grid-template-areas: 'a b c';
❸    grid-template-columns: repeat(3, 1fr);
}
```

Two of these rules should be familiar now: line ❶ sets the element to act as a grid container, and line ❸ creates three columns of 1fr each. Line ❷ uses the grid-template-areas property to name each of the columns: each identifier in the space-separated string (*a*, *b*, and *c*) is matched to the columns, in turn. This output is shown in Figure 17-7.

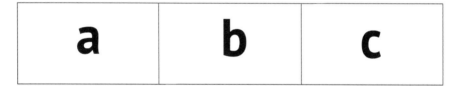

Figure 17-7: Three columns made with named areas

To place an item using a named area, you use the area's identifier as a value for the grid-area property. For example, to place an item in the middle (*b*) column of my example grid, I use this:

```
F { grid-area: b; }
```

You don't have to use single characters to name areas, as I've done here; you can use any string of characters, as long as they don't contain a space. For example, to make your content more human-readable, you may want to describe the purpose of each area. Here's an example:

```
E { grid-template-areas: 'nav main side'; }
F { grid-area: main; }
```

Each string of identifiers represents a grid row, so to add a new row, you just add a new string. If you use the same identifier multiple times in the same string, the area will span that number of columns. If you use the same identifier in the same position in different rows, the area will span that number of rows. You can see what I mean in the following code; in the first row, one column is called *nav* and two are called *head*, so the *head* area will span two columns; the second row also has a first column called *nav*, so the *nav* area will span two rows:

```
E {
    display: grid;
    grid-template-areas:
        'nav head head'
        'nav main side';
    grid-template-columns: repeat(3, 1fr);
    grid-template-rows: 80px auto;
}
```

Using this code, you can place grid items into areas that span multiple tracks. In the following snippet, element *F* is placed into the *head* area, meaning it spans the second and third columns of the first row, and element *G* will be placed into the *nav* area, making it span the first and second row in the first column. This is shown in Figure 17-8.

```
F { grid-area: head; }
G { grid-area: nav; }
```

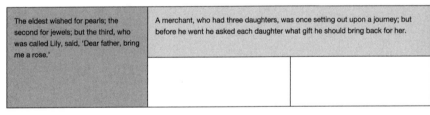

Figure 17-8: Items placed on the grid in named areas (lines added for clarity)

If you use multiple string identifiers, you must use the same number of columns in each grid; otherwise, the rule will be declared invalid and be ignored.

The grid-template Shorthand

To avoid having to write three separate rules to define a grid (grid-template-columns, grid-template-rows, and grid-template-areas), you can use the grid-template shorthand. This shorthand makes defining your columns and rows, without named areas, simple. Here's an example:

```
E { grid-template: grid-template-columns / grid-template-rows; }
```

To use the property with named grid areas, you add the identifiers after the slash, as in this example:

```
E { grid-template: repeat(3, 1fr) / 'nav head head'; }
```

And if you also want to define heights for the rows, you can add the length value of the row after each identifier string. Let's look back at the full grid defined in the previous section:

```
E {
    grid-template-areas:
      'nav head head'
      'nav main side';
    grid-template-columns: repeat(3, 1fr);
    grid-template-rows: 80px auto;
}
```

Here's how that grid looks if written using the grid-template shorthand:

```
E {
grid-template: repeat(3, 1fr) / 'nav head head' 80px 'nav main side';
}
```

NOTE *I don't declare the row height after the second named area string because it defaults to auto.*

Implicit Grids

Implicit grids are defined by their contents, rather than the specified length values of explicit grids. When you don't care how many rows or columns there are in your grid, only that each item in the grid has a place, you can use the grid-auto-columns and grid-auto-rows properties. Each property takes a single value to specify the width of the row or column. For example, this code says that any created columns should be 1fr wide, and that any new rows should be 80px:

```
E {
    display: grid;
    grid-auto-columns: 1fr;
    grid-auto-rows: 80px;
}
```

Now any item with a grid-column or grid-row value will be placed in the grid, and the grid will automatically adjust its size to accommodate the items, keeping all columns and rows at the set size. For example, the following code shows a grid item set to start in the second column of the first row, and to span two rows and two columns. The grid will expand to fit this item, as you can see in Figure 17-9.

```
F {
    grid-column: 2 / 4;
    grid-row: 1 / span 2;
}
```

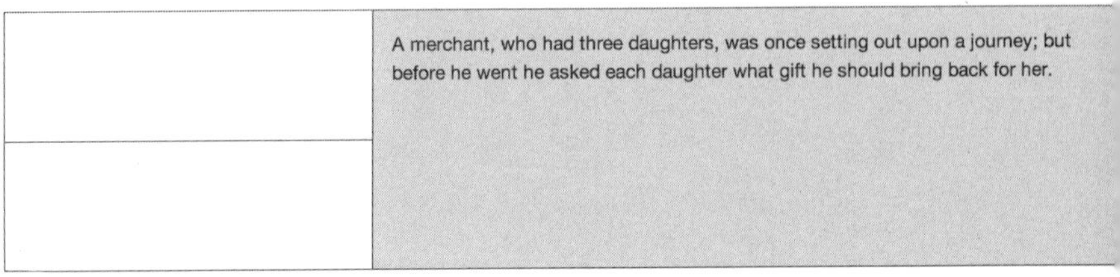

A merchant, who had three daughters, was once setting out upon a journey; but before he went he asked each daughter what gift he should bring back for her.

Figure 17-9: An implicit grid created by the item it contains (lines added for clarity)

Grid Items Without a Declared Place

What happens to children of the grid container that have no declared place in the grid because they don't have either `grid-column` or `grid-row` values? They fall back to the default values of 1 and are stacked into the same cell at row one, column one.

You can alter this default behavior with the `grid-auto-flow` property, which ensures that any items without an assigned place are inserted into the grid where space is available. You can also add a level of control over where they're placed. Here is the basic form of this rule:

```
E { grid-auto-flow: keyword; }
```

The keyword can be `column` or `row`. If you use `column`, items will fill empty cells in columns, moving down the column; if you use use `row`, the items will fill empty rows, moving across the row. For example, in Figure 17-10, the container on the left has a `grid-auto-flow` value of `column`, so the items that haven't been placed fill the cells of each row down the current column and then skip up to the next column when the first column is filled. On the other hand, the container on the right has the value of `row`, so the items are placed across the row until the row is filled, at which point the items move to the second row.

A merchant, who had three daughters, was setting out on a journey.
But the third, who was called Lily, said, "Dear father, bring me a rose."
The eldest wished for pearls; the second for jewels.
A merchant, who had three daughters, was setting out on a journey.
The eldest wished for pearls; the second for jewels.
But the third, who was called Lily, said, "Dear father, bring me a rose."

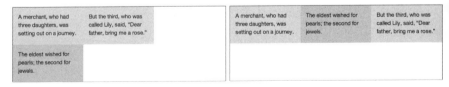

Figure 17-10: Comparing automatic flow: (left) items flowed into columns and (right) items flowed into rows

Combining Explicit and Implicit Grids

When you create explicit grids, you may find that the number of available grid tracks is fewer than you need for your items. Say you have a three-column grid, but a grid item is supposed to span four columns:

```
E { grid-template-columns: repeat(3, 1fr); }
F { grid-column: 1 / 5; }
```

In this case, the grid will expand to contain the tracks created by the item; an extra column will be added to the grid, making four in total. You can set the size of these extra tracks with the grid-auto-columns and grid-auto-rows properties.

The following code creates an explicit grid of three columns and two rows and allows for any items exceeding this explicit grid by adding an implicit grid. The extra columns in the implicit grid are defined as 1fr wide, with extra rows being 80px high:

```
E {
    grid-template-columns: repeat(3, 1fr);
    grid-template-rows: repeat(2, 80px);
    grid-auto-columns: 1fr;
    grid-auto-rows: 80px;
}
```

Now any items placed in this grid will fill an area that matches the dimensions of the explicit grid.

The grid Shorthand

Defining a grid with both explicit and implicit properties can lead to a large list of rules. For example, the following code shows an element with rules to create an explicit grid with named areas, as well as implicit grid properties to allow for any items that might extend the grid, giving you a total of six rules:

```
E {
    grid-template-areas: 'a b b' 'a c d';
    grid-template-columns: repeat(3, 1fr);
    grid-template-rows: 80px auto;
    grid-auto-flow: row;
    grid-auto-columns: 1fr;
    grid-auto-rows: 80px;
}
```

Fortunately, a shorthand property is available for this list of rules. The shorthand is called grid—however, you can only use it to set either explicit or implicit grids, not both. To use it to set implicit grids, use this syntax:

```
E { grid: grid-auto-flow grid-auto-columns / grid-auto-rows; }
```

So here is the shorthand for the implicit grid rules shown in the previous code:

```
E { grid: row 1fr / 80px; }
```

The grid syntax for setting explicit grids is exactly the same as for the grid-template property you saw earlier in this chapter. That being the case, here is the shorthand for the explicit grid rules shown at the start of this section:

```
E { grid: repeat(3, 1fr) / 'a b b' 80px 'a c d'; }
```

You might find it strange that two shorthand properties do exactly the same thing. I can only agree with you.

Grid Item Stacking Order

When placing items on a grid, areas will sometimes overlap. To handle such an eventuality, you can create a stacking order to define the way that items are stacked in the grid. For example, you could say that items that start in the third row should be stacked on top of items that start in the first row, regardless of their order in the DOM.

You can change the stacking order with the z-index property. The items with the highest z-index value will be stacked above all others. For example, the following markup shows two div elements that will become grid items:

```
<div class="grid-item item-one">...</div>
<div class="grid-item item-two">...</div>
```

I'll place both items in the grid, but by adding the following code I ensure that item-one will be stacked on top of item-two by making its starting column and row greater than those of item-two:

```
.item-one {
    grid-column: 2 / 4;
    grid-row: 2;
}
.item-two {
    grid-column: 1 / 3;
    grid-row: 1 / 3;
}
```

You can see the result in the example on the left of Figure 17-11: *item-one* is stacked above *item-two*. But if you increase the z-index of *item-two* like so:

```
.item-two { z-index: 2; }
```

you'll see that *item-two* is now stacked above *item-one*, as shown on the right of Figure 17-11.

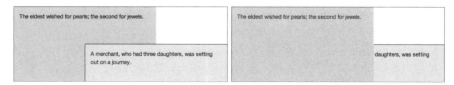

Figure 17-11: Comparing stacking order: (left) stacking follows placement, (right) stacking set by z-index

An alternative approach uses the order property, introduced as part of the Flexbox Module (see Chapter 15). In explicit grids, this property acts exactly like z-index, changing the stacking order; in implicit grids, however, it also changes the order in which items are placed in the grid.

You can see this in action in Figure 17-12, where I've flowed three grid items (*item-one*, *item-two*, and *item-three*) into a grid with a grid-auto-flow value of column. In the left grid, the items are flowed into the grid in the order in which they appear in the DOM, but in the right grid, the order of two of the items is changed, as shown in Figure 17-12.

```
.item-one { order: 2; }
.item-two { order: 3; }
```

Figure 17-12: Stacking with the order property in implicit grids: (left) in DOM order and (right) order set with the order property

Internet Explorer's Grid Layout Syntax

Internet Explorer 10 was the first browser to implement the Grid Layout properties, although with a syntax that has since become outdated. So you can replicate certain grid layouts in IE10 and IE11 if you use caution, but with very strict limits—the most notable being that you can only create explicit grids.

All of the IE grid properties use the -ms- prefix, as does the value of the display property:

```
E { display: -ms-grid; }
```

You create tracks with the -ms-grid-columns and -ms-grid-rows properties, which are analogous to grid-template-columns and grid-template-rows. The difference is in the way you repeat track lines: When designing for IE, you put the width values in parentheses, followed by the number of repetitions in square brackets:

```
E {
    -ms-grid-columns: (1fr)[3];
    -ms-grid-rows: (80px)[2];
}
```

Grid items are placed with the -ms-grid-column and -ms-grid-row properties, which function like grid-column and grid-row, but only allow a single numeric value. To span items across multiple cells, you must use -ms-grid-column-span and -ms-grid-row-span to set the number of tracks an item should span (like the span keyword.)

That being the case, the rules applied to elements E and F in this code block are identical in function:

```
E {
    -ms-grid-column: 1;
    -ms-grid-column-span: 2;
    -ms-grid-row: 2;
    -ms-grid-row-span: 3;
}
F {
    grid-column: 1 / span 2;
    grid-row: 2 / span 3;
}
```

As of this writing, the IE syntax has no named areas, nor does it have anything equivalent to grid-column-end or grid-row-end.

Summary

Grids are the first step toward a whole new way of laying out content on the Web. The combination of Grid Layout, Flexbox positioning, and Media Queries makes possible rich layouts that you can adapt to many different devices and viewports, ushering in a whole new world of web design, free from the constraints of float hacks and restrictive markup.

Grid Layout: Browser Support

	Chrome	Firefox	Safari	IE
Grid layout	No*	No	No	IE10†

* Implemented but off by default
† Syntax different from the spec; with vendor prefix

18

BLEND MODES, FILTER EFFECTS, AND MASKING

The majority of today's browsers—desktop and mobile—support the *Scalable Vector Graphics (SVG)* format. SVG differs from image formats such as GIF, JPEG, and PNG (known as bitmap images), as SVG is made up of a markup language (similar to HTML) that describes points, or vectors, rather than the grids of pixels that make up bitmap images. One advantage that SVG has over bitmap images is that, as a vector format, it scales well to fit screens of any resolution. In addition to this, the SVG format offers a built-in array of rich graphical effects previously available only in image-editing software such as Photoshop, GIMP, and Sketch.

Until recently, however, using those graphical effects in browsers wasn't practical; live image effects are computationally intensive, and using them on the Web would have negatively affected performance. Today, however, browsers have become much faster and more capable, with almost all rendering graphics directly on the device's GPU. This advance allows for the hardware-accelerated display of transformations and animations and unlocks the potential to use the rich graphical effects of SVG.

As browsers implemented SVG graphics effects, it became somewhat of a no-brainer to also give other web technologies access to them. So, in this chapter, you'll learn about three features that make SVG's graphical potential available to CSS: *blend modes, filter effects*, and *masking*. These non-destructive effects only alter the way images are displayed on the page; they don't modify the source images.

NOTE *Many SVG effects involve variations of color, which are very difficult to portray in black and white. I strongly encourage you to see examples of the effects yourself at http://thebookofcss3.com/.*

Blend Modes

If you've used professional-grade image-editing software like Photoshop or GIMP, you may already be familiar with blend modes. Blend modes are a way to mix an image into a solid color or another image so the two appear merged or blended.

Various blend modes are available, each of which blends images in different ways, according to various algorithms. The available modes in CSS are defined in the Compositing and Blending Module (*http://www.w3.org/TR/compositing-1/*). I can't cover all of the modes in detail due to a lack of space, so I'll concentrate on three:

Screen In this mode, whites remain white, whereas black lets the background color show through. As a result of applying this mode, images tend to become lighter.

Multiply This mode tends to produce darker images. Blacks remain black, whereas whites let the background color pass through.

Overlay The Overlay mode strikes a balance between the Screen and Multiply modes. Highlights and shadows are preserved, increasing contrast.

The remaining blend modes are generally variations on these three. You can read a full explanation of each in the spec or see a good visual introduction on *http://dev.opera.com/articles/getting-to-know-css-blend-modes/*.

background-blend-mode

The background-blend-mode property is used to blend the background layers of an element; for example, you might use it to blend the background color with the background image. This property works solely in the context of the element: Only the background layers are blended; the element itself doesn't blend with any part of the page below it. The property requires as a value the keyword of the blend mode you want to use, such as screen, multiply, or overlay. For example, here's how to apply the Multiply blend mode:

```
E { background-blend-mode: multiply; }
```

The default value of `background-blend-mode` is `normal`, which leaves the background layer unblended.

Blending an Image and a Color

The simplest way to show how background blend modes work is to blend a background image with a background color. The following listing has an element with a background image and color applied and is set to use the Screen blend mode:

```
E {
    background: url('foo.png') #f00;
    background-blend-mode: screen;
}
```

Figure 18-1 shows the result of this and other blend modes. Image (A) at top left has no blend mode applied and is provided as a reference. The other images each have a different blend mode keyword applied, namely screen (B), multiply (C), and overlay (D). (Note that in this case the Overlay mode just puts a solid color over the image, which is far from ideal; Overlay blend modes are much more useful when blending two images.)

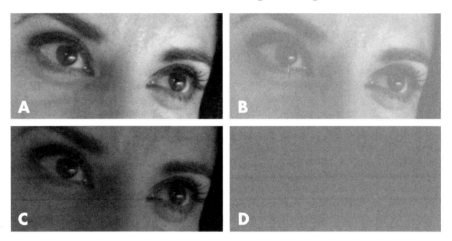

Figure 18-1: Comparing different blend modes applied to a source image

Blending Two Images

In addition to blending a background image layer with a color layer, you can also blend a background image layer with other background image layers. To do so, apply multiple background images (as discussed in Chapter 8) and then set the blend mode as before:

```
E {
    background-color: transparent;
    background-image: url('foo.png'), url('bar.png');
    background-blend-mode: multiply;
}
```

Figure 18-2 shows examples of blending two images. Each image has different blend mode keywords applied. From left to right, these are screen, multiply, and overlay. (If you're looking at the example files using a desktop browser, hover your mouse over the elements to show the two different background images that I've used.)

Figure 18-2: Blending multiple background image layers

Notice that I've set a transparent background color on the element. If I hadn't, the multiply keyword would have made the lower background image layer blend with the background color and then blend with the other image layer, creating a different effect than what I intended.

Multiple Blend Modes

Since you can add multiple background images to an element, it follows that you can apply a blend mode to each layer. To do so, you need only list the required blend modes in a comma-separated list of values.

In the following code, the element has three background layers: two images and a color. I've applied two blend mode keywords: Multiply mode will be used to blend the background color with *foo.png*; the result will be blended with *bar.png* using the Screen blend mode.

```
E {
    background-color: #f00;
    background-image: url('foo.png'), url('bar.png');
    background-blend-mode: multiply, screen;
}
```

NOTE *As with the other multiple background properties, having fewer values on the background-blend-mode property than there are background layers will make the value list loop.*

Varying the blend modes can produce dramatically different results. For example, Figure 18-3 shows a number of combinations applied to different elements with identical background layers. The element on the left uses the Screen mode on the top image layer and Multiply mode on the lower; the element in the middle uses Multiply mode on the upper image layer and Overlay on the lower; and on the right, Overlay mode is applied on the upper and Screen on the lower. As you can see, the results are quite different.

Figure 18-3: Applying multiple blend modes in different combinations

mix-blend-mode

Although blending background layers is undoubtedly useful, the real power lies in blending one element with another. In CSS3, you do this with the mix-blend-mode property. When applied to an element, this property blends the content of the element with the content and background of any elements that are directly behind it on the screen.

To understand how this differs from background-blend-mode, let's see a quick example. In the following listing, I apply a background image to element *E* and the Multiply blend mode to element *F*, nested inside *E*:

```
E { background-image: url('foo.png'); }
F { mix-blend-mode: multiply; }
```

Figure 18-4 shows the result, along with other blend modes for comparison. The element at top left (A) has no blend mode applied and is used as a reference; the remaining three each have blend mode keywords applied: screen (B), multiply (C), and overlay (D).

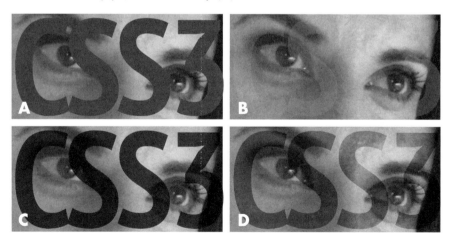

Figure 18-4: Different blend modes applied to the text element, mixed with the background of its parent

isolation

When using `mix-blend-mode`, be aware that it will blend with *every* visual element drawn behind it on the screen, which can cause unintended consequences. For example, say you have the following markup structure, in which an `img` element is nested inside a `div`, inside the body:

```
<body>
    <div>
        <img src="foo.jpg">
    </div>
</body>
```

Now you set a background image on the body and the `mix-blend-mode` property on the `img`:

```
body { background-image: url('bunny.png'); }
img { mix-blend-mode: screen; }
```

In this case, the `img` will blend with the body because the `div` is transparent, as shown in the example on the left of Figure 18-5.

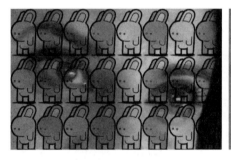

Figure 18-5: Isolating an element to set a new stacking context

If the result isn't exactly what you want, you can make an element create a new stacking context,[1] similar to the way setting `position: relative` on an element resets the coordinates for absolute positioning. When blending, this process is called *isolating* the element, and you use the isolation property:

```
E { isolation: isolation-mode; }
```

The default value is `auto`, but to create the new stacking context, you must use the alternate value, `isolate`:

```
div { isolation: isolate; }
```

---

1. If you need a refresher on stacking contexts, go to *https://developer.mozilla.org/docs/Web/Guide/CSS/Understanding_z_index/The_stacking_context/*.

You can see the difference in the example on the right of Figure 18-5. The div is isolated and a new stacking context created, so the img is blended only with the transparent parent. As a result, you don't see the background image of the body as in the example on the left.

Filter Effects

Like blend modes, filters are a common part of professional image-editing software. Filters are used to change an element's appearance before it reaches the page, and unlike blend modes, they don't rely on the interaction of two components. CSS filters are defined in the CSS Filter Effects Module (*http://www.w3.org/TR/filter-effects-1/*) and are applied using the filter property, shown here:

```
E { filter: function; }
```

The *function* value is at least one of a range of nine filter effect functions. Each accepts a single argument, except when a series of arguments is required (in a space-separated list). I discuss each one here.

blur()

Applies a blur effect to an element. The argument for the blur() function is a unit of length that controls the radius of the blur. The effect is called *Gaussian blur*—a kind of image smoothing that reduces noise in the image. The higher the radius value, the greater the blur effect. For example, to create a blur of radius 10px, you use this code:

```
E { filter: blur(10px); }
```

You can see the blur effect in action in Figure 18-6. The unfiltered image is on the left; the blur() filter has been applied to the image on the right.

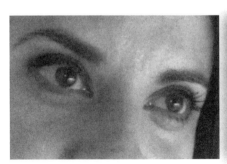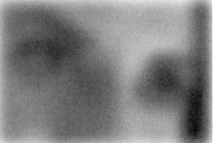

Figure 18-6: Applying a Gaussian blur filter

brightness() and contrast()

The brightness() function changes the brightness of an element, whereas the contrast() function increases or decreases the contrast between the dark and light of an element. Both functions take a percentage as an argument. Here's an example:

```
E { filter: brightness(50%); }
E { filter: contrast(50%); }
```

In both cases, an argument of 100% leaves the element unchanged. An argument of 0% for brightness() makes the element fully black, and 0% for contrast() makes the element fully gray. You can use values in excess of 100% to increase the brightness and contrast as necessary.

NOTE *You can also use a number for this function, with 1 being equivalent to 100%, 1.5 to 150%, and so on. The same applies to all other functions that accept percentage values.*

Figure 18-7 shows examples of both functions. The first image has no filter applied and is shown as a reference. The middle image has the brightness() function applied, and the image on the right has contrast()— each function has an argument of 50%.

Figure 18-7: Adjusting brightness and contrast with CSS filter effects

grayscale(), sepia(), and saturate()

The next three functions all deal with color. The grayscale() function gives you a way to replace colors with shades of gray so you can convert images to black and white. The sepia() toning function is similar to grayscale(), except it uses a gold tint to produce a vintage photo effect. Finally, the saturate() function controls the color intensity.

Each of the functions accepts a percentage value as an argument:

```
E { filter: grayscale(100%); }
E { filter: sepia(100%); }
E { filter: saturate(200%); }
```

A value of 100% for the grayscale() function makes an image completely black and white. Passing 100% to the sepia() function makes an image fully sepia toned. In the case of both functions, a value of 0% leaves the image unchanged, whereas values greater than 100% are treated as 100%.

The `saturate()` function also accepts a percentage as an argument, but it works differently from `grayscale()` and `sepia()`. A value of 0% makes an image appear fully unsaturated—or grayscale—whereas values greater than 100% oversaturate the image.

NOTE   *To see these functions in action, view example file 18-a on this book's companion website* (http://thebookofcss3.com/).

hue-rotate()

The prosaically named `hue-rotate()` function is used to rotate the hue of an element. Recall from "Hue, Saturation, Lightness" on page 116 that color hue is calculated from an angle around the axis of the color wheel. Therefore, the required argument to the `hue-rotate()` function is a degree, like this:

```
E { filter: hue-rotate(45deg); }
```

Applying `hue-rotate()` actually shifts the hue of all colors in an element around the color wheel by the same amount. To see this function in action, view example file 18-b on this book's website.

opacity()

The `opacity()` function works the same as the `opacity` property introduced in Chapter 10. The function accepts a percentage value as an argument, with 0% equal to fully transparent and 100% equal to fully opaque:

```
E { filter: opacity(25%); }
```

Values greater than 100% are treated as 100%.

If the result of the `opacity()` function is identical to that of the `opacity` property, why bother using it at all? Because you can combine it with the other filter effect functions, as you'll see shortly in "Multiple Filter Effect Functions" on page 234.

drop-shadow()

At first, the `drop-shadow()` function may seem to be the same as the `box-shadow` property, introduced in Chapter 9. Indeed, it even takes the same values as arguments: an x-offset, y-offset, blur radius, and shadow color. Here's an example:

```
E { filter: drop-shadow(5px 5px 3px gray); }
```

The biggest difference between the two is that the `drop-shadow()` function is aware of any alpha value (opacity) in the target element. You can see the difference clearly in Figure 18-8. The target image has a transparent background, so in the image at left (which has the `drop-shadow()` function applied), the drop box follows the outline of the image. The image on the right, however, has the box-shadow property applied. Because the box-shadow property doesn't care about alpha transparency, the shadow follows only the outline of the box.

Figure 18-8: Comparing the drop-shadow() filter (left) with the box-shadow property (right)

Multiple Filter Effect Functions

You can apply multiple filter effect functions to an element by simply listing them in a space-separated list. For example, you could add both blur and a drop shadow to an element:

```
E { filter: blur(5px) drop-shadow(5px 5px 3px gray); }
```

The order in which you list the functions is important, as that's the order in which they'll be applied. For example, in this next listing two filter effects are applied, but I've changed the order: in the first, the gray-scale() function is applied before sepia(), and in the second, I've reversed it:

```
E { filter: sepia(100%) gray-scale(100%); }
E { filter: gray-scale(100%) sepia(100%); }
```

In the first example, the sepia() function will be applied and then grayscale(), so all the colors of the sepia() filter effect will be converted to grayscale. In the second, the grayscale() function will be applied and then sepia(), so the colors of the sepia() filter effect will show. Example file 18-c on this book's website shows how this appears.

Like CSS Transforms (introduced in Chapter 12), when you list multiple functions in the filter property, any functions not in the list will have their values returned to the default. For example, in the following listing, the element loses its sepia() filter effect on hover:

```
E { filter: sepia(100%) blur(2px); }
E:hover { filter: blur(5px); }
```

Filters in SVG

Recall that CSS filter effects are simply shorthand for SVG filter presets. The Filter Effects Module shows the markup equivalents for all of the CSS functions. For example, the SVG markup for the blur() filter looks like the following (the *blur-radius* value is a unitless number):

```
<filter>
    <feGaussianBlur stdDeviation="blur-radius" />
</filter>
```

You can create your own filters in SVG and apply them in CSS by using an ID reference. The first step is to add an ID value to your filter:

```
<filter id="blur">...</filter>
```

Then refer to it in your CSS using the url() notation, containing the ID reference, as a value for the filter property. If your SVG is in line with the markup in your document, you need only the ID reference:

```
E { filter: url('#blur'); }
```

If your SVG is in an external asset file (say, *filters.svg*), state the path to that file followed by the ID reference:

```
E { filter: url('filters.svg#blur'); }
```

Unlike CSS filter effects, this technique only works for a single filter. To apply multiple filters to an element, you have to combine them in the SVG markup first.

Masking

Masking is a technique in which certain parts of an element are hidden from view. There are two approaches to masking: clipping, where the area that's hidden is set by a polygonal shape that's overlaid on an element, and image masking, where an image's alpha channel is used to set the hidden area.

Clipping

Clipping is the simplest form of masking. When clipping, a shape is laid over an image and any parts of the element that are behind the shape will be shown, while any parts outside the boundaries of the shape will be hidden. The boundary of the shape is called the *clip path* and is created with the clip-path property:

```
E { clip-path: shape; }
```

The *shape* can be one of four basic types, each of which is represented by a function: circle(), ellipse(), inset() (for rectangles), and polygon(). Each function takes a number of arguments, which define the clip path. For example, to create a circle, you supply three arguments to the circle() function, using a syntax like that for radial gradients (see Chapter 11):

```
E { clip-path: circle(r at cx cy); }
```

The *r* represents the radius of the circle, and *cx* and *cy* are the coordinates of its center. So to clip an element to a 100px circle positioned at the center of the target, you use these values:

```
E { clip-path: circle(100px at 50% 50%); }
```

The ellipse() function is very similar, requiring only an extra argument to set the radii of the ellipse:

```
E { clip-path: ellipse(rx ry at cx cy); }
```

Here *rx* is used to represent the *x*-axis of the radius, and *ry* the *y*-axis. To create an ellipse with a radius of 50px and 100px, again at the center of the target, you use these values:

```
E { clip-path: ellipse(50px 100px at 50% 50%); }
```

To see how these appear in practice, take a look at Figure 18-9. The example on the left uses the circle() function with the values used earlier, and on the right, ellipse(), also with the values used earlier.

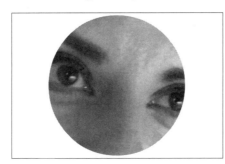 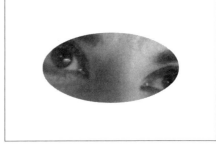

Figure 18-9: Function values for the clip-path property: circle() (left) and ellipse() (right)

As mentioned earlier, the inset() function is used to create a rectangle that is inset from the border of the element to which it is applied. It can accept up to 12 (!) arguments. The first four arguments set the distance that each side of the rectangle is offset—just like the border-image-slice property (see Chapter 9). So a single value will set the offset distance equally on all sides; if two values are supplied, the first will set the top and bottom and the second the left and right; and so on.

If we were to use all four values, the syntax would look like this:

```
E { clip-path: inset(o1 o2 o3 o4); }
```

Each *o** represents an offset value (the top, right, bottom and left, respectively).

In its simplest format, a single value would create four equal offsets, as in this case, where each offset value is 2em:

```
E { clip-path: inset(2em); }
```

You can also round the corners of the clip path, which is where the remaining arguments come in. Following the round keyword, you can use syntax identical to that of the border-radius property (see Chapter 9) to define a radius for each corner—with up to eight values for fine control. To prevent my having to repeat the explanation of the border-radius shorthand here, this example shows how you'd set a radius of 20px on each corner of the inset rectangle defined earlier:

```
E { clip-path: inset(2em round 20px); }
```

See the result in Figure 18-10. The example on the left shows a rectangle with right-angled corners, and on the right, a rectangle with rounded corners.

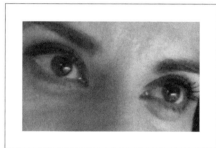

Figure 18-10: The inset() function without (left) and with (right) border radius values

You can use the polygon() function to create more complex clip paths. This function takes an unlimited number of arguments, in pairs, in a comma-separated list. Each pair creates a coordinate value, and the full set of coordinates is used to draw the required clip shape. As a very simple example, this syntax defines the three points of a triangle:

```
E { clip-path: polygon(0% 100%, 100% 0%, 0% 0%); }
```

The triangle's points are at the left top, left bottom, and right top of the target element. You can see how this is clipped in Figure 18-11.

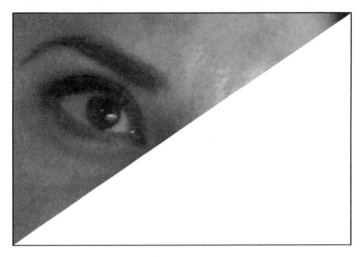

Figure 18-11: A triangular clip path made with the polygon() function

NOTE *Clipping an element only changes its visual appearance—the dimensions and box model of the element that's clipped will be unmodified. For a suggestion of how this may change in the future, see "Shapes" on page 246.*

Implementation of clip-path in Safari

The clip-path property was implemented in Safari 7, with a vendor prefix, but using a now-outdated version of the syntax (the updated syntax was implemented in Safari 8). The polygon() function works in the same way, but the others are slightly different; for example, the circle() function looks slightly different, requiring three comma-separated arguments:

```
E { -webkit-clip-path: circle(cx, cy, r); }
```

Similarly, the ellipse() function accepts four arguments:

```
E { -webkit-clip-path: circle(cx, cy, rx, ry); }
```

The inset() function is known as inset-rectangle(), and it requires a minimum of four comma-separated values to represent the offset distances:

```
E { -webkit-clip-path: inset-rectangle(o1, o2, o3, o4); }
```

You can round the corners, but the values must be the same for each corner—you can't set an individual value per corner. You can, however, set x-axis and y-axis values to make irregular radii:

```
E { -webkit-clip-path: inset-rectangle(o1, o2, o3, o4, rx, ry); }
```

The biggest difference from the standard is in the rectangle() function; this was originally defined in the spec but has since been pushed back to a future version. The rectangle() function also lets you create rectangular clipping shapes but using coordinates rather than offset values. It accepts up to six arguments:

```
E { -webkit-clip-path: rectangle(x, y, w, h, rx, ry); }
```

The first four arguments are required: x and y set the x- and y-coordinates of the top-left corner of the shape, relative to the top-left corner of the target element; and w and h set the width and height, respectively, of the shape. The optional rx and ry arguments can be used to set the border-radius of all corners of the clip path. (You can use one value to make an equal radius, but you can't set each corner individually.)

Figure 18-12 shows how these six values set the clipping area of an image.

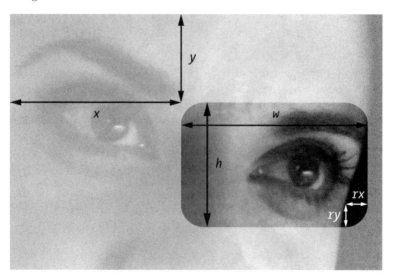

Figure 18-12: Six values for the rectangle() shape function that set the clipping area

If we combine these options as shown in the following listing, we would create a clip path 10px from the top left of the element it's set on, with a width of 50 percent, a height of 100px, and corners with a radius of 20px on both axes. Figure 18-13 shows what this would look like.

```
E { -webkit-clip-path: rectangle(10px, 10px, 50%, 100px, 20px); }
```

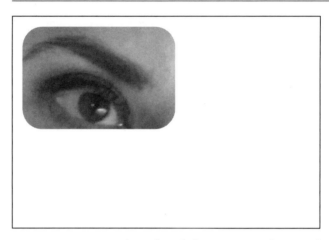

Figure 18-13: A rectangle made with the rectangle() function of -webkit-clip-path

Animating Clip Paths

Because clip paths are defined using coordinates, animating them to create impressive effects is easy. For example, you can take the triangle polygon defined in the previous section and transition it on hover:

```
E {
    clip-path: polygon(0% 0%, 0% 100%, 100% 0%);
    transition: clip-path 1s;
}
E:hover { clip-path: polygon(100% 100%, 0% 100%, 100% 0%); }
```

In this animation, two points of the triangle stay in the same position, while the third switches to the corner diagonally opposite. This is animated with a transition, causing the effect you see in example file 18-d.

Clip Paths in SVG

You can also create clip paths in SVG and apply them to an element using CSS. To do so, you first define your clip path markup and then assign it a unique ID. For example, the following listing creates a circular clip path using the clipPath element at the center of the element, with a radius half the width and height. It has an ID of clipping.

```
<defs>
    <clipPath id="clipping">
        <circle cx="0.5" cy="0.5" r="0.5" />
    </clipPath>
</defs>
```

Once defined, I apply this clip path to my element using the `clip-path` property, with a value equal to the `url()` notation containing the ID of the clip path:

```
E { clip-path: url('#clipping'); }
```

Unfortunately, this method has drawbacks. For one, as of this writing, it only works in Firefox. Also, you can't animate these shapes without using JavaScript.

Image Masking

In addition to clipping an element with geometric shapes, you can also mask one image with another, using the alpha value of the mask to determine how much of the target will be visible. (This process is similar to the way blend modes work, except that it uses alpha rather than black and white.) The mask is applied using the `mask` property, which takes these values:

```
E { mask: image position / size; }
```

The *image* value is the `url()` notation with a path to the image to be used as a mask. The properties *position* and *size* work the same as the background-position and background-size properties (see Chapter 8). For example, the following code will set an image called *mask.png* at the center of an element, with the mask filling the width of the parent while maintaining its original aspect ratio:

```
E { mask: url('mask.png') 50% 50% / 100% auto; }
```

Figure 18-14 shows the three steps in masking. The target image is on the left; the image to be used as a mask is in the middle; and the mask applied to the target is on the right.

Figure 18-14: The three steps of image masking

This is a simple mask. The syntax is much more flexible than this, although a bit too complicated to explore in detail in this book.

The mask property is shorthand for a whole range of subproperties, including mask-image, mask-position, and mask-size. You can use many more properties in addition to these, and the full mask shorthand looks like this:

```
E { mask: image mode position / size repeat origin clip composite; }
```

Let's take a brief walk through the unfamiliar properties. The mask-mode property determines whether the mask should work on the default alpha channel or through *luminance* (lightness); mask-repeat tiles the mask image just as background-repeat; mask-origin and mask-clip also work like their background equivalents (background-origin and background-clip in Chapter 8); and mask-composite controls how multiple mask-image values should interact if they overlap.

Border Masking

In Chapter 9, I introduced the border-image property, which is used to apply images to the borders of an element. You can use the same basic method of slicing an image that we discussed in that context to apply a mask to the border of an element.

The properties involved in border masking are mask-border-source, mask-border-slice, mask-border-repeat, mask-border-width, and mask-border-output. Each can be included in the mask-border shorthand, and each is identical in function to their border-image-* counterpart. For example, to set an image *mask.png*, with slices of 40px each, which repeats along each side of an element, you use this syntax:

```
E { mask-border: url('mask.png') 40px repeat; }
```

Unfortunately, as of this writing no browser supports this in accordance with the spec (though Chrome and Safari support a similar but outdated property called -webkit-mask-box-image), so I won't spend any more time discussing border masking.

Masking in SVG

You can use SVG to mask images, much as you might clip them. To do so, you define the mask in markup and then apply it using a CSS property (mask). For example, the following listing creates a mask of a black box with a white ellipse in the center:

```
<defs>
    <mask id="masking">
        <rect y="0.3" width="1" height=".7" fill="black" />
        <circle cx=".5" cy=".5" r=".35" fill="white" />
    </mask>
</defs>
```

The next step is to apply the mask to the target element, using the mask property with a url() notation containing the ID of the mask element (masking):

```
E { mask: url('#masking'); }
```

NOTE *For a more in-depth look at masking in SVG and CSS, see Dirk Schulze's "CSS Masking"* (http://www.html5rocks.com/en/tutorials/masking/adobe/).

Combining Filter Effects and Masking

Should you want to combine filter effects with masking on the same element, it's important to know that they will be applied in a specific order: filter effects are applied first, followed by clipping, then masking, and finally opacity. To see the consequence of this order, consider the following listing that applies a drop shadow filter and circular clipping path to an element:

```
E {
    clip-path: circle(50% at 50% 50%);
    filter: drop-shadow(5px 5px black);
}
```

In this code, the effects are applied to the image in this order: first, the drop shadow is applied; then the image with the drop shadow applied is clipped into a circle. To avoid the clipping of the drop shadow, you can apply the filter effect to a parent element:

```
D { filter: drop-shadow(5px 5px black); } /* parent */
E { clip-path: circle(50% at 50% 50%); } /* child */
```

This works because of the way browsers parse the DOM for rendering. The clipping of the child element will occur before the filter effect that is inherited from the parent. (Figure 18-15 compares the two methods.)

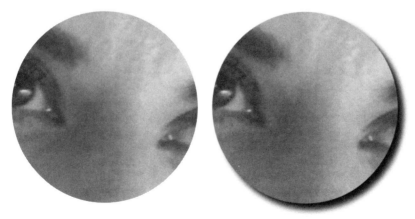

Figure 18-15: Comparing rendering order of graphical CSS effects

Summary

Blend modes, filter effects, and masking provide access to web browser features that were previously found only in professional photo-imaging software. Each is useful on its own, but combine them and designers and developers get a whole new way to approach visual design on the Web.

The ability to use graphical effects like these comes thanks to the widespread implementation of SVG. The markup that describes an SVG image is already closely tied with HTML (it can be dropped into HTML and will be parsed as part of the document), and in the future you should see SVG and CSS become much more closely tied—we've seen that with the graphical effects in this chapter, and modules currently in development also describe a shared implementation of the animation properties described in Chapter 14.

Blend Modes, Filter Effects, and Masking: Browser Support

	Chrome	Firefox	Safari	IE
background-blend-mode	Yes	Yes	Safari 8	No
mix-blend-mode	No[*]	Yes	Safari 8	No
isolation	No[*]	No	Safari 8	No
filter	Yes[†]	No[‡]	Yes[†]	No
clip-path	Yes[*]	No	Safari 8[§]	No
mask	Yes[†]	No	Yes[†]	No

[*] Implemented but off by default
[†] With vendor prefix
[‡] Can use filters defined in SVG
[§] With vendor prefix; implemented with outdated syntax in Safari 7

19

THE FUTURE OF CSS

In this final chapter, we'll look at some more experimental CSS3 features. As you'll see, these features range from ones that greatly extend your ability to lay out pages (to rival those of printed magazines) to ones that bring you powerful methods and functions found in other programming languages.

I must state up front that these features have limited implementation and, as I write this, are defined in modules that have yet to complete the W3C recommendation cycle; these two facts mean that the future of the features in this chapter is uncertain. Because these features are in such a state of flux, I'll discuss each briefly, without the level of detail used throughout the rest of this book.

Shapes

One limitation of CSS is that all elements are rectangular. Even if you use rounded corners or clip an element (as discussed in Chapter 18), the underlying box is still rectangular. So, for example, content floated around a rounded or clipped element will follow the rectangular outline of the element's bounding box, as you can see in Figure 19-1.

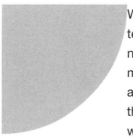 While I watched the tempest, so beautiful yet terrific, I wandered on with a hasty step. This noble war in the sky elevated my spirits; I clasped my hands, and exclaimed aloud, "William, dear angel! This is thy funeral, this thy dirge!" As I said these words, I perceived in the gloom a figure which stole from behind a clump of trees near me; I stood fixed, gazing intently: I could not be mistaken.

Figure 19-1: Although the element here has rounded corners, content floated around it follows its rectangular bounding box.

The CSS Shapes Module (*http://www.w3.org/TR/css-shapes/*) addresses this problem by allowing you to apply geometrical shapes to elements, so inline content can flow around the outline of these shapes, rather than the original bounding box. The shape-outside property defines the shape to be applied to an element:

```
E { shape-outside: shape-function; }
```

The *shape-function* value can be any of the functions allowed on the clip-shape property (introduced in "Clipping" on page 235): inset(), circle(), ellipse(), or polygon(). For example, this code creates a circle with a radius of 100px and a center at the top left of the element it's applied to:

```
E { shape-outside: circle(100px at left top); }
```

When this element is floated, any inline content around it wraps around the outline of the circle, as shown in Figure 19-2.

Note the shape applies only to the element's float outline; the background color, images, and borders will still respect the element's box. As you can see in Figure 19-3, I've removed the border-radius value from the floated element, and the text overlaps the element's box. To avoid this problem, you could consider using a clip path (see "Clipping" on page 235) that matches the defined shape.

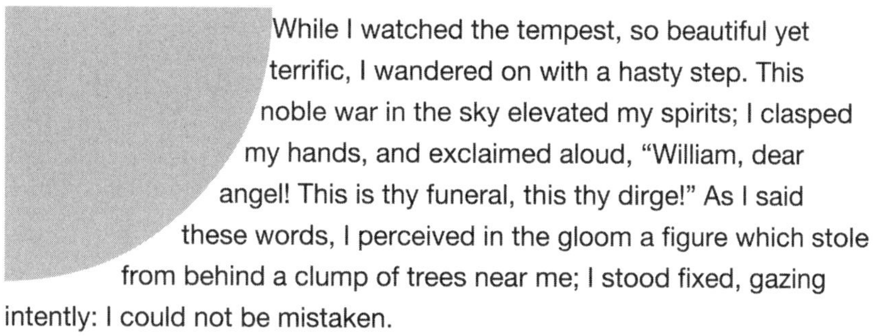

While I watched the tempest, so beautiful yet
terrific, I wandered on with a hasty step. This
noble war in the sky elevated my spirits; I clasped
my hands, and exclaimed aloud, "William, dear
angel! This is thy funeral, this thy dirge!" As I said
these words, I perceived in the gloom a figure which stole
from behind a clump of trees near me; I stood fixed, gazing
intently: I could not be mistaken.

Figure 19-2: An element with a CSS Shape applied. Content flows around the defined circular outline rather than the bounding box.

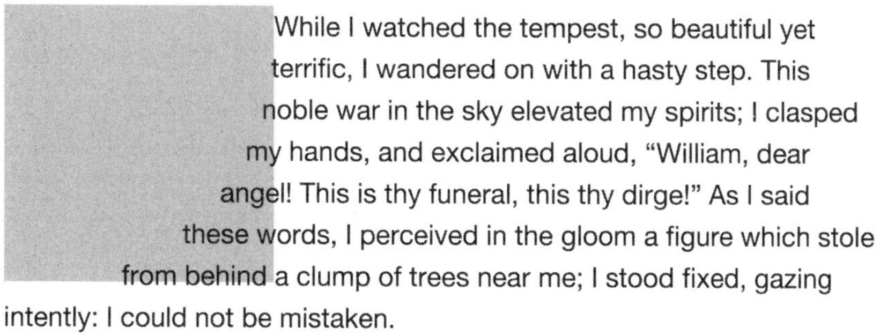

While I watched the tempest, so beautiful yet
terrific, I wandered on with a hasty step. This
noble war in the sky elevated my spirits; I clasped
my hands, and exclaimed aloud, "William, dear
angel! This is thy funeral, this thy dirge!" As I said
these words, I perceived in the gloom a figure which stole
from behind a clump of trees near me; I stood fixed, gazing
intently: I could not be mistaken.

Figure 19-3: Without a matching border-radius value, floated text overlaps the background color of the shaped element.

To create extra space between the edge of the float shape and the content flowing around it, you can use the shape-margin property. This property accepts any length value. For example, this code adds an extra 0.5em around the shape:

```
E { shape-margin: 0.5em; }
```

Note that, unlike the margin property, you can only add a single margin value that applies evenly to all sides of the shape.

Exclusions

As of this writing, in order to have content flow around an element you must make the element float. The drawback is that an element can only be floated to the left or right; you can neither position it in the middle of text nor do you have much fine control.

The CSS Exclusions Module (*http://www.w3.org/TR/css3-exclusions/*) addresses this problem. CSS Exclusions defines a way to flow text around any element, regardless of whether the element itself is floated. Figure 19-4 shows an element positioned over some text. In the example on the left, the element doesn't interact with the text, but on the right, it acts as an *exclusion element*—it behaves as if it was floated, and the text flows around it on both sides.

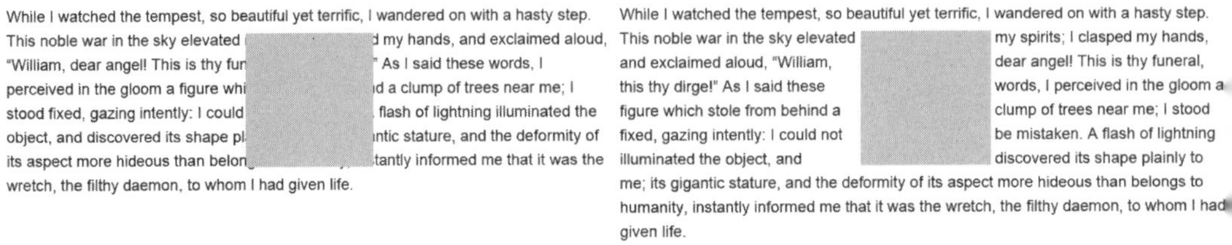

While I watched the tempest, so beautiful yet terrific, I wandered on with a hasty step. This noble war in the sky elevated [ ] my hands, and exclaimed aloud, "William, dear angel! This is thy fun[ ]" As I said these words, I perceived in the gloom a figure whi[ ]d a clump of trees near me; I stood fixed, gazing intently: I could [ ] flash of lightning illuminated the object, and discovered its shape pl[ ]ntic stature, and the deformity of its aspect more hideous than belon[ ]tantly informed me that it was the wretch, the filthy daemon, to whom I had given life.

While I watched the tempest, so beautiful yet terrific, I wandered on with a hasty step. This noble war in the sky elevated [ ] my spirits; I clasped my hands, and exclaimed aloud, "William, [ ] dear angel! This is thy funeral, this thy dirge!" As I said these [ ] words, I perceived in the gloom a figure which stole from behind a [ ] clump of trees near me; I stood fixed, gazing intently: I could not [ ] be mistaken. A flash of lightning illuminated the object, and [ ] discovered its shape plainly to me; its gigantic stature, and the deformity of its aspect more hideous than belongs to humanity, instantly informed me that it was the wretch, the filthy daemon, to whom I had given life.

Figure 19-4: On the left, an element is positioned above text; on the right, a floating exclusion element has text flowing around it.

You create an exclusion element with the wrap-flow property, which accepts a single keyword value:

```
E { wrap-flow: flow-direction; }
```

The *flow-direction* keyword sets the sides of the element around which any inline content flows. You can control the flow with one of several values; each of these is shown in Figure 19-5:

- The clear value means content will not flow around either side of the exclusion element (A).
- The both value flows inline content around both sides (B).
- The start value means inline content flows around the left side of the element (if the writing direction of the document or element is left-to-right), leaving the right side empty (C).
- The end value does the opposite of start: Inline content flows around the right side of the element, leaving the left side empty (D).

The minimum and maximum keywords flow content around the side of an element with either the lesser or greater (respectively) distance between the side and the nearest side of its containing element. Using the examples in Figure 19-5, maximum would be equivalent to start (C) and minimum to end (D).

The default keyword value is auto, which means no exclusion will be created—the content flows beneath the element, as shown on the left in Figure 19-4.

As I write this, Internet Explorer 10 and 11 support CSS Exclusions, using the -ms-wrap-flow property and without the minimum keyword value.

While I watched the tempest, so beautiful yet terrific, I wandered on with a hasty step.

This noble war in the sky elevated my spirits; I clasped my hands, and exclaimed aloud, "William, dear angel! This is thy funeral, this thy dirge!" As I said these words, I perceived in the gloom a figure which stole from behind a clump of trees near me; I stood fixed, gazing intently: I could not be mistaken. A flash of lightning illuminated the object, and discovered its shape plainly to me; its gigantic stature, and the deformity of its aspect more hideous than belongs to humanity, instantly informed me that it was the wretch, the filthy daemon, to whom I had given life.

A

While I watched the tempest, so beautiful yet terrific, I wandered on with a hasty step. This noble war in the sky elevated my spirits; I clasped my hands, and exclaimed aloud, "William, dear funeral, this thy dirge!" As I said these gloom a figure which stole from behind a I stood fixed, gazing intently: I could not be lightning illuminated the object, and plainly to me; its gigantic stature, and the deformity of its aspect more hideous than belongs to humanity, instantly informed me that it was the wretch, the filthy daemon, to whom I had given life.

B

While I watched the tempest, so beautiful yet terrific, I wandered on with a hasty step. This noble war in the sky elevated my spirits; I clasped my hands, and exclaimed aloud, "William, dear angel! This is thy funeral, this thy dirge!" As I said these words, I perceived in the gloom a figure which stole from behind a clump of trees near me; I stood fixed, gazing intently: I could not be mistaken. A flash of lightning illuminated the object, and discovered its shape plainly to me; its gigantic stature, and the deformity of its aspect more hideous than belongs to humanity, instantly informed me that it was the wretch, the filthy daemon, to whom I had given life.

C

While I watched the tempest, so beautiful yet terrific, I wandered on with a hasty step. This noble war in the sky elevated my spirits; I clasped my hands, and exclaimed aloud, "William, dear angel! This is thy funeral, this thy dirge!" As I said these words, I perceived in the gloom a figure which stole from behind a clump of trees near me; I stood fixed, gazing intently: I could not be mistaken. A flash of lightning illuminated the object, and discovered its shape plainly to me; its gigantic stature, and the deformity of its aspect more hideous than belongs to humanity, instantly informed me that it was the wretch, the filthy daemon, to whom I had given life.

D

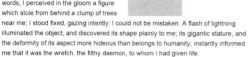

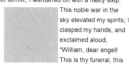

Figure 19-5: Content flows around an exclusion element based on the use of various keyword values.

Regions

Chapter 7 explained CSS columns, the method of flowing content across multiple sequential columns. The CSS Regions Module (*http://dev.w3.org/csswg/css-regions/*) extends this idea, allowing content to flow into multiple regions, which aren't required to be consecutive in layout order, and regardless of their position on the page. Think of a long magazine article that continues across multiple, though not necessarily sequential, pages.

CSS Regions makes this possible by defining an area of content and assigning it a unique identifier, known as a *named flow*, with the `flow-into` property:

```
E { flow-into: foo; }
```

Once this identifier has been assigned, the content of element *E* can flow into multiple regions. To do this, use the named flow as the value of the `flow-from` property; for example, if you wanted to flow the contents of *foo* into the elements *F* and *G*, this is the code you'd use:

```
F, G { flow-from: foo; }
```

The content of *E* flows into *F* first because it's listed first in the code. If the content overflows *F*, the overflow goes into *G*. Figure 19-6 shows content flowed into three independent areas. (I've added background shading to make each area easier to identify.)

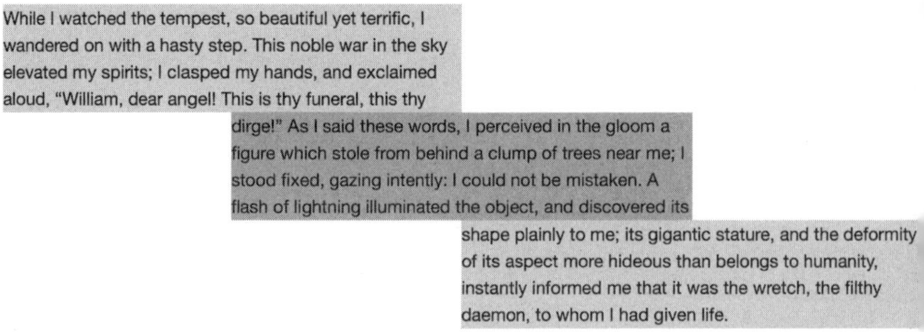

> While I watched the tempest, so beautiful yet terrific, I
> wandered on with a hasty step. This noble war in the sky
> elevated my spirits; I clasped my hands, and exclaimed
> aloud, "William, dear angel! This is thy funeral, this thy
> dirge!" As I said these words, I perceived in the gloom a
> figure which stole from behind a clump of trees near me; I
> stood fixed, gazing intently: I could not be mistaken. A
> flash of lightning illuminated the object, and discovered its
> shape plainly to me; its gigantic stature, and the deformity
> of its aspect more hideous than belongs to humanity,
> instantly informed me that it was the wretch, the filthy
> daemon, to whom I had given life.

Figure 19-6: Text flows into the first box, overflows into the second box, and then over-flows into the third.

The elements *F* and *G* can be placed anywhere on the page; they do not need to be contiguous (though you should, of course, make it easy for the user to follow the visual flow of the content).

As of this writing CSS Regions is implemented in Safari 6.1 and above, using the -webkit- prefix. CSS Regions is also in Internet Explorer 10 and 11, using the -ms- prefix and with the added proviso that the element from which the content flows must be an iframe.

Variables

Almost every programming language can define *variables*—symbolic names to which you can assign values and that can be referenced or updated later. Part of the reason for the wild popularity of CSS preprocessors such as Sass is that they allow the use of variables in CSS. This popularity has led directly to the creation of *custom properties*—a limited variable-like feature in the native CSS language. These are introduced in the CSS Custom Properties for Cascading Variables Module (*http://www.w3.org/TR/css-variables-1/*).

You define a custom property in three steps: by setting its *scope* (the range of values to which it can be applied), creating a unique identifier, and then assigning that identifier a value. Here's how that looks in code:

```
❶ :root {
❷     --fooColor: #f00;
  }
```

Leaving aside ❶ for now, look at ❷, where I've defined the custom property using the unique identifier --fooColor. (CSS variable names must be a string of characters with no spaces and prefixed with a double hyphen to avoid conflict with other defined values.) I've assigned the color value #f00 to the custom property, but any valid CSS property value is permitted.

Once the custom property has been defined and given a value, you can use it as the value of any other property. The value assigned to the custom property is used as the value of the property that refers to it by using the unique identifier as an argument in the var() function. For example, to call this value on a border-color and color, you write the following:

```
E {
    border-color: var(--fooColor);
    color: var(--fooColor);
}
```

Here, the value of the custom property --fooColor (namely #f00) will be used as the value of the border-color and color properties of E. Of course, the value of the custom property must be valid when applied to the property that refers to it: there would be no point in using a color value for the width property. If you do use an invalid custom property in a rule, the rule will be ignored.

Now, let's return to ❶ in the code shown earlier. This line sets the scope of the variable. In my example, the scope is the :root selector, which means the variable has *global scope* that can be applied to any element, regardless of its position in the DOM. If you prefer the custom property only be valid when applied to a subset of elements, you can limit this scope. For the custom property to be valid only when applied to h1 elements, for example, you set its scope like this:

```
h1 { --fooColor: #f00; }
```

Having restricted the scope in this way, a reference to the custom property from any h1 selector displays it with the color value #f00:

```
h1 { color: var(--fooColor); }
```

But if you refer to the custom property from an element outside the scope, like an h2, the custom property is unknown, so the following rule will be ignored:

```
h2 { color: var(--fooColor); }
```

As of this writing, custom properties are available in Firefox 31 and above and are implemented in Chrome behind a flag, but they may not be enabled as there are certain performance concerns. As such, custom properties face an uncertain future.

Feature Queries

Media queries, introduced in Chapter 2, have transformed our ability to make sites work responsively across many different screen sizes and resolutions. Their power is partly due to their logical simplicity: If the conditions of the query are met, the rules defined within the query's declaration block are applied. This idea is developed further in the CSS Conditional Rules

Module (*http://www.w3.org/TR/css3-conditional/*), which extends queries not only to use conditions based on device/UA properties such as dimension and resolution, but also to allow the definition of CSS rules that only apply if a particular CSS feature is supported.

These new conditional rules, known as *feature queries*, are defined with the new @supports rule. The @supports syntax is similar to @media, except it requires a CSS property-value pair (or pairs) as an argument. If the browser supports the property-value pair, the defined rules are applied.

For example, to test if a browser supports Flexbox, the conditions of the test are that it recognizes the display property with a value of flex:

```
@supports (display: flex) {...}
```

In a modern browser that has implemented Flexbox (and @supports, of course), the property-value pair is recognized, and the rules in the curly brackets are applied. Older browsers without Flexbox support won't recognize that combination of property and value and will skip the rules.

As with media queries, you can use logical operators—and, or, and not—with feature queries. For example, to see if a browser supports both Flexbox and Transitions, you use and:

```
@supports (display: flex) and (transition: 1s) {...}
```

If a property has multiple implementations using vendor prefixes and you want to test that the browser has any one of those implementations, you use or:

```
@supports (animation-duration: 1s) or (-webkit-animation-duration: 1s) {...}
```

And to see if a browser doesn't support a particular property, you use not:

```
@supports not (display: flex) {...}
```

As of this writing, the @supports rule is implemented in Chrome and Firefox and listed as "In Development" for Internet Explorer. Webkit has implemented it experimentally, but as of this writing it is not listed for release in Safari 8. In these browsers, rules inside the @supports declaration block will be ignored.

Device Adaptation

One critical part of implementing responsive design with media queries is the ability to set viewport properties, using the viewport meta tag (see "Device Width and Height" on page 15). Unfortunately, the viewport meta tag is not without its problems—not least of which is that the initial implementation was undocumented, meaning other browser vendors had to reverse-engineer it, leading to small interoperability issues. The CSS Device

Adaptation Module (*http://www.w3.org/TR/css-device-adapt/*) attempts to address these interoperability problems by translating the viewport meta tag properties into native CSS, and documenting and standardizing features as well as adding new ones.

The Device Adaptation Module reimplements the viewport meta tag with a new at-rule, `@viewport`:

```
@viewport {...}
```

The `@viewport` rule accepts numerous property-value pairs or *viewport descriptors*, which set the parameters of the viewport. Some of these descriptors are existing CSS properties, whereas others are unique to `@viewport`. In many cases, these descriptors are not the same as the arguments used in the viewport meta tag, but they perform the same role. For example, to set the width equal to the device width in the meta tag, you write this:

```
<meta name="viewport" content="width=device-width">
```

To perform the same operation with the `@viewport` rule, you use the width property, with a value of 100vw—the full viewport width (the vw unit was discussed in Chapter 16):

```
@viewport {
    width: 100vw;
}
```

The best part of the `@viewport` rule is you can combine it with media queries, creating custom viewports for different device configurations. For example, you can set the width equal to the device width only on small screens:

```
@media (max-width: 480px) {
  @viewport {
      width: 100vw;
  }
}
```

As of this writing, the `@viewport` rule is implemented in Internet Explorer 10 and 11 as the `@-ms-viewport` rule. It's also implemented in Chrome, although not currently enabled by default.

Sticky Positioning

A fairly common web design pattern is to make elements *sticky* so they stick to the top or bottom of the viewport as the page is scrolled. Stickiness has usually been accomplished by setting the fixed value on the position property using scroll events in JavaScript, but CSS3's Positioned Layout Module (*http://dev.w3.org/csswg/css-position-3/*) introduces a native sticky value for the position property to do the same thing.

Sticky positioning is a kind of hybrid of relative and fixed positioning. An element's position is relative until it reaches a *sticky threshold* value, which is a preset scroll position of the viewport. For example, in the following listing, element *E* becomes sticky when the viewport scrolls down 20px from the top:

```
E {
    position: sticky;
    top: 20px;
}
```

As of this writing, sticky positioning is in Safari from 6.1, with the value -webkit-sticky, and unprefixed in Firefox. Chrome is expected to implement sticky positioning, and it is listed as "Under Consideration" in Internet Explorer.

And Much, Much More

CSS is a living standard, undergoing constant development, whether driven by the W3C, browser vendors, interested parties like Adobe, or the web development community. In addition to the new features discussed in this chapter, many more exciting CSS developments are being proposed, debated, and developed. Some of these include, but are not limited to, the following:

- The ability to set different shapes for corners and allow clipped or partial lines for borders
- The ability to apply the position keywords from Flexbox (Chapter 15) to any element, causing big changes in the way elements are positioned
- Color functions that allow colors to be tinted or shaded easily and that provide easier grayscale manipulation
- Extending the idea of custom properties to include custom selectors or functions
- Grids based on lines of text, which are designed to allow better placement of elements in content with a vertical rhythm
- Image values including sprites and fallbacks, and ones that can use elements as backgrounds

These features are mostly still at the theoretical stage, but they should give you some insight into the level of thinking that's going into the future of CSS. And such is the rapid rate of change in the web industry, that within a few months of reading this, doubtless many more novelties will have been proposed.

Conclusion

CSS is clearly evolving. From its humble beginnings as a way to provide simple decoration to text documents, CSS is moving toward a future where it becomes almost a language in itself, capable of adapting to the many devices that we will use to access the Web in the future.

I've learned in my years of working with and writing and talking about CSS that change comes from unexpected directions. Certain seemingly useful modules or properties will remain unimplemented for many reasons—whether because of business decisions, resources, or just plain politics. And change is driven by different sources: from the W3C and browser vendors to companies like Adobe that want to shape the web in their own image to the development community that builds tools to meet the demands of web development. You just never know where the next big shift will come from.

I haven't covered everything in the CSS3 modules in this book, but I hope I've covered enough to at least make you curious about some of the new technologies you can start using today, as well as what lies on the horizon for CSS. I urge you to stay connected to the conversation that surrounds styling elements for the Web, to download preview releases of browsers, to create your own experiments, and to let the browser makers and the W3C know the results of your experiments. CSS3 has (mostly) been molded around the desires of web developers, and your opinions and feedback are vital.

Future CSS: Browser Support

	Chrome	Firefox	Safari	IE
Shapes	Yes	No	Safari 8[*]	No
Exclusions	No	No	No	IE10[†]
Regions	No	No	Yes[*]	IE10[‡]
Variables	No	Yes	No	No
Feature queries	Yes	Yes	No	No[§]
Device adaptation	No[ǁ]	No	No	IE10[†]
Sticky positioning	No	Yes	Yes[*]	No

[*] With vendor prefix
[†] With vendor prefix; no support for minimum value
[‡] With vendor prefix; only an iframe can be used as the content source
[§] Currently listed as "in development"
[ǁ] Implemented, but disabled by default

A

CSS3 SUPPORT IN CURRENT MAJOR BROWSERS

This appendix collects the browser support tables that are shown at the end of each chapter, providing an at-a-glance summary of the implementation of the CSS3 properties and rules featured in this book.

This listing is somewhat complicated by two factors: The first is that, as I've mentioned repeatedly, CSS3 is still in a state of flux, and some properties are still very subject to change; the second is that new versions of browsers are released regularly and consistently, and each release sees a host of new implementations.

In the following tables, I indicate implementation status in the four major browsers: Chrome, Firefox, Safari, and Internet Explorer. I haven't included Opera, as that's now based on Chrome and has broadly the same feature list. Unless otherwise indicated, the mobile version of each browser has the same feature set as the desktop version.

Chrome and Firefox are *evergreen* browsers: they update automatically and version numbers are only used for internal reference. Internet Explorer and Safari continue to release versions at regular intervals; as I write this, IE11 and Safari 8 are the most recent versions.

In the support tables below, where a *Yes* is used it means that the feature is supported either in an evergreen browser or in at least the last three versions of Safari (6–8) or IE (9–11). Otherwise, a version number will be shown. With regards to IE, it's safe to presume that, with a very few exceptions, almost nothing in this book is implemented in IE8 or below.

I keep updated versions of these tables on the website that accompanies this book (*http://www.thebookofcss3.com/*), so check there regularly for the most up-to-date implementation status.

Media Queries (Chapter 2)

	Chrome	Firefox	Safari	IE
Media queries	Yes	Yes	Yes	Yes

Selectors (Chapter 3)

	Chrome	Firefox	Safari	IE
New attribute selectors	Yes	Yes	Yes	Yes
General sibling combinator	Yes	Yes	Yes	Yes

DOM and Attribute Selectors (Chapter 4)

	Chrome	Firefox	Safari	IE
Structural pseudo-classes	Yes	Yes	Yes	Yes
:target	Yes	Yes	Yes	Yes
:empty	Yes	Yes	Yes	Yes
:root	Yes	Yes	Yes	Yes
:not()	Yes	Yes	Yes	Yes
Pseudo-elements (:: syntax)	Yes	Yes	Yes	Yes
UI element states	Yes	Yes	Yes	Yes
Constraint validation	Yes	Yes	Yes	IE10*
::selection	Yes	Yes	Yes	Yes

* Does not support :in-range, :out-of-range

Web Fonts (Chapter 5)

	Chrome	Firefox	Safari	IE
@font-face	Yes	Yes	Yes	Yes
font-size-adjust	No	Yes	No	No
font-stretch	No	Yes	No	Yes
font-feature-settings	Yes	Yes	No	IE10
font-variant-*	Yes*	No	Yes*	No

* Requires vendor prefix

Text Effects and Typographic Styles (Chapter 6)

	Chrome	Firefox	Safari	IE
text-shadow	Yes	Yes	Yes	IE10
text-overflow	Yes	Yes	Yes	Yes
text-align (new values)	Yes	Yes	Yes	No
text-align-last	Yes	Yes*	No	Yes†
overflow-wrap	Yes	Yes‡	Yes	Yes‡
hyphens	No	Yes*	Yes*	IE10*
resize	Yes§	Yes	Yes§	No

* With vendor prefix
† Without the start and end values
‡ As word-wrap
§ Not in mobile browsers

Multiple Columns (Chapter 7)

	Chrome	Firefox	Safari	IE
column-count	Yes*	Yes*	Yes*	IE10
column-width	Yes*	Yes*	Yes*	IE10
columns	Yes*	Yes*	Yes*	IE10
column-fill	No	Yes*	No	IE10
column-gap	Yes*	Yes*	Yes*	IE10
column-rule	Yes*	Yes*	Yes*	IE10
column-span	Yes*	No	Yes*	IE10

* With vendor prefix

Background Images (Chapter 8)

	Chrome	Firefox	Safari	IE
background-position (edge values)	Yes	Yes	Yes	Yes
background-attachment	Yes	Yes	Yes	IE10
background-repeat (new values)	Yes	No	No*	Yes
background-repeat (two values)	Yes	Yes	Yes	Yes
Multiple background images	Yes	Yes	Yes	Yes
background-size	Yes	Yes	Yes	Yes
Updated background property	Yes	Yes	Yes	Yes
background-clip	Yes	Yes	Yes	Yes
background-origin	Yes	Yes	Yes	Yes

* The values are recognized but don't display correctly.

Border and Box Effects (Chapter 9)

	Chrome	Firefox	Safari	IE
border-radius	Yes	Yes	Yes	Yes
border-image	Yes	Yes	Yes	IE11
box-shadow	Yes	Yes	Yes	Yes

Color and Opacity (Chapter 10)

	Chrome	Firefox	Safari	IE
opacity	Yes	Yes	Yes	Yes
RGBA values	Yes	Yes	Yes	Yes
HSL values	Yes	Yes	Yes	Yes
HSLA values	Yes	Yes	Yes	Yes
currentColor value	Yes	Yes	Yes	Yes

Gradients (Chapter 11)

	Chrome	Firefox	Safari	IE
Linear gradients	Yes	Yes	Yes	IE10
Repeating linear gradients	Yes	Yes	Yes	IE10
Radial gradients	Yes	Yes	Yes	IE10
Repeating radial gradients	Yes	Yes	Yes	IE10

2D Transformations (Chapter 12)

	Chrome	Firefox	Safari	IE
2D transformations	Yes	Yes	Yes*	IE9*, IE10

* With vendor prefix

3D Transformations (Chapter 13)

	Chrome	Firefox	Safari	IE
3D transformations	Yes	Yes	Yes*	IE10†

* With vendor prefix
† No support for the preserve-3d value for transform-style

Transitions and Animations (Chapter 14)

	Chrome	Firefox	Safari	IE
Transitions	Yes	Yes	Yes	IE10
Animations	Yes*	Yes	Yes*	IE10

* With vendor prefix

Flexbox (Chapter 15)

	Chrome	Firefox	Safari	IE
Flexible box layout	Yes	Yes	Yes*	IE10†, IE11

* With vendor prefix
† Supports an older syntax, with vendor prefix

Values and Sizing (Chapter 16)

	Chrome	Firefox	Safari	IE
Root-relative units	Yes	Yes	Yes	Yes
Viewport-relative units	Yes	Yes	Yes*	IE9†, IE10‡
Calculated values	Yes	Yes	Yes	Yes
Box sizing	Yes	Yes	Yes	Yes
Intrinsic/extrinsic sizing	Yes§	Yes§	Yes§	No

* Buggy support for vh in iOS
† Supports vm instead of vmin, no support for vmax
‡ No support for vmax
§ With vendor prefix

Grid Layout (Chapter 17)

	Chrome	Firefox	Safari	IE
Grid layout	No*	No	No	IE10†

* Implemented but off by default
† Syntax different from the spec; with vendor prefix

Blend Modes, Filter Effects, and Masking (Chapter 18)

	Chrome	Firefox	Safari	IE
background-blend-mode	Yes	Yes	Safari 8	No
mix-blend-mode	No*	Yes	Safari 8	No
isolation	No*	No	Safari 8	No
filter	Yes†	No‡	Yes†	No
clip-path	Yes*	No	Safari 8§	No
mask	Yes†	No	Yes†	No

* Implemented but off by default
† With vendor prefix
‡ Can use filters defined in SVG
§ With vendor prefix; implemented with outdated syntax in Safari 7

Future CSS (Chapter 19)

	Chrome	Firefox	Safari	IE
Shapes	Yes	No	Safari 8*	No
Exclusions	No	No	No	IE10†
Regions	No	No	Yes*	IE10‡
Variables	No	Yes	No	No
Feature queries	Yes	Yes	No	No§
Device adaptation	No‖	No	No	IE10†
Sticky positioning	No	Yes	Yes*	No

* With vendor prefix
† With vendor prefix; no support for minimum value
‡ With vendor prefix; only an iframe can be used as the content source
§ Currently listed as "in development"
‖ Implemented, but disabled by default

B

ONLINE RESOURCES

In this appendix, I list some useful articles, resources, and tools for finding out more about each of the new CSS3 features listed in this book. A million and one sites offer demonstrations and tricks; throw a stone at Google and you'll hit 500 pages of them. Although some are useful, many are notably less so, so I've tried to steer clear of "30 Awesome Things You Can Do with CSS3!" blog posts and offer, instead, resources that I think are of more practical value.

This list is very much a work in progress, and I aim to keep an updated list on the website that accompanies the book: *http://www.thebookofcss3.com/*. If you know of any resources that you think I should add, get in touch through the website and let me know.

General CSS Resources

Before I get into specific articles, I want to recommend a couple of sites that have been absolutely invaluable to me while writing this book. Without these, my job would have been exponentially harder, so I must give huge thanks to the authors.

Probably the most useful site on the Web, and certainly the one I refer to most, is the Mozilla Developer Network (MDN). Written by volunteers, this site is the best resource for HTML, CSS, and JavaScript, with clear descriptions of every property: *https://developer.mozilla.org/*.

Alexis Deveria's site, Can I Use… is an amazing set of tables of data about implementation of emerging web platform features across different browsers. If you want to know how widespread support for a feature is, this is the only place to go: *http://caniuse.com/*.

Chapter 2: Media Queries

- Essential Considerations for Crafting Quality Media Queries: *http://zomigi.com/blog/essential-considerations-for-crafting-quality-media-queries/*
- 7 Habits of Highly Effective Media Queries: *http://bradfrostweb.com/blog/post/7-habits-of-highly-effective-media-queries/*
- Use CSS Media Queries for Responsiveness: *https://developers.google.com/web/fundamentals/layouts/rwd-fundamentals/use-media-queries/*

Chapters 3 and 4: Selectors, and Pseudo-classes and Pseudo-elements

- IE Test Drive – CSS3 Selectors: *http://ie.microsoft.com/TEStdrive/HTML5/CSS3Selectors/*

Chapters 5 and 6: Web Fonts, and Text Effects and Typographic Styles

- A More Modern Scale for Web Typography: *http://typecast.com/blog/a-more-modern-scale-for-web-typography/*
- The Elements of Typographic Style Applied to the Web: *http://webtypography.net/*
- Google Web Fonts: *https://www.google.com/fonts/*
- Font Squirrel: *http://www.fontsquirrel.com/*

Chapter 7: Multiple Columns

- Simple Grids with CSS Multi-Column Layout: *http://dbushell.com/2014/02/03/simple-grids-with-css-multi-column-layout/*
- IE Test Drive – Hands On: Multi-column Layout: *http://ie.microsoft.com/testdrive/graphics/hands-on-css3/hands-on_multi-column.htm*

Chapters 8 and 9: Background Images, and Border and Box Effects

- CSS Sprites: What They Are, Why They're Cool, and How To Use Them: *http://css-tricks.com/css-sprites/*
- The Humble `border-radius`: *http://lea.verou.me/humble-border-radius/*
- `border-image` Generator: *http://border-image.com/*

Chapter 10: Color and Opacity

- Which CSS Color System to Use Where: *http://demosthenes.info/blog/781/Which-CSS-Color-System-To-Use-Where*
- HSL Color Picker: *http://www.workwithcolor.com/hsl-color-picker-01.htm*

Chapter 11: Gradients

- CSS3 Patterns Gallery: *http://lea.verou.me/css3patterns/*
- IE Test Drive – CSS Gradient Background Maker: *http://ie.microsoft.com/TestDrive/Graphics/CSSGradientBackgroundMaker/*

Chapters 12 and 13: 2D and 3D Transformations

- CSS3 Transformations: *http://www.sitepoint.com/series/css3-transformations/*
- Transforms Playground: *http://www.westciv.com/tools/transforms/*
- Understanding the CSS Transforms Matrix: *http://dev.opera.com/articles/understanding-the-css-transforms-matrix/*

Chapter 14: Transitions and Animations

- All You Need to Know about CSS Transitions: *http://blog.alexmaccaw.com/css-transitions*
- Ceaser – CSS Easing Animation Tool: *http://matthewlein.com/ceaser/*
- Animate.css – Just-Add-Water CSS Animations: *http://daneden.github.io/animate.css/*

Chapter 15: Flexible Box Layout

- Solved by Flexbox: *http://philipwalton.github.io/solved-by-flexbox/*
- Leveling Up with Flexbox: *http://zomigi.com/blog/leveling-up-with-flexbox/*
- Fibonacci – Flexbox Composer: *http://maxsteenbergen.com/fibonacci/*

Chapter 16: Values and Sizing

- There's More to the CSS rem Unit than Font Sizing: *http://css-tricks.com theres-more-to-the-css-rem-unit-than-font-sizing/*
- Using vw and vh Measurements in Modern Site Design: *http://demosthene .info/blog/660/Using-vw-and-vh-Measurements-In-Modern-Site-Design/*
- Design from the Inside Out with CSS Min-Content: *http://demosthenes .info/blog/662/Design-From-the-Inside-Out-With-CSS-MinContent/*

Chapter 17: Grid Layout

- Grid by Example: *http://gridbyexample.com/*
- How to Create an Adaptive Layout with CSS Grid: *http://msdn.microsoft .com/en-us/library/ie/jj553856%28v=vs.85%29.aspx*
- Giving Content Priority with CSS3 Grid Layout: *http://24ways.org/2012/ css3-grid-layout/*

Chapter 18: Blend Modes, Filter Effects, and Masking

- PhotoShop in the Browser: Understanding CSS Blend Modes: *http:// demosthenes.info/blog/707/PhotoShop-In-The-Browser-Understanding-CSS -Blend-Modes/*
- Understanding CSS Filter Effects: *http://www.html5rocks.com/en/tutorials, filters/understanding-css/*
- CSS Masking: *http://www.html5rocks.com/en/tutorials/masking/adobe/*

Chapter 19: The Future of CSS

- Creating Non-rectangular Layouts with CSS Shapes: *http://sarasoueidan .com/blog/css-shapes/*
- Understanding Reference Boxes for CSS Shapes: *http://razvancaliman .com/writing/css-shapes-reference-boxes/*
- The CSS Exclusions Module—Letting Your Content Flow: *http://www .vanseodesign.com/css/exclusions/*
- Coming Soon: CSS Feature Queries: *http://blogs.adobe.com/webplatform/ 2014/08/21/coming-soon-css-feature-queries/*

INDEX

dots per centimeter (DPCM), 14
dots per inch (DPI), 14
dots per pixel (DPPX), 14
double colon (::), for
        pseudo-elements, 45
drop-shadow() function, 233–234
drop shadows, 65–68, 107–109, 233–234
dynamic columns, 77–78

E

ease-in keyword, for transition-timing-
        function property, 168
ease-in-out keyword, for transition-
        timing-function property, 168
ease keyword, for transition-timing-
        function property, 168
ease-out keyword, for transition-timing-
        function property, 168
elements. *See also* pseudo-elements
    resizing, 72–73
    size of, 203–207
    spanning multiple columns, 82–83
    text flow around, 248
ellipse() function, for clip-path, 236
ellipse keyword, for radial gradients,
        127–128
ellipses
    percentage values on
        border-radius for, 101
    quarter, 98
ellipsis keyword, for text-overflow
        property, 69
em (relative unit), 199, 200
Embedded OpenType (EOT)
        format, 52
:empty pseudo-class, 41
enabled elements, 43
:enabled pseudo-class selector, 43
Ending Substring Attribute Value
        selector, 25–26
end keyword
    for animation, 171
    for text-align property, 70
    for wrap-flow property, 248
EOT (Embedded OpenType)
        format, 52
equal sign (=), as Exact Attribute Value
        Selector, 22
even keyword, 33
ex (relative unit), 199
Exact Attribute Value Selector, 22

Exclusions Module, 247–249
    browser support, 255
expand keyword, for animation-name
        property, 177
explicit grids
    creating by setting track size, 211
    vs. implicit grids, 221–222
    placing items in, 214–215
expression, evaluating, 11
extent of gradient, 128
external style sheet
    @import rule for, 10
    link element for, 9
extrinsic sizing, 204–207

F

FaaS (Fonts as a Service), 53–54
farthest-corner keyword, for radial
        gradient, 128–129
farthest-side keyword, for radial
        gradient, 128–129
feature queries, 251–252
    browser support, 255
    logical operators for, 252
file-type extensions, rules for, 26
fill keyword, 206–207
    for border-image-slice property, 104
filter effects, 231–235
    blur() function, 231
    brightness() and contrast()
        functions, 232
    browser support, 244, 262
    combining with masking, 243
    drop-shadow() function, 233–234
    grayscale(), sepia(), and saturate()
        functions, 232–233
    hue-rotate() function, 233
    multiple functions, 234
    online resources, 266
    opacity() function, 233
    in SVG, 235
Firefox
    background images, 87
    column-fill property, 79
    column layout, 76
    font-feature-settings property in, 61
    font formats, 52
    font-size-adjust property, 57
    font-stretch property, 58
    images in column layout, 82
    and legacy gradient syntaxes, 131
    min-content and max-content, 205

Firefox *(continued)*
 prefix for, 5
 resize property, 73
 resolution media feature, 15
 ::selection pseudo-element, 46
 text-overflow property, 70
 web fonts, 47
:first-child pseudo-class, 33
::first-letter pseudo-element, 45
::first-line pseudo-element, 45
:first-of-type pseudo-class, 37–38
fit-content keyword, 206
fixed keyword, for background-
  attachment property, 86
Flash of Unstyled Text (FoUT), 55
flat keyword, for transform-style
  property, 161
Flexbox. *See* Flexible Box Layout
  Module
flex container
 alignment inside, 193–197
 creating, 186
 width of, 189
flex-direction property, 186
flex-end value
 for align-items property, 194, 195
 for justify-content property, 193
Flexible Box Layout Module, 185
 alignment, 187
  inside container, 193–197
  of multiple lines, 196–197
 browser support, 197, 198, 261
 declaring model, 186
 flex-basis property, 191–192
 flex-direction property, 187
 flex-flow shorthand, 196
 flex-grow property, 189–190
 flex shorthand, 192–193
 flex-shrink property, 191
 fully reordering content, 188–189
 online resources, 265
 reversing content order, 187–188
 wrap and flow, 195
flex items, adding to container, 186
flex-start value
 for align-items property, 194
 for justify-content property,
  193, 194
flex-wrap property, 196
flow-from property, 249
flow-into property, 249
Fontdeck, 54, 57

@font-face rule, 47, 48–51
 bulletproof syntax, 51–53
font-family property, 48
font features, 59–61
font-feature-settings property, 59
font-kerning property, 61
fonts
 controlling loading, 55
 defining different faces, 49–50
 finding name, 49
 formats, 52
 licensing for web use, 53–54
 OpenType fonts, 58–61
 true vs. artificial faces, 50–51
 x-height, and ex, 199
Fonts as a Service (FaaS), 53–54
font-size-adjust property, 56–57
font-size property, 199
Fonts Module Level 3, 48
Font Squirrel, @font-face Generator, 5?
font-stretch property, 58
font-variant-* properties, 61
forwards keyword, for animation-fill-
  mode property, 180
FoUT (Flash of Unstyled Text), 55
fraction unit (fr), 211
 vs. percentages, 213

G

Gaussian blur, 231
General Sibling Combinator, 28–29
global scope, for variables, 251
Google Fonts, 54
gradians, 124
gradient line, 122
gradients, 121–133
 browser support, 133, 260
 linear, 122–127
  setting direction, 122–123
 multiple, 132
 online resources, 265
 radial, 127–131
graphics. *See* images
grayscale() function, 232–233, 234
grid-area rule, 216
grid areas, 210
 names for, 217–219
grid-auto-columns property, 219, 221
grid-auto-flow property, 220
grid-auto-rows property, 219, 221
grid-column-end property, 215
grid-column-start property, 214

trigonometric functions, 145–146
TrueType font format, 52
Typekit, 54
type selectors, 21
typographic styles
    browser support, 74, 259
    online resources, 264

U

UI element states, 43–44
url() function
    for borders, 102
    filter ID in, 235

V

:valid pseudo-class, 44
values and sizing, browser support,
        208, 261
Values and Units Module, 199
    angle units, 124
    calculated values, 202–203
    relative length units, 199–202
        root-relative units, 200
        viewport-relative units, 200–202
variables, 250–251
    browser support, 255
    online resources, 266
Verou, Lea, 170
vertical alignment, with align-items
        property, 194–195
vertical axis, translateY() function for
        movement on, 140
vertical pipe (|), as Language Attribute
        Selector, 22–23
vertical value, for resize property, 73
vh (viewport height), 201
viewport
    descriptors, 253
    of media type, width, 12–13
    meta tag, 16
    of mobile device browser, 16
    setting properties, 252–253
viewport height (vh), 201
viewport-relative units, 200–202
@viewport rule, 253
viewport width (vw), 201
visible keyword, for backface-visibility
        property, 162
vmax, 201, 202
vmin, 201, 202
vw (viewport width), 201

W

Web Font Loader Library, 55
web fonts, 47–62
    browser support, 62, 259
    @font-face method, 47, 48–51
    licensing, 53–54
    online resources, 264
    real-world example, 54–55
WebKit, syntax for linear gradients, 131
-webkit-clip-path, in Safari, 238
-webkit- prefix, 5, 149
    for transition properties, 166
Web Open Font Format (WOFF), 52
web pages, layers, 165
websites
    devices for accessing, 7
    mobile-friendly versions of, 8
web use, licensing fonts for, 53–54
weight of fonts, 49–50
Westciv, 3D effects test page, 151
width
    of flex container, 189
    of text column, 77–78
width media feature, 12–13
width-to-height ratio, for media
        queries, 17–18
WOFF (Web Open Font Format), 52
words, hyphenation, 72
word-wrap property, 71
Working Draft status, 3
wrap-flow property, 248
wrap value, of flex-wrap property, 196

X

x-axis, 64
x-height, 56
x-offset, 66
    for text shadow, 68

Y

y-axis, 64
y-offset, 66
    for text shadow, 68

Z

z-axis, 64, 149, 150
zebra striping for tables, 35–36
z-index property, 222–223

The Book of CSS3, 2nd Edition is set in New Baskerville, Futura, Dogma, and TheSansMonoCondensed. The book was printed and bound by Lake Book Manufacturing in Melrose Park, Illinois. The paper is 60# Husky Opaque Offset Smooth, which is certified by the Sustainable Forestry Initiative (SFI).

The book uses a layflat binding, in which the pages are bound together with a cold-set, flexible glue, and the first and last pages of the resulting book block are attached to the cover. The cover is not actually glued to the book's spine, and when open, the book lies flat and the spine doesn't crack.

UPDATES

Visit *http://nostarch.com/css3_2e/* for updates, errata, and other information.

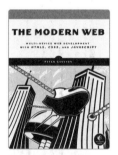
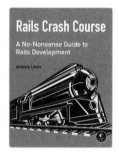